# Between You and Me

# Between You and Me

## PEARL BAILEY

# A Heartfelt Memoir on Learning, Loving, and Living

Thorndike Press • Thorndike, Maine

**Library of Congress Cataloging in Publication Data:**


Bailey, Pearl.
    Between you and me / Pearl Bailey. -- Large print ed.
    p.   cm.
    Reprint. Originally published: New York : Doubleday,
    1989.
    ISBN  0-89621-950-X (alk. paper : lg. print)
    1. Bailey, Pearl. 2. Singers--United States--Biography.
I. Title.
[ML420.B123A3    1990]                          89-48686
782.42164'092--dc20                             CIP
[B]                                             MN

Thorndike Press Large Print edition published in 1990 by
arrangement with Doubleday and Company.

**Cover photo by Deborah Feingold.**
**Cover design by Karen Katz.**

This book is printed on acid-free, high opacity paper.

# *Contents*

TWO
# THERE'S NOBODY HOME
### DEDICATED TO MY FAMILY — AND YOURS

THREE
# REFLECTIONS AT SEVENTY
### PEARL'S GEMS

# Prologue

Many things happen in one's lifetime. I've already written several books, but I haven't said it all. Some *thoughts* and incidents I've been carrying in my head started to hang heavy. I picked up my pen again, trying to get it all out, so I could replenish my brain for another decade; searching for new avenues and adventures to relate. Along came a publisher (Doubleday), a lady senior editor, Pat Kossmann, who listened to my ideas, and the emptying and reloading began.

Pouring out one's insides may sound easy but it comes hard — especially when expressing personal feelings — in truth. As a celebrity who's had a good relationship with the public for so long, I did not want to "glitz" it up. The public and I have been related so long. I want to speak for myself, not through a "ghost writer," one who can often stifle a writer's personality.

And so, for better or worse, you'll find in this book the entertainer, cook, housekeeper, wife, mother, philosopher, needlepointer, traveler, four-time public delegate to the U.S. Mission to the United Nations. Oh yes! Let's add also the author, poet, and "Medal of Freedom" recipient. Whomever you've known all these years, I hope you'll meet here.

I want to speak from the depth of my soul of joy, pain, and loneliness, a void no one but God understands that has filled all my life.

It's all here and it is yours to seek and find. Three "books" are entwined. I hope "Go for It, Honey" is an incentive for others, particularly older people like myself, to return to school, and perhaps pursue those goals once dreamed of but put aside. Sure, there are difficulties involved in this; but don't let them turn you off. I could have dressed it all up and made it look like "a piece of cake," but that wouldn't have been honest. Younger people than I have waded through it easier. Sometimes we wish our brain were sharper, our muscles stronger (to carry the books) and even our relationships more enlightening. But we must remember that everything worth having comes with a price to pay.

You will feel all of this should you ever take on the challenge of going to or staying in school. Many times I said to myself, "Pearl, you've bitten off more than you can chew." But I kept re-chewing my cud until I was able to swallow. I encourage you, dear reader, try it

10

too. Just "Go For It, Honey," and rejoice at your success.

I'm glad I "went for it" — and stuck with it — to receive a college degree from Georgetown, at the age of sixty-seven! My family's support kept me going. My husband Louie was always there for me. I've had a lot of time since graduating to sit back and think about *family*. It means *that much* to me. But many things I've seen over the years tell me that *family* — family life in America — is hurting.

I knew I had to put my feelings on paper. In "There's Nobody Home," I talk about why I think things are falling apart on the home front. Maybe you'll recognize your family in here. What to do, things to expect, some remedies; some hope on *how* we might save it.

We're at a frightening period in America. The decline in family life is slowly sapping the strength of our nation. Long ago at the United Nations (1976), I met a magnificent person, a man named Cheik Guy, from Senegal. His family and Louie and I became close friends. His children called me Aunt Pearl.

On a trip to Senegal for a conference on Ecosoc (Economic and Social) affairs I had a great opportunity to observe Africa. Walking the streets, visiting the hospitals, was quite an experience. I absorbed much wisdom. I even

11

received an award-winning book of poetry from their President Felix Houphouet Boigny (for which he won the Nobel Prize). In it he had inscribed, "I am watching you give love."

I enjoyed seeing families walking together, little ones hanging on to their mother's skirt feeling safe and secure. Whenever you spoke to a little one, his mother gave a small nudge on the shoulder and the little hand shot out to meet yours, with warmth. There in Senegal I was overwhelmed with a nostalgia for *how our families used to be in America.*

On returning to America, sitting with Cheik in the delegate's dining room at the UN, I learned more about family together-ness in Senegal — and in Africa as a whole. Through his eyes I began to recall my own upbringing, and longed, once again, to see it back. I thought something must be done or we will be destroyed as a nation. That feeling has intensified through the years. I realize now that we can grow closer as families if we keep our sights on God and live as a nation under Him.

That encounter with African wisdom was just one of *many* that I would have in years to come. People, places, experiences, that have enlarged my life *so much*. I began to record my recollections — and before I knew it, there

12

were tablets filled with stories. Recollections of things and places, past and present, which have helped make my life worthwhile. I've met many people; been many places; learned many lessons. Laughed, pained, and cried. *I even died (clinically) in 1972.* Why am I alive to write, dear readers, I cannot answer. I choose to believe that God saw fit for me to hang around until I fully start to understand all of His goodness and pass it on to my fellow man.

I believe that, being seventy years old, I'm allowed to reflect on these special moments. And I share "Reflections at Seventy: Pearl's Gems" in a spirit of friendship. This whole book, in fact, is intended as nothing more than an informal exchange between friends. And it comes straight from my heart to you; I ask only for your prayers.

With love from

*Pearl*

# *ONE*

Go for It, Honey
*On to Georgetown*

# The Beginning

Things were going along fine in my career — no job problems, no marriage hang-ups, and thank God, no health problems. Life was fine. Then I got the letter. From Georgetown University in Washington, D.C.

"What now?" I thought. A concert perhaps for the students. Was I wrong! These people were asking if I would accept an "honorary degree in the arts." Would I accept? I wasted no time. *Yes; definitely, yes.* This was brand new to me. I wondered, "Now who stirred up this idea?"

I'd seen Georgetown occasionally in my life; it was in the section we used to call "Foggy Bottom." That big imposing building had stood there almost two hundred years. (The two-hundredth anniversary was October 1, 1988.)

I was now about to reach another milestone. "What had I done to deserve it?" I asked them. "Many things," the answer came back. So I decided to "go for it."

17

All the details were spelled out; soon the day arrived. Pearl was going to enter a school yard. How many years had it been since I'd really been a part of any school? More than that, I thought, "How many years had passed since I sat in a classroom?" The night before my honorary degree was to be presented I looked back *and remembered.*

Strangely enough it was in Washington, D.C. (where we came when I was three years old, from Newport News, Virginia), that I first had attended school. Garnett-Patterson on Tenth and U Streets. My brother Willie (Bill Bailey, the dancer) and sister Eura went to Garnett; Virgie, my oldest sister, did not attend school in Washington at all. Garnett and Patterson were only feet apart from each other. I went to Patterson.

I remember vividly the principal's name and appearance. Mrs. Lewis was a large lady, with gray hair and the most beautiful face I had ever seen. Years later, to be near my sister Virgie, we would come to live next door to Mrs. Lewis on Georgia Avenue. Across the street they were digging a huge excavation site that eventually became Banneker Center — named after the man who was the surveyor for Washington, D.C. What many today do not know is that Mr. Banneker was a Negro.

18

It appeared to this little girl that we moved to many houses while I was growing up. I do not know why; we were not ducking the landlord. Papa always paid the rent on time. He was a preacher, went to church every night. Papa was also a hard carrier (cement worker) by day. Because we moved so often, I went to many schools: Cleveland, John F. Cook, Lucretia Mott, Slater-Langston; I also still remember some principals — Mrs. Cook, Mrs. Wilson, Mrs. Slaughter.

Then came another move, a drastic one. I was eight at the time. Mama and Papa separated. Mama went to Philadelphia. At ten, so did I (in a strange way). Eura followed but Virgie remained in D.C. Mama used to come to Washington from Philadelphia on Sunday excursions; one Sunday she didn't. That day Willie, who was all of fourteen, had left early in the morning on his bicycle for Philadelphia — and Mama. He must have left around 5 A.M., because Papa always arose at 6 A.M. for work or church. No one in the household had any idea of his plans. And to top things off, Willie did not have Mama's address. Virgie had it.

How long it took him, heaven only knows. Philadelphia is at least two hundred miles from Washington — and remember there were no freeways then. Maybe some trucker drove him part of the way. Anyhow, he finally arrived and by a quirk of fate went to a drugstore at Twenty-first and Norris streets. He asked the druggist, a Mr. Schlesinger, "Do you know where a lady lives around here — I think it's Twenty-second Street — named Mrs. Bailey or Mrs. Robinson?" (Mama had remarried.) "She is very pretty with real, I mean real, deep dimples." Great description of Mama; she was all he said. Mr. Schlesinger asked, "Would her first name be Ella?" "Yes," Willie answered. "Well, young man, a lady like you've described lives at 1936 North Twenty-second Street on the third floor. She comes in and does work for me twice a week," Mr. Schlesinger told the excited Willie.

He jumped on his bike, pedaled around the corner, found the house, and rang the third-floor bell. Mama always used to tell us the story so well. She said, "No one in the house was awakened, but me. Only God could have done that because had anyone else answered, Willie may have gone away and been truly lost." She looked out the window and — I can hear her now — in that soft lilting voice, she asked, "Who is it?" Willie heard her "Mama, Mama, it's me." Mama was scared half to death. Willie stayed a week and returned on the excursion train to D.C.

Willie had it all figured out, "The baby

[me] belonged with Mama." Virgie was now married with her own new baby boy, Junior. She lived at 429 Elm Street, we lived with Papa at 15 Q Street, N.W. I remember another time while everyone was asleep — Virgie, I know now, was in on this — when Willie woke me up, a sleepy child of ten. He sneaked me over to Virgie's house where we stayed until 7 P.M., train time to Philadelphia. Eura told me, "When Papa woke up, he seemed to realize at once where Willie and you had gone." She said, "That's the only time I think Papa wept; you were his baby."

Willie returned to D.C. and shortly thereafter, with Papa's approval, returned to Philadelphia with Eura.

I entered the fifth grade at Joseph Singerly, on Twenty-second and Berks, right across the street from our apartment. My behavior at that school, as you might guess, was exceptional; it had better have been, because of how close to home I was. In those days the teachers reigned supreme. They had the school's and your parents' permission to (a) keep you after school, (b) send you home with a note in a *sealed envelope* (you didn't dare change a word), (c) use the pointer or the twelve-inch ruler to give you a tap or two on the knuckles, (d) suspend or expel you. No parent would come forth to save you. Your prayer was, "Lawdy, don't let the folks find out I got a lick from the teacher," because you knew they would double the punishment — and not just on the knuckles. Far worse than any of these things was having to bring your parents to school. That's the day you wished you'd never been born. The memory of it still makes me tremble.

In passing to the eighth grade we all transferred to John F. Reynolds, on Twenty-fifth and Jefferson. That was a heartbreaker. Not only was I in love with Singerly, but I had been close to home and adored my teachers. My favorite was the tallest lady I'd ever seen, Mrs. Faison. She was at least five-eleven or six feet.

Mrs. Faison taught sixth grade; she gave me my first pair ever long stockings. They were white, silk stockings. You should have seen this eleven-year-old child opening that long, thin box, glimpsing those fabulous creations. You ask what had I worn before? What else — socks; didn't we all? They were held up by garters which we had made ourselves, with elastic bought from the 5 & 10.

One special Sunday Mama allowed me to wear them. I headed for the beautiful Catholic church on the corner. I'd never been in there before, plus we were not Catholics. No one

22

will ever know how proud I was of those stockings. Me, a little child, walked proudly into that big church and sat hoping that as I had marched down the aisle everyone had seen "the long, white, silk stockings."

Not being used to the ceremonies, I watched carefully out of the corner of my eye. Everything they did, I did. When the people dipped their fingers in the water, knelt, I did the same. Dip, up, down, down, up. I had no idea what the others were praying for; Pearl just wanted everyone to see those "white stockings."

Arising from one of my "kneeling sessions," I looked down; heavens to Betsy!! There was a huge hole in the knee of my stockings. Who could I blame? Surely the Lord was not punishing this child for being in a church not of her faith. My heart was shattered. This group had lost me as a potential Catholic! The Pentecostal religion instilled in me was still firmly in place. I tried carefully to stitch the hole but the stockings developed run after run. My beautiful stockings were ruined. I did not tell Mrs. Faison. I was too crushed.

William Penn High School, on Fifteenth and Wallace, was next on the agenda. The years passed; I loved school more and more. To go to school, many of us girl students walked down Ridge Avenue to Fifteenth Street, then turned on to Wallace. Of course what helped make the trip pleasant was the boys who walked in that direction going to Central High (an all-boys school). When I passed the Pearl Theater at Twenty-first and Ridge Avenue, sometimes I would see the name "Bill Bailey" on the marquee. I was so proud of my brother; he was a sensational tap dancer. To many minds, in fact, he was surpassed only by Bill "Bojangles" Robinson, the best in the world. Anyway, here I was, the schoolgirl going off to school, so I could someday become "a school teacher."

Now in 1978 I was reliving those years and the walk down Ridge Avenue. It was a strange sort of feeling. I was being given an honorary degree by one of the most prestigious schools in the country, Georgetown University.

On that spring day I was attended by my husband, Louie Bellson, noted drummer; the great Don Redman's wife, Peetney; Blanche Shavers, wife of Charlie Shavers, "Undecided" writer; Ambassadors Ardeshir Zahedi of Iran, Ashraf Ghorbal of Egypt, Abdullah Salah of Jordan, and Yagub Khan of Pakistan (now Foreign Minister). These were my guests. Mrs. Rose Kennedy, Senator Ted Kennedy, and many of their family were there to see one of their young ones graduate.

There's a room at Georgetown in the Healy building (the main building) where the "biggies" congregate before affairs. This particular day there were "academia people" in long, black robes, and square hats with tassels, chatting away so comfortably, while I was shaking. Our little group of show business folks huddled together; the ambassadors were outside. I was *numb*. "Is it going to be like this all the way?" "What do we do next?"

A man came into the room and said, "Okay, it's time to go." They gowned me, gave me my cap, and coached me once more. I thought I looked "spiffy," and my Louie just beamed at his wife. A professor extended his arm and out we marched, leaving my friends to follow. I was being taken into another world. Around the circle, down the graveled walk we marched, smiling, waving at the cameras. The lawn was packed with graduates, anxious parents (glad to be free of some financial burden), and friends.

Folks were applauding, screaming. My stomach felt funny, like big waves were coming in and going out. My knees shook and my heart was beating an unknown tempo. Louie's drum never made a sound like my heart. However, nothing deterred Pearl from her march. Finally we came to a large platform. Seated there were all these black-robed people; I didn't know whether to go up there or grab Louie's hand, run, and head for home. Thank God I continued. My last look back met Louie's smiling face, urging me to carry on.

On the platform was Father Healy, a tall, handsome, imposing man. He has been president of Georgetown since 1976 and is highly respected by all who have ever met him. His eyes fairly twinkle when he talks to you; he comes across as a man of courage and convictions. And Father Freeze, who by the time I enrolled had become the provost, was also on the platform. Father Freeze has a laugh that tinkles like ice in a glass. We became very close friends through the years. There was also "Gentle" Dean Davis — and he is such a gentleman — who sat there basking in the warmth of it all. (These three men were to have a strong impact on me, spurring me on to enroll and acquire that higher education.)

The time to receive my honorary degree had arrived. Father Healy put the hood over my head, fairly beaming yet not outsmiling me. A few shivers ran through me; then slowly my body settled down. I eased into the "thank you"; this was my element. I had a written speech, but quickly discarded it. I began winging it. I felt like I was "home free." The press had a field day.

Then came the unexpected. A surprise

even to me. Without forethought, out of my mouth came these words: "Who knows, folks. I may be coming to this school." There was an uproar from the audience. What had I said? Whatever it was, I did it — the next year. I entered Georgetown University as a freshman.

# The Entrance

As you come under the arch at Thirty-seventh and O Street, N.W., a huge, gray, antique building looms into view. It has the look of an ancient Gothic cathedral. In front of Healy stands a stern statue of John Carroll. I checked him out right away. Walking around him two or three times, I had the feeling he was watching me. Ah! I saw parking spaces. I thought, "Great, this will be ideal, less walking." Little did I know then that my full course load would mean many times walking between those buildings. Nor did I dream they would put up so many new structures, each time eliminating parking spaces. I ended up walking my buns off. In snow, rain, and heat.

There is a cemetery and a chapel located in back of Healy. I stood there many times when I needed quiet moments. It worked. To the left of Healy is White Gravenor where I spent most of my hours. Dean Davis, the dean of Arts and Sciences, had his offices there; that became my haven when I needed those academic and soul-searching answers. Dean Davis is soft-spoken and gentle. I'll never forget him advising me after I'd been in school for a while; he must have sensed an inner turmoil. "Pearl," he said (in that pacifying voice), "marriage is an education too. You could spend more time with Louie and do a bit more of your life's work." How right he was. After all, tuition and expenses get heavy. "Take off a semester," he said. I took his advice — but I was back for more the next semester.

White Gravenor has a large stone porch with a wide stone railing. That's where we students gathered, sat, and discussed our pains and pleasures. We'd chat, pray, sack out our papers, discuss the professors, or sip coffee before entering the building. Some would take their coffee and a snack inside. I'd always think back to when I was in school and this was never allowed. Oh well, maybe I hadn't gotten collegiate enough yet.

Large windows overlooked the porch. Those windows gave the perfect view whenever Dean Davis wanted to observe us. His assistants, Barbara and Gwendolyn, sat out front and in a smaller room to their left was Assistant Dean Carey. The room was small; she is small — but is she mighty! Not only did this lady fill that office, she filled her classroom

29

with an inner strength few knew was in that small body.

Directly across from Gravenor was Lauinger. The library was in that building — more about that later. Then there was Old North and Old South, buildings on Thirty-sixth Street. Georgetown is spread out — especially to this girl who was then pushing sixty. To her, it was a complex and exciting world.

To digress a bit: After receiving the honorary degree and before entering Georgetown University I went to Pierce Community College in California. Louie and I were sitting at the kitchen table one day (I was reading as always) and I saw an ad that stated you can "come to Pierce and take one or two courses, or enroll full time." "Louie," I said, "I'm going up there tomorrow and sign up for a couple of courses so that I can get the feel of going to college." I did. I signed up for French, my favorite language (after English of course). Geography, which I thought I could really sink my teeth into, was next. But it wasn't the geography I had expected. It was about clouds. Some of the homework was making graphs. I had detested making graphs when I was twelve. Cumulus clouds. Take 'em or leave 'em. By the end of the term I had an "A" in French. And that summer I had my teacher come over to do a tutorial, for which I enough with the Greek philosophers. No! In my senior year, I dared to take on the Arabic philosophers. "A real cinch," thought I, since I'd been many times to the Arabic world. Aha! But I found that our stern, no-nonsense, cute-as-a-button lady professor really had the knowledge of those Arabic masters to lay on us. Many times I longed instead to go back to dear Socrates and his friends.

To help me remember the philosophers Tūsî, Rāzî, Ibn Khaldūn, and Maskawa, I had to devise another clue. This time it was "TRIM" (how one would like to look after the SPA). Oh, I had all kinds of things working to achieve my goal. It's easy, especially after hanging out with the students. Those young ones love to teach *you* the "tricks of the trade." It's the one chance they get to tell you something.

Professor Druart, who taught the course, and I developed a warm spirit between us. Little did she know many times I would linger in class until she had gathered her material just so I could strike up a conversation with her. I liked her and knew she had so much to give us. I knew that I wanted to learn even more from this dear lady. One day, she told us how she made this "chocolate mousse." I asked her to bring some in some time. She did. I thought that was pretty special. But my

received another "A." The clouds final, however, never came off. The flu came on . . . I think. Shame on me. However, I did well enough in class that I can always go back and take a final. And I will. The course helped me see and understand more clouds.

My mind might have been foggy then, but the fog was surely lifted at GU. Now I was ready. Bring on the big stuff.

As a freshman I was just one of the kids — and there were hundreds of us. The isolation didn't last long. We were all steered into the gym to have our photos taken for our I.D. cards. Funny, because I had company I.D. and Social Security I.D. cards that were older than most of these children. The press were there en masse to see if this was some big publicity stunt. Stunt! *I don't do stunts.* (Six years later they were back at Georgetown to see the end of that little "caper": Pearl finishing in style. There was no way to put measures on "my scale of joy.")

We were all nervous enough the first day. Students became more excited by the presence of a celebrity. They got over that soon — and went on to spend their parents' tuition money. This was no lark for me. It was all business and a yard wide. The world of show business and other things aside, I had walked under that "arch" with a strong determination to be a "student" all the way. Louie, at my side, said, "Honey, I'm proud of you." That was all I needed. January 18, 1979, was my day.

The first subjects I selected were philosophy, English, French art (of which I was no connoisseur), and a subject everyone at GU must take once, religion. I thought, with Papa having been a reverend, that would be a breeze. It was — but a very strong breeze. No light stuff. I was going for the *goal*. The religion course involved the Bible, prophets, religious writers, different versions of what I'd learned with Papa. I thought, "How holy do I want to get here?"

Philosophy always fascinated me, studying and reading about great thinkers. Socrates was and is my favorite. How was I to know then that a woman, Diotima, taught him of love. By the time I left Professor Desan's class, I learned to love and respect others.

Professor Desan is a rare man. Our class was huge; everyone obviously had heard so much about him they wanted to be a part of his life. He is a small man, keen-eyed, and quick-witted. One couldn't stop long enough to concentrate on his physical appearance because he kept growing taller as he talked to you. About the middle of the term he dubbed me the "Pascalian Woman," woman of faith.

*That* I am; I kept the faith that I could make it through Georgetown University.

My mind and eyes were really enlarged when Desan took us into Plato's world. I entered "the Cave." But the more Desan said about it the worse I got. Nothing was wrong with Plato, Desan, or "the Cave." It was Pearl. Now, older, I'm back into Plato's *Republic*. Either Plato is now explaining it better or I'm understanding him better. "The Cave," to me is life; lived.

One night Professor Desan and his wife, Betty, decided to accompany me on one of my rare nights out. Louie's group was playing at Blues Alley, and we took off. Imagine this great philosopher and the "Jazz Artist." Professor Desan listened intently, never taking his eyes off Louie, fascinated by the drums. To this day he says, "Never did I see anything like what Louie did on those drums." What amazed him — from a philosophical point of view — was the relationship of the man to the instrument. I could have told him he had gazed upon what we in our industry call all musicians, "a rare breed of men."

When I think of philosophy, I always remember the "Big Three": Socrates, Plato, and Aristotle. I'd remember their names with "SPA" (where fat people go to get thin).

Anyway, you would think that I had had

real dessert from her was a nice, hard-earned passing mark, plus her respect and love.

A gentle giant, Professor Rocco Porreco, taught me ethics. His kindly face belies the grade you'll receive if you don't study. His way of addressing the class is so smooth and quiet, one thinks, "I'm not going to be interested in this." But I was. He guided us through the term. You could relax in his class, but not too much — or you'd perhaps lose an "A."

# Moving On

Between the second and fourth semesters I got well seasoned — in fact roasted and well done. English classes are an experience you *must* have, if only to contemplate, "Did I ever know anything about the use of the English language?" Back in grade school English was my pet subject. I loved poetry and writing compositions. In penmanship I got an "A+" — we learned the "Palmer Method." I remember the teacher reminding us, "top on six," "bottom on seven," "lip on eight," "stem on nine." "Hold the pencil lightly, rest on three fingers," etc. I did that. She used to walk up and down the aisle, peering over our shoulders, stopping to correct us. As soon as she went back, I'd grab that pencil tightly, drop my wrist, and go to town writing comfortably. But that training has paid off. I often wonder, why can't most doctors and dentists write? We'd cure ourselves.

All this grade school teaching prepared me for Professor Knoll's class. Knoll is a very intense man who studies each person carefully; he is very precise and to the point. No halfway thoughts in his class: you had to deliver back the exact message you received from your readings. It was assumed, of course, that all the basics of English had long ago been mastered.

I had picked the heavy stuff, wanting to go beyond myself, though many times I wished I hadn't. I'm glad I persevered. I got a "B" in the course. A "B" with Professor Knoll made you think heaven was close. Not that a higher mark wasn't attainable — it was, but for those more astute than Pearl was in that class. English class was a marvelous challenge; a chance to learn from a great scholar, a master of his trade. GU is full of masters — and mistresses, too!

There was one very young, quiet lady, whom I will always remember. She taught Greek and loved it as though it were her native land. Her name was Professor Victoria Pedrick. Dean Davis had suggested, because of a time-scheduling problem, that I take a tutorial; perhaps try a course about the Greek wars. That fascinated me, for once again here was a subject that I liked back in high school more than forty years earlier. However, Pearl didn't realize that time can make even a "Greek war" slip away.

There was a small office under the Lauinger building. I walked in one day and there sat this young girl. Initially I was going to wait in the hall since she was there first. "Come in," she said, "I'm waiting for you." *She* was waiting for *me*. "Good gracious," I thought, "this must be the teacher." By the time she finished filling my head, *I knew*, definitely, she was the teacher. During my junior semester I took on Greek Love Poems. I became a shy, blushing girl (in her sixties). The students might have thought I was *real hip,* but I was constantly being amazed at "those Greeks," and those students.

Pedrick was all of twenty-six or twenty-seven years of age, although being small she looked ten. When I finished Love Poems *I* was ten. I shall never forget the day we were to bring in some clippings suggesting the word "erotic." Oh, boy! Did those young ones find photos; probably one of their happiest assignments, and not X-rated.

We sat in a circle with our photos, passing them around so we could discuss them individually. As the explanations progressed, my blood pressure rose, but since it's usually very low, I survived. We did get quite a few laughs from the theories. I might have been wiser and older, but the young were more daring. After the recovery from Greek love, I thought,

"Pearl, these kinds of classes could *make* you young again, or make you *wish* you were young again." All the while we went into our great theories of what these people meant to express in those "erotic" photos, our dear teacher (bless her heart) was like a stone angel, watching us all squirm. Inwardly I felt she wanted to burst with laughter at our sometimes silly antics. Mercy, was I unprepared for the Greeks. Lord, I am glad that I met that dear young lady to whom I owe so much, in so many ways. Poetry and love merged in that class.

As I have said, it is mandatory to take a religion course at Georgetown. I wound up pursuing this study. At first my major was going to be French, but I switched to theology. When people ask me, "Pearl, why did you switch?" I tell them, "Because it's easier to know the Lord than it is to know French!"

My first choice was Rabbi White's class, Hebrew Religious Thought. I thought, how hard could it be? My papa was a reverend, the Bible was read at breakfast and dinner, we said grace at meals, and we went to church. So this would be a cinch, I thought.

Let me say here that the young are not always the kindest, nor the most unbiased. My first time in the class (which was packed) was a lesson in the cruelty some young students can face in college, and not be able to deal with. Some started to snicker, and I knew exactly why. I took the last seat, and that row kept up their snickering. What a pity that some people would laugh or resent one walking in on another's belief in God. It was handled well, believe me. In soft yet deep tones came the words "We'll have none of this." And it stopped, *forever*.

The rabbi had been speaking of Abraham and his discussions with God: Abraham asks God if He will also destroy the righteous with the wicked. I was sure in my mind that the rabbi used the word "argue" or "argument" with God. That did it. Let me get out of this room or "Papa will come back from the grave and kill me." The idea of someone arguing, or for that matter even discussing, heavy issues with God blew my mind. I stared at this new preacher (the rabbi-teacher) and listened some more. Yes, he had referred to an argument. Raising my hand, I asked, "Do you mean, sir, that Abraham really argued with God?" My feathers were sort of ruffled, but more in puzzlement than anger. "Rabbi," I asked again, "are you meaning that there was a *discussion* between God and Abraham?" "Yes, Pearl." The word "discussion" sat well with me. I thought everyone now and then needs to have a conversation with God. Couldn't hurt.

I never imagined what the study of biblical things would involve. Each religion has its own theories and I learned more in that class than I did growing up in Papa's church. Things that I had never understood started to become clear. The rabbi took things apart and put them back together so that there was no mistaking the message. Regardless of the personal religion of anyone in that class, each of us walked away feeling blessed with much knowledge of God's plan. Religion and philosophy started to interrelate for me.

I learned still more when, through Georgetown's Overseas Studies Plan, I was able to be tutored by Chaim Herzog and Jonathan Magonet (now principal), at Leo Baeck in London, while working there. My sponsor was Lord Jamison, the oldest living Zionist, and certainly one of — if not the — oldest member of Parliament. It felt strange going into a school where young men were studying to be rabbis. I met Dr. Albert H. Friedlander, the president of Leo Baeck, and formed other friendships that are still lasting. Rabbi White sat with me so many hours in tutorial classes, filling my soul.

"What path," I thought, "should I take next to enlighten my soul?" Where was I to go after all these classes? To "The Brains." Dr. Michael Berenbaum, whom I now consider a son, shook the foundation of mental learning for me as Rabbi White had shaken my religious and spiritual base. The wisdom I gained from Berenbaum's class is priceless. He is young, aggressive, tough, wise as some sages of yore, and as brilliant as a diamond. When class ended, you felt *filled*, *drained*, and *filled* again. He would surge into the classroom as if he'd just arrived by Amtrak, put down his bundle of papers, and get started. We didn't open copy books right away with him; he preferred you to listen, question him, discuss. Then we could make notes according to what we felt would be important in a paper or test later on.

Studying the great Martin Buber continued from Rabbi White's class into Berenbaum's. Buber has had a large effect on my life. We went through the pains of the Holocaust, so eloquently expressed in all of Eli Wiesel's books that we read. At the "Soviet Jewry" affair on December 6, 1987, in Washington (two days before the visit of Gorbachev), I sat beside the honored man, Eli Wiesel, thanking him for helping us to understand more about the miseries of his people, of humanity as a whole.

Sometimes questions were asked which might have turned off some teachers, or thrown them a curve. I'll never forget one fellow who asked a question (strongly, since he was a Negro speaking of the Negro race) which stopped Berenbaum for a moment. The fellow, who was about thirty, I'd say, referred to the fact that our race was in the same plight as the Jewish people in the Holocaust. He said, in part, "You have to understand that as the Jewish people were mistreated so were our people. What about those made slaves, killed, dragged from their homes and families? It's the same, or at least isn't one thing as bad as another?"

Berenbaum paused, then spoke. "Yes, in a sense it is the same, yet there is a difference. The Negro people were treated in a manner such as the world hopes will never happen again. Their masters saw a value in these people, that they were able to work, produce, and be used to further themselves. As such, even though slaves, they were a 'commercial commodity.' The Jew was seen as one to eliminate: a useless person, to be erased entirely; a 'piece of merchandise,' a piece of 'nothing.' " The professor then expressed everyone's feelings that such horrors should never recur. Berenbaum was never off guard, always quick to answer our most twisted questions.

These lessons proved invaluable to me on future travels in the Middle East. They helped me to expand my knowledge about

43

this exciting part of the world. The words of the *Koran* now flow like music. When I read them I feel poetic waves go in and out of my heart. I'm always trying to learn more, to open doors to better understanding of the Arabic people's thinking, living, and beliefs.

Studying with Professor Ibrahim Raouf of Egypt gave me much of this knowledge so that I could see these lands physically and spiritually. Jordan (Petra and Jerash), Egypt (Cairo, Alexandria), Kuwait, Abu Dhabi (United Arab Emirates), Bahrain, Oman, Lebanon, Dubai (United Arab Emirates). I ate at Raouf's home, drank the Arabic coffee he brewed, practiced Arabic writing on a little blackboard he bought just for our lessons, and stretched my mind and heart. Thank God.

Between other subjects I sandwiched in Father James Redington's class, Hindu Path of Love. And listened to Father Robert Lawton give the Catholic perspective of truth. I didn't want to skip anything! I was in school and wanted to grab all that I missed years ago.

I remember one day when Father Redington was not there when we assembled for our Hindu class. As folks will do, after a delay of five minutes or more, the students started to squirm. A few of the restless decided to leave. Some griped that they paid for that class, so "Where was he?" The patient waited. I suggested, "Why don't we do the class ourselves? One of us start; he'll be here." Then some protests. "Have we given any thought that this man could be ill?" I asked. "We'll be the losers if we go." A couple of smart alecks said, "I'm due this time." "So sit," I said, "and enjoy what you're paying for." A couple left, but the rest stayed.

I was asked to start the discussion. The vision of being a future Georgetown professor loomed in my head (*I was into it now*), when oops! in walked Father Redington, smiling. He always smiles. Recently he wrote me a letter about those days. I couldn't believe that he would even remember this student, although, often on campus, we met and chatted. I don't think I know a more peaceful man.

By now, French — which was my first major — had become my minor. However, I always had great love for my teacher, Madame Soudée; she's my Aries sister now. Darling Thérèse, my first French teacher, was accidentally electrocuted at her home in France, while on vacation. I recall many hours of happiness with her learning and sipping *cappuccino* (she exposed me, of course, to the French label).

Madeline Soudée and I had three sessions together. She's a taut, sharp, swift-talking, and conscientious woman. As with all the

French, she wants her students to be precise in the work assigned. They regard her highly, as she takes time to make sure you get everything correct. There is no time for fooling around in her class. She seldom laughs much, but one can always see a twinkle in her eyes when we struggle with her language. I'm sure she enjoyed the "Southern" flavor I gave to French. Every moment in her class was like a trip to Paris.

Recently, I was asked by the USO to go to Paris for a gala benefit, to be held in the garden of the American embassy. Having never played Paris, though I'd traveled there, and relishing the opportunity to help an organization I'd been associated with for years, we all went (the Quartet and I). Ambassador Rogers of Tennessee (a good ole Southern boy — we mentioned grits, cornbread, and black-eyed peas *even* in Paris) and his charming wife had a turnout that included every high dignitary in Paris. The evening was a smashing success, raising $650,000 for our boys and girls in the services. At another USO gala in Washington, D.C., on December 8, 1988, $1 million was raised so groups of all kinds could let the boys know the folks at home cared. (When it comes to helping the USO, though, *no one* can or will forget the great one, Bob Hope.)

When I wondered what I could do to put

"the icing on the cake" at the Paris concert, I immediately thought of Madame Soudée. I got in touch and asked her what song was sure to touch the heart of every Frenchman. She wrote me, naming three but recommending "l'Hymne à l'Amour" as the favorite. She put down on paper her idea of the American translation (although the French words were already there). Soudée was probably thinking, "Please, oh, please dear sister Pearl, don't go to Paris and foul up the language and then proudly announce, 'My French teacher taught me.'" They would have given her and me the lash. As soon as the pianist played the first eight bars I said, "I know that song, it's very popular here; that's Edith Piaf, the great love of France." Need I tell you as the *pièce de résistance*, that night, with sheet music in hand, (no mistakes for me in front of all those Frenchmen) I sang a bit in French — then in English:

## L'HYMNE À L'AMOUR

If the sun should tumble from the sky;
If the sea should suddenly run dry,
If you love me only love me,
Let it happen, I don't care.

They chewed on it — and ate it up. I was

"total French," if only for a short time.

An encyclopedia is the only way I can describe Professor Foley, my history teacher. Tall, lanky, direct, stern, fierce (in a loving way), he spouted out a few choice words every now and then. He was a handsome man, like the "salted sailor of the academic world." The religiousness within him made him literally glow. Foley thought he hid it within his other aforesaid qualities; he didn't, at least not for this old owl. Constantly during the lessons he would tell a story of his mother, father, wife, or children, pause, then move on. It was as if he was touched by a spell to talk about them. You could sense the love in his voice. Foley was the most forceful teacher I had. History was his passion, and in his class it became yours.

I didn't think I'd make it out of class alive. Dreams of "failure" were written boldly on my brain; not because of lack of effort, but because by now (the first half of senior year) I was older and getting tired. How you treated the little blue test books was a reflection of how he taught you. After the final exam (I was terrible on the midterm), he called me up to his office. He had spoken to different individuals in class, but this was a call to his office. "Lawdy," I thought, *"this has to be the end of me.*" My arthritic, dancing knees were shaking. Here was I, inches away from graduating and this man told me, "Come to the office." I felt, "Mercy, have mercy, this is it; failure."

There he sat; by now he looked eighteen feet tall. Again the conversation about his family, his parents. Then he said, "Pearl, when you came into class I was sort of thrown off — this woman of experience and fame, here in my class." "*You* were thrown off, Professor?" I almost screamed at him, "I have been sitting a whole semester, scared to death of you . . . The children," I hesitantly told him, "had *warned* me what to expect, and when you went into your first act, fear struck and *never* left me."

Reaching casually into his desk drawer he withdrew — lawdy! *The blue book.* This was it. All that buildup, now came the "Georgetown Slam Dunk." Well, I had passed with a high "C." And I gazed up and thanked my Maker. I know for sure that however much our teachers loved us, there was *no* favoritism. We smiled at each other and he said, "Pearl, send my mother and dad a photo, please." Two grown-ups with a deep respect — teacher and pupil.

The last time I saw Professor Foley was in the library on a very warm day. As I pored over my books, a voice broke into my thoughts,

"Pearl, I see you're still at it." It was Professor Foley. "I'm going on a sabbatical," he said. "Oh, Professor, I was going to take History II with you in my last half here." He laughed, "You want me again?" Yes, dear Professor, I certainly did, dear teacher; you were *all* teacher, and a yard wide.

Professor Foley did not come back to Georgetown. There is a plaque on campus, at the foot of a tree, for Professor Michael Foley. Georgetown and those students whom he taught will never forget him. How could we forget, he left us so much. He once told me his mother said, "Mike, don't be too tough on Pearl, she's in there trying." I felt like crying.

I received a nice note from his mother in July 1983. She had written, in part:

Pearl, we admire you for your desire and perseverance in seeking a higher education. That is something that can never be taken away from you and the day you receive your degree we will try to get to Georgetown. We are pleased to know you will be taking another course from Mike. You'll be in good hands.

My reply was short:

I never had another class with your

dear son, Mrs. Foley. He left us all — too soon.

Love and thank you,<br>PEARL

History II was a must for me in order to graduate. The class was conducted by a most thorough feminine historian, Assistant Dean Claire Carey. She would stand on an elevated platform, then get off, then get back on. She was always checking things on her podium. Michelle (my play-niece, with brains *and* beauty) and Cathy (flutist with the band for athletics) kept me sane. How I respect these young ladies; one has gone to *law* school and the other to *medical* school.

Michelle lived across the street from me and so became my riding companion to school; she was never absent or late. Dean Carey was for-ever in our conversation. (Michelle had taken Carey's class before.) Sometimes I would call her in the middle of the night, "What was she saying today?" She threw me off by all her movements; but it was fascinating to watch her teach. "She's not tough," Michelle said. "Hah! Hah!" laughed Pearl. "Dig her," Michelle said. "I do dig her, little niece, but I can't keep up with her."

Gradually I did fall in to that class; and because of that dear, dancing lady I was

51

recently asked to return to Georgetown to lecture about life in "the world outside of academia." Dean Carey must have thought, "Pearl too, has a *history*."

What I most enjoyed about studying art were the visits to museums. I could walk around in the quiet and lose myself. It is even more exhilarating when you know something of what you're viewing, and the human being who created it. My professor, Cara Ferguson, took me deep into the world of beauty. Thanks to her great knowledge, I discovered the work of genius in the beauty of ancient places in Italy, Germany, France, Egypt, Turkey, and Greece. But the best treasure is the friendship I have today with Cara Ferguson.

# The Pangs That Pay Off

*Lectures*

It starts with taking notes until your arthritic fingers almost drop off. Take heart, would-be student of any age, they'll be functional. This book was written and rewritten in *long hand*. Instead of walking through the Yellow Pages, your fingers will crawl through those classes. Press on, my dears; be determined. "No one *will* or *can* outtalk my fingers," you say? You're lying. *They can, and they do.*

In my first semester there were composition books piled so high I could have reached heaven. The opening days, I sat high and tall, ready with "Palmer Method" fingers, alert ears cocked to catch every word. Forget it. By the end of the week, my back was in a half-upright position, ankles crossed, catching and writing every *tenth* word or so, if lucky. I had decided my fingers, and my professors' mouths, did not coincide.

What puzzled me were the students who were so laid back, jotting down things effortlessly, as if this was all happening in *slow motion*. Were they so smart that they didn't have to listen? No; definitely not. They were using the "shorts." Pearl was using the "longs." Let me hip you about the "shorts." The children (oops! I must say young adults) taught me. For example, use a "w" for *with;* "w/o" for *without;* "a/k/a" for *also known as,* "dba" for *doing business as,* "re:" for *regarding,* "fpo" for *for purpose of,* "b/o," for *because of,* and so on. They had tons of them. Their notebooks were filled with these shorts, and many more which they created for themselves as they went along. All the time I had been spelling out every darn thing at racetrack speed.

Once the shorts were conquered, I felt better. I didn't need as much "Ben-Gay" as before; copying was easier. The bad part of this was that the darn kids had turned me on to a method of relaxation that, at my age and stage, would make me sleepy. Still, I wanted to be "the coed." I figured this school business could be a blast. I was always curious about what would come next.

*Tests: Terror Time*

It begins with the misery of "midterms." This is the first half of your possibly going *berserk*. These tests show whether *you are sure of* what you *thought* you were sure of. It's a paradox. It can be a tragedy to overstudy for a test. You will cram your skull until it almost pops, or until you awaken to the fact that all that *enters* does not *stay*. It leaves by some "unseen door." It does not leave by your ears, because they are too filled with the lectures; nor by your eyes, which are filled with the readings, nor by your mouth, which has asked already a thousand questions. *It just disappears.* Where? I've looked up in a daze at ceilings, seeking answers, both at home and at school. Day and night my search went on for that lost knowledge. What I had *copied* and *studied* seemed to have disappeared. Charlie, my cocker spaniel, often opened his large eyes from a beautiful sleep and I'd ask him, "Where did it go?" He went back to sleep. The dog was smarter than I.

Dear ones, I got into bed early the night before a test. I believe in "brain rest" — for students of any age. Sleep would come and go; it was hopeless. My mind was a jumble of mismatched facts. "Dear Lord, make the nights longer; the school disappear; make this all a dream; or a play I am performing. It's not true, is it, Lord?" *"Yes, Pearl, it's true, you're in school, so get your act together, lady."*

I'd always have to get up and go to the bathroom just as an answer I'd been searching for popped into my head. I'd start to doze in the bathroom. A hour later: *"Come out, Pearl."* That voice again. "There are no answers in there." So I would make one last appeal to my Maker. "How about my calling a fellow student?" *"Why? They're probably more scared than you."* Squeezing my eyes to conjure up a vision, I'd fall asleep.

Next day, on the way to school alone (this was before I met Michelle), I would still be trying to sort it out. Why was this happening to me? Show business was easy compared to this. I blamed the traffic, talked to myself in the car (folks looked across at me strangely, then drove off in high gear, perhaps thinking, "She's either mad as a hatter, or reached that age where things go like a 'bump in the night.'"). I even went into the local butcher shop, "Neams," to see my Lebanese friends and order my groceries with no money. They just said, "See you later, Pearl." I think they loved me and knew my agony.

Sitting in the car, watching students go by, I could tell who had tests that day. Not the happy ones. Their turn hadn't come. I started getting temptations: "Glue the answers to your shoes, eyeballs, hands, in your bosom."

56

All good, but useless ideas. Those professors had eyes behind their backs. What would be the use, anyhow, when we didn't know the questions? I was lost, but went into class with hope in my heart. I would try to do my best. And I did. God always heard my prayers.

Before I knew it, though, came the "finals." Lawdy, not again so soon. This test is *two to four* questions requiring an essay response that is fully detailed. The teacher places a time upon the blackboard (usually an hour or ninety minutes) and you're *off*. What a mistake should you take fifteen minutes to *decide* your subject (there was usually a choice of questions), *ten minutes* to bite the pen or pencil, fifteen *more* to read over your first essay, then erase because you think it's wrong. Every time the teacher rises from her/his desk your stomach does a queer flip-flop because you know it's another "countdown" on the board. It's a frantic race until you realize, "I'm *home free*." That's the moment the professor writes a large *5 minutes* on the board. Time to pray again before closing the book!

The book, by the way, is the "little blue book." There must be thousands of them, I think. It's really odd, this tiny book scares the hell out of you. Upon entering the classroom for your test, you pick up one or maybe two from the teacher's desk. The professors are so kind, offering "as many as you wish, should you need them." Need them? More? Gracious me, I didn't want *the one* I had. What in the world would I put in it? If at midterms *I thought my brain was dying,* by finals it was stone-cold *dead.*

For one end-term, I had spent weeks of cramming. That meant more boiled dinners for Louie, unopened mail, no ball game looking or listening. Life stopped. Without fail, the things that I had pinned down (and that I gloated about knowing), were the things the teacher *did not ask.* "Unfair," I screamed inside, "it is unfair. The professors changed it, I know they did." Not so; I found it was all in the wording of the questions. A simple thing such as, "How did Socrates die?" became "What possibly could Socrates have drunk which brought on his demise?" At least it sounded like that to me. Clear as a bell, I knew it was "the hemlock"; instead of answering that, my confused self and I wanted to elaborate on whether he *willingly drank it* or it *was poured down his throat.* You people who know me have no idea what Pearl lived *inside* during her school years. Now it's a laugh; then it was pain and joy mixed. But I don't regret a bit. I went for it, honey, because I wanted it. Sometimes I'd think, "Shouldn't I be somewhere, on some date, singing and dancing?" No sir. I belonged here, thinking.

Undergoing the trauma of tests made me grow and appreciate the pain of the younger students. For those who make it, let's give a "hip, hip hooray," and then some. Remember, my dear readers, in school we all had that contagious disease called Get An "A." The young who failed would send a letter home: "Dear Mom and Dad, Give me another chance."

I shared the same anxieties as the youngsters. But I still encourage people I meet — especially older ones — to *press on.* Tuition costs can run high, but most of us throughout our lives have wasted money on things a lot less important than education.

After one of my trying times my good friend Howard Cosell (who's also a lawyer and author, by the way) said in a crowded Yankee clubhouse room, "Pearl, you've done something rare. You've transcended your profession." Not quite understanding his words I asked him to clarify that. He said, "I mean you've gone on and above your show business career, which brought you success, and did more." It was the tests, dear Howard, my insides said, "It was the '*tests.*'" Also, an anonymous fan wrote, "Pearl, you've become a rare individual, all of America saw that and you made that remarkable difference. I rejoice in your accomplishment." It's something when you read those words on paper.

... Speaking of "paper," that evokes another pang.

*Creating a Masterpiece*

"Lightning Time" strikes at least two or three times in a semester. Term papers count heavily in your grade. Show me all the intellectuals, and I make a bet there will be few who will say, "I was sensational at papers." Most of the bright ones grimace. Those who don't are obviously leaning toward "genius." Mind you, a paper is quite different from a test. It takes *will power* personified. This is where your creative self springs forth. The papers put you on another plane. I learned the hard way how to get the big "A": (a) lose sleep, (b) do research, (c) use tablet after tablet of paper, (d) rewrite until your tongue hangs out.

Sometimes, I felt a clash between my formal and informal training. Daring to exercise too much freedom of mind, failing to do research, can be your downfall. Get ready to burn the midnight oil — and candles. This will be no ordinary feat you're attempting.

Rabbi Abramowitz, a good, stern, toe-the-mark teacher, wrote on my first paper, "Pearl, I loved your thinking, emotion, handwriting" (Boy was I beaming!). Then the blow. "However, Pearl, you need to clarify exactly what the person in the book is really saying — not what you think he's saying." My feathers fell. I was a "downed bird."

The first time a person of my age group reads something like this, it's a bitter pill. It goes into the pit of the stomach with the taste of gall because we have so long grown out of being reprimanded. Ride it through, honey; you're having fun growing up twice. Here was I, an older-than-everybody-including-the-rabbi student being scolded. Well — corrected, anyway. I felt ten years old. This struggling student recovered quickly, though, because I respected the rabbi. Also I am in a business where you *must* recover quickly or life will run right over you while you're lying on the ground screaming and kicking. In show business, if you don't get applause for one song, you move on to the next. Keep moving so the thrown eggs (silent or loud) won't hit you. To this very day my routine flows; one number, many times, rides over the next. *Life is a flow.* Anyway, thanks to student friends, I learned how to organize a paper and improvement set in. On to a passing grade I went.

Papa and Mama taught us to "Swallow hard

and try again." A loving "B" was my reward in Rabbi Abramowitz's class. He met my husband at Kennedy Center after one of our concerts and said, "She got a 'B,' but she's an 'A' thinker." Again, those cotton-picking papers; yet later they helped me so much in trying to write books. Five. So, as the saying goes, we take the bitter with the sweet. We learn: time takes care of all. And while I couldn't do without formal education, the informal had often given me the fortitude to carry on.

What we older ones learn on the bricks many times far surpasses anything of the young. I would advise any older person to return to school and experience what is going on now in the field of education. *Formal training* can bring you a sense of order and discipline in many ways different from our workplaces. My life became a seesaw. "The *studied* life versus the *lived* life." Both require patience, learning, and loving.

Theatrical work demands much. We act and react simultaneously. We must feel the emotions of the audience. "What do they want (more? or less?)? Are they listening or asleep? Have I touched them?" Sounds easy. It's not! It comes with experience and time. Once learned, though, it is a jewel in a perfect setting, and it will work for you in any profession. As Miss Ethel Waters taught me, *"It's* ever I went on a job, at least two tote bags of books and paper came along. People have asked me how I got it done. On trains, in the car, in hotel rooms and motel rooms, and, if warm enough, sitting on the grass under a pleasant shade tree. If I missed any exams (papers were not), they were made up. In my years at Georgetown I had to make up only three. School was my love; there was no way I would mistreat it.

I remember my first winter on campus. Marching into class the first cold day of my first semester, I asked, "Where can I hang my coat?" The class broke up. "Hang what coat?" "Well," I said, "when I went to school we had a cloakroom." They couldn't relate to that. "Two places are available, Pearl," one said smiling, "the back of the chair, or the floor." Initially I resisted — "My nice coat, on the *floor?*" Then I folded it neatly and laid it on top of my book bag — on the floor. From that day on, I wore sneakers, pants, and sweaters (and actually felt better). Only on bitter cold, snowy, or rainy days did I wear my coat again; then, like everyone else, I hung it on the floor.

Finally — and you should know this should you decide to enroll at Georgetown — there are the *stone steps.* They will live forever, not

*keeping your fingers on the pulse of the audience.*" For anyone returning to classes there are adjustments to many changes; but you will find it a terrific challenge and the results lasting. To my junior *and* senior readers, I say: "Go for it, honey." Follow through. You'll find that pot at the end of the rainbow. That's why I stayed in Georgetown. We older ones, honey, have guts and stamina.

## Things Between
## (Advantages and Disadvantages)

Examinations and papers come and go but classes go on forever. For me, trying school again after more than forty years out was worse than working out for the Olympics. It was especially hard when I'd have to go off on an engagement. I would arrive back in D.C. very tired. From my years of work and travel, rising at seven in the morning had gotten to be a ritual. Still, I found at least a few things about going to school that were irritating. For instance: Why were the buildings at Georgetown always over the hill, far away? I found that the walk from one building to another could be long or short, depending on: (1) How many books you were carrying. (I carried a ton until I got wise and brought only the ones needed. In the beginning I must have thought it made you look studious to carry a lot.) (2) How bad your feet hurt (for me, tennis shoes, boots, flats — they all hurt). (3) If you had arthritis or a backache. (4) How much sleep you had the night before (not enough, usual__ in my case). (5) How absorbed you were in t__ recurring thought, "What the hell am I doir__ here?"

"Treatment" was available in some cases__ (1) soak the feet nightly; (2) use the hydroco__ lator pack under the back and elsewhere; (3__ stop thinking *where* am I or *why* am I in school? Think positive. You are not alone. *The young ache, too.*

For a student like Pearl, the inevitable housework creeps in — and family life still goes on. In my case (my real home being in Arizona) I lived in a hotel suite off campus complete with kitchen. Though a lot was taken care of for me, I still had things to do. And your marriage has to be watched *carefully*. "Conversation" is nonexistent — except for occasional grunting and mumbling. Though lack of communication can be a real problem, in our household things went efficiently. E.B., my road manager, did his theatrical business tasks; Dodi, my secretary, who lives on the West Coast, was handling the office; and of course Louie kept traveling.

There were tons of mail every week, which I had to sort, answer, and return to Dodi for typing and mailing. It was a busy, almost im__ possible routine; however, we did it. When

only in my thoughts, but in my *bones*. It seemed no matter what class I was going to or coming from, they loomed in front of me. *The Stone Steps. The Monsters.* With knees aching and heavy book bags in tow, I made the first landing. I would stop to rest at a concrete bench there. It must have been put there for tired students like me. I tried to resist sitting because I would never have gotten up again. So it was "plod onward and upward." Having had a chest condition, it was not safe for me to climb those stairs. Many times I felt a tremendous pull inside, and my breathing was labored. I was frightened, though I never told Louie. I'm sure he would have insisted I stop.

By the time I reached my junior year, some of the kids who used to laugh at me trudging up those stairs (they must have thought I was acting) began to stop; and before I realized it, they had taken the load out of my hands, without a word, and brought the bags to the top of the stairs. Bless their hearts, then and now. Dear ones, know that if Pearl had possessed some "holy water" I would have sprinkled you until you were wet with its goodness.

"Did you have to climb those stairs?" people ask me. "Yes." It was that or climb a steep incline up to the front gate. Besides, they were the quickest way to the *library*, where all a stu-

67

dent's troubles were either made or solved. There, too, peace was found, and friends met for the "dreaded research."

# The Library Scene

Libraries have always been my haven. At Georgetown, the library became my first and second home. Both my "haven" and "hell."

On weekends I punished myself terribly, gathering books — any books — that I thought related in *any* way to my subject matter. Then I'd need to make two trips to the car. I really was trying to be a top student. Avrom, one of my classmates, was such a fantastic student (straight "A's") and spent ten to twelve hours in the library sometimes. He just "had to be," he said, "all A's." I told him once when he looked ill, "Avrom, better be a healthy 'B', than a *dead* 'A'." Now here was I, pushing myself in the same way. And often it involved a frantic search.

Books that were torn and tattered fascinated me most, because in my opinion the older the book, naturally the older the author, which made him *know more* than the young ones. Stupid me. I quickly discovered that the professors also knew those authors and did not agree with their theories. No wonder they advised us to stick with *their* book list.

Early in your college career (maybe the first day), you'll be told by the teacher that if you yield to temptation and cheat in any form, you will be expelled. Plagiarism is *out*. I truly believe those professors know every darn word of every book in that library. Should you not heed this advice, you will have to answer to the following: (1) Where did you find this? (2) Who recommended this particular book? (3) Why do you think it's true? (4) Can you fully explain the theory of the author? (5) Do you *know* the author? It isn't worth chicanery, honey.

I could never understand why — even when I had an early start — the book I needed was gone from the library. And for how long, there was no way to tell. Everyone just happened to need that *same book*, at the *same time*. In a situation like this, you began to panic, wondering, "When will it be returned?" Then you were told there were fifteen on the list ahead of you. Your heart stopped for a moment. Should I go to the last person's house and read over his shoulders? Did I know him? Maybe I should buy the book.

If, and when, the book you were seeking was found (usually on the wrong shelf in the wrong area), you tried to find a nice, lonely spot to get into it. Libraries are invariably warm with a lot of cozy spots. You sat, opened your book, and immediately went to sleep. *A cat nap.* I know cat naps that have lasted an hour. No problem. You said to yourself, "I deserved that."

Libraries are indeed special places. I'm so proud that on September 12, 1988, a "Pearl Bailey Branch Library" was officially opened in my old hometown — Newport News, Virginia. Now I can search, research, and sleep in peace.

# The Bookstore

The Georgetown bookstore is located under the library building. If you're planning a visit, take money, credit card, and a shopping list for the week. This is not a bookstore; it's a department store. Everything you brought or wished you had brought from home is found in this place. I call it "Temptation Alley."

A student, of course, has to have this stuff — especially the things stamped with your school name, or in your school colors (blue and gray). I was a Hoya, and I wanted the world to know.

It was no different when I took seminars at Oxford and Canterbury. At these two schools Pearl went broke on banners, sweaters, etc. I needed that job in London to pay for the luxury of showing everyone when I returned home that I'd been to these famous schools. Buying for myself was not enough. Louie, E.B., Dodi, her son Michael, my daughter DeeDee and son Tony — everyone had to be a Georgetown Hoya. Here was a mother be- having like a child. I was broke, but happy.

# The Sports Lady —
## The Athletic Pearl and Friends

The GU Hoyas were the coming team when I entered Georgetown. John Thompson, the basketball coach, was one of the best in the country. When the season opened the school would go "bananas." The championship loomed large for them. I went a bit crazy when the team was on TV; my studies slowed down. Talk about a fan. I crocheted blue and gray caps for the team on weekends (Who asked me? *Nobody.*).

One thing John Thompson (molder of good young men) demanded was that *school* and *sports* go hand in hand. He is to be credited for having all or most of his boys graduate. I was proud to have graduated in May 1985 with a few of them. Pat Ewing and I were a part of the two-hundredth anniversary gala for Georgetown in 1988. He looked so handsome in his tuxedo while I strutted in my gown.

You haven't lived until you catch this girl on the gym floor (once) with the cheerleaders doing her thing. I'm a dancer, true, but, honey, my "high kicking time" was years ago. An exciting moment sent the leg too high, and Ben-Gay and hot packs had to be called into action. The cheerleaders went on dancing; Pearl sat, and screamed for her boys.

One year at play-off time in Philadelphia, my happiness was complete. My classmate (in French) from Egypt, named "Happy," and I headed for Philly. Pom-poms were waving in the breeze as we went up the highway, eating our crab cakes and yelling out the window at our Maryland rivals, also headed for the play-offs. Two young coeds were on their way to cheer our team on to the championship. Never had I experienced anything like this. My fans should have seen me.

By now, I knew all the GU players. Often we'd stop on campus and chat awhile. I also knew players from other colleges. It is so nice that many of these young players have gone into professional basketball. There's: Pat Ewing (my hero), New York Knicks; Eric "Sleepy" Floyd (now a Houston Rocket); from the University of Maryland, Bernard King; The Pearl (Syracuse), Dwayne Washington; the soaring eagle of North Carolina, Michael Jordan (Chicago Bulls); James Worthy (North Carolina) Lakers; Ralph Sampson (was Houston); Isiah Thomas (Pistons); and David Wingate

('76ers). Yes, I am an older part of those boys.

We — and that included the teachers — were so obsessed about our team, that one day, during play-off time, only seven students showed up in ethics class. Nat Hyman, my play-nephew, who has a superb mind, asked, "Professor, how about us going across the street to my house and watching the game?" Professor Porreco thought a brief moment, smiled, and agreed. So off we went, eight strong, including Porreco.

Nat was my tormentor, we were always kibitzing over "Who was the smartest?" We'd meet in the library and help each other. He taught me the correct way to study and I was able to help him in some of his subjects by teaching him to apply some elderly wisdom in his work. We were a pair. We were and are still Nephew Nat and Aunt Pearl. Nat was also a dapper dresser. Always the right sweater with the right pants. A classy dude.

We trooped across the street to his little gray house on the corner, which he said he shared with other tenants. After turning on the TV, he asked, "Does anyone want coffee?" "Oh, Nat," I said, "that would be fine." Hearing him fumbling around in the kitchen, I thought, "What does this boy know about making coffee?" I went into the kitchen to help. There was the biggest mess I had ever encountered. Dishes were piled as high as the windowsills; those that someone had pretended to wash lay in the rack; there were dirty pans. Retreating through the dining room, I saw newspapers mixed with books and heavens knows what else piled on the table. This was a "war zone."

"Nat, come in here." "What's up, Aunt Pearl?" Not only did I *show* him what was up, I promised to report this to his parents. "Oh no!" he screamed. Meanwhile the company was sitting in the living room enjoying the game, oblivious to what I now noticed were newspapers scattered on the sofa and chairs as well.

I sent him back, red-faced, to enjoy the game in the living room. I began to clean a saucepan for coffee; I didn't trust the coffee-pot. Every dried-up coffee ground in that pot looked like a *bug*. While awaiting my coffee, I washed dishes, picked up newspapers, all the while mumbling about "lazy, but brilliant children." Then I dumped the garbage. The game had ended by the time I sat down with my coffee.

Aunt Pearl asked him, "How can you wear those sharp gray silk slacks and live in this dirty house?" Nat said, "Aunt Pearl, I will show you my room upstairs; it's neat. It's the tenants." "Well," I said, "if you're considered the landlord, throw them out. Warn them, then throw them out. I'll be back to check this out, then I'm writing your parents." I never did go back, but I'd bet that house is clean.

What a love he is. After working on Wall Street, where he did well, he is now in Palm Beach, Florida, doing quite well in his own jewelry business. School has given me many lovely new children.

The last sports laugh was not mine. One day I was wearing my Hoya sweater so proudly — as most everyone else was. As I passed the steps of Healy Hall, a few boys yelled, "Pearl, that's a crazy sweater you're wearing, where did you get it?" "At the book-store, boys." "Hot dog," I thought, "the kids really dug me being a 'real coed.'" Two or three classes later (having passed by Healy each time), I got the same thing. "Gee whiz," I thought, "these young folks sure are stupid not to know their own school store; their parents are wasting their money." Turning to give them a hard look, I caught them laughing, making gestures across their chests. *Dirty rascals*. They were putting my *breasts* on.

# Campus Cruelty

While there's a lot of fun at schools, there's much anger too. Vehemence, real terrifying vehemence. It seems all campuses suffer from it. What a pity. At Georgetown we had so many students from other lands. There's a huge School of Foreign Service. Politics, activists, and evil have pervaded the campus. Whether those at the top were aware of all of it, I do not know. It was frightening to me to think young minds could think and do terrible things. Who or what had taken over their minds? Silently sometimes, loudly at other times, I heard and witnessed it. I can't believe we are allowing this sort of thing to invade our schools.

Some students have a "built-in hatred" against their fellow students. "It is their right to have their political voices heard," some say. I agree, but not if it destroys fine minds of the young, without giving them a chance at "loving." Their right to happiness is being drained. There were several incidents of religious and other bias on campus, particularly over the Arab-Israeli conflict.

Then there was the time I bought some cookies from a friend outside the library. When I offered one to a friend of another nationality he went "ape." He began hurling tirades and insults against "the cookies" and the cookie seller. He finally got on my nerves. "Those cookie seller sons of b —." "Listen," I said, "the flour came from the mills of the West, raisins from California, spices from India, even the oven was made someplace else. Now which one of these places and people do you also hate?" "None," he said. "Then eat the darn cookie, be grateful to God that I gave it to you, and shut up," I said to him in no uncertain terms. He made me ill. He looked at me with an evil glare, I reached out to him with cookie in hand; he took it, and ate it. Not one did he eat, but many. Lesson One in Bigotry Loss. He probably still hated the salesman, but he adored the cookie. Around campus I used to see this guy and he'd always say, "Lady, do you have any more cookies?" We'd both smile over that.

Once a group of girls approached me — beautiful Negro girls of all shades. There were not many of us on campus. "Join our sorority," they said, "because we feel alienated, and you, being a celebrity, will bring them to us."

They looked helpless, but were very intelligent. "Dear girls," I said, "they may not be in love with me. You're basing my importance to you on the basis of my being a celebrity. Aren't you putting me in the same bag they're placing you? Don't let this celebrity bit throw you off. Would you have invited me into your sorority if I were not a celebrity?" I asked that because unfortunately many times on campus a few of them had looked down their noses, as I walked along with other classmates.

Going on with my studies, I pitied their ignorance. "You're bigots," I said, "because I did not come here to alienate myself or be alienated against. Those who wish to join the human race, welcome aboard. You girls know what and who we are; you know what you deserve, and I'm sure you must have been aware, when you left home, there were some who would ignore or pass you by. Some of those who are looking down their noses at us will, someday, have to smile; if not they'll keep sniffing until they smell themselves, the odor of hatred will stifle them. Hatred thrives on hatred; love overcomes it. Ignorance fans bigotry. Intelligence smothers it.

"Smother them in class; the time you spend on sitting in the sorority worrying about them, you should spend on your lessons, or how to make a more joyous time for yourselves.

When, and if, you really need me, I am here. For everyone."

No one said they were in love with me either, but by going about my business, using the same facilities as they were to better myself, I might even sneak on by and be able to look back and say, "Come on, love, catch me and enjoy."

Those girls went merrily on their way; I later saw them more and more on campus, sometimes strutting. No, it was not right to give these girls the treatment; then reflect back to the "cookie boy." There but for you go I, friend. Bigots are miserable people who keep busy finding other people to hate. Stomp on them, honey, with love and intelligence; and stand tall if they offend you.

Unfortunately, there are hate groups or gangs in the streets of every city. You kids who are coming out in this world, be ready for them; and if all of us put more practice into dropping the *labels* we use, we'd be better off.

The problem of drugs — and alcohol — only intensifies the feelings of ill-will on campus. I am not a prude, but I think that drinking gets out of hand. Obviously, it's the parent in me. The concerned parent.

One day on campus coming from French class I saw a gorgeous girl, her hair streaming in the wind, wearing a long white dress. She was making her way to "somewhere." I noticed she was wearing *nothing* underneath the dress. Did she know it? Who could tell. Students were staring at her as she passed. Finally, someone guided her to her dormitory. It's nice that in general the young will look after each other. Seeing that girl wrenched my heart; for in her at that moment I could see all of our children.

I'm proud that Father Healy did not allow issues to get too far out of hand at Georgetown. He grabs things and deals with them quickly. This man is the epitome of "a decent human being." Should he miss the mark, Father Freeze is right there to pick up the slack. Our faculty (at least those I dealt with and met) practiced compassion and understanding for breakfast, lunch, and dinner. Granted, I did not meet all the people there, and I can't say, "It's sheer perfection at GU." But I do pray for all of them. And they should, too.

# *Family on Hold?*

Your big concern will be, "Suppose I do go back to school? I have a family; how will that work?" It can work nicely if you get a routine, develop patience, sit down and explain it to the family, hear their side — and hope for the best. Selfish motives, as to why you should not attend, may creep into the conversation. *Listen. Hear.* But also ask yourself, "Where will *they* all be if I'm sitting home twiddling my thumbs?" Be considerate, but take a chance, *live a little*.

Maybe you will have to go to a community college and take one course at a time; maybe you'll even resort to taking an at-home college course. However it works, try once more. I think I might have continued with college courses — even after acceptance by Georgetown — had *someone* in my family joined me.

I had taken a summer-school class in English with a major at Cal State, Northridge. DeeDee, my daughter, decided she would finally join me (show business, of course, was her thing but education got a break because at that time singing jobs were not too frequent). DeeDee had heard, through the student grapevine, who were the easiest teachers. I could have told her: *none*. Oh well, let 'em learn. I picked the hard major. I mean he was (once) an honest-to-goodness Army major. His message was clear the first day: "We are here to work hard or you will know it by your mark." The major laid this out in an exact, concise voice. *No smiles.* At the end of the semester DeeDee got a "C" (at least she went and tried school); Mama got an exciting "A" from a brilliant teacher. The major was an angel. My secretary, Dodi, even caught the fire and took a couple of courses, on top of all her family and work duties. A good example of "it *can* be done."

In our thirty-six years of marriage I've seldom missed having Louie's dinner ready on time. At Georgetown my courses were set so that only twice a week we ate a 6 P.M. dinner; otherwise it was 5:30 P.M. I managed to do most of the cooking the night before, while studying. We had a lot of spaghetti sauce, roasts, beans, corn (always), chicken soup (a must), fish, greens. Food was either broiled or boiled, seldom fried. If there were not enough pots, I'd borrow E.B.'s from his kitchen. Louie and E.B. called me the fastest cook in the *East* or *West*.

I'd crash in the door, remove my shoes, put the pots on (especially the corn for Louie, *every* day, winter and summer), put on my worn housecoat, set the table. All of this before removing my stocking cap. Nothing hindered me because Louie and E.B. disappeared. Mama said to us from childhood, "Do not allow anyone in the kitchen while you are cooking; you'll burn the food if you talk." I've burned a bit and it always happened when I started to chitchat; about what else? *School.*

After dinner, I *did not* participate in the dish-washing episode. That was Louie's gig (when he was in town); otherwise it fell to E.B. I think the easiest way to get husbands to do dishes daily is to sweet-talk a bit, moan about all the homework pushed upon you by those cruel professors, talk about the miserable kid next to you, act exhausted (you are), and cry if necessary. I did almost anything — but the dishes. After Louie did his chore he disappeared into the other room to write music or take a rest. If the ball games were on TV he'd watch while writing music.

Things actually ran pretty smoothly. I knew what had to be done — how do you get it in your head, if you don't study? Often I wondered where my love life had gone. I'd peek in the room at Louie; we'd wave at each other, smile, and return to our individual labor. He wanted me to do my best and I wanted the same for him. When he'd be into "deep" stuff musically, I returned the favor.

In the midst of schoolwork I was sometimes distracted with concerns about members of my family. Even at school Tony and DeeDee came between the pages of my books. There were aggravations, too, over other things. I'd ask myself, "Am I avoiding something or someone?" "Am I crowding in too much?" "Instead of filling my mind with Greek history or English, shouldn't I attend to so-and-so's problems?" "*No,* " my mind said.

This was ten years ago, when Tony was twenty-four and DeeDee eighteen, and both were no longer in the house. When I was young my mother and father never left us alone at night. In the same way, Louie and I had someone in our home at all times if we were out of town. To me that was a *must.* "So what concerns you, Pearl?" I wondered.

"They need me," the answer came. Heh! What does Pearl need? In always remembering others, I had forgotten myself. Didn't my going give them the "space" they needed to grow? Didn't it give them the chance to "find themselves"? It sounded great, but usually it felt awful. Who was the lonely one? I found out.

We can all get very busy in life and forget to do the basic "niceties" that we were taught. We forget basic manners like *calling, writing, touching,* coming to visit Mom and Dad. *There was absolutely no excuse* for the lack of communication between my children and us; and I paint no rosy pictures of it. I cannot recall getting any phone calls unless there was a problem; it was either something that blew my mind or, in my son's case, a matter of "the mighty loan" (that was never repaid).

Whenever we did talk, it seems I was always reminding them to remember people, to send thank-yous for favors, to send cards on holidays — Mother's Day, Father's Day. It was in vain. I ofttimes used to ask myself, in my loneliness, "Are these the people I gave my all for?" I'm sure now they truly regret their lack of compassion and love. But it's their shame, not mine; they have to live with it. What I feel is sadness.

All this could be swept under a rug; but that's not necessary in my family because we were taught to grow with experience and time. I would be lying if I did not say, "It pained." My children were into "their things," getting on with their lives, assuming that Louie and I were okay. To them, I suppose, we didn't need these "old-fashioned love touches." But, children of ours, *we did.* I know *I* did. I could only put my feelings into a "pot of stew," where they simmered, boiled over, and got done. I missed the children, but I plodded on in Georgetown.

I realized how, especially on "heavy study days," we can take each other for granted. We *do* love each other, but . . . Patience and tolerance carried Louie and me through it all.

# Staying Power

I'll admit that school is a difficult experience for an older person, but so is it for the young. I have advice for those like me who want to give it a try. We have to mingle with each other — especially in the classroom. The initial sensitivity we feel soon wears off. Keep telling yourself, "Their mom and pop are paying for these kids; I'm paying for mine." It's sacrifice and love entwined. But most of all, it's a game of *guts*.

Your teacher most likely will be younger than you; you'll have to cope with the ways and whims of people whom you have surpassed in life experience. You'll be like an alien to them. The young student will picture you as their "mom" or "pop," sitting next to them. They'll withdraw; so will you. Take it all in stride. Get into your slacks, sweater, and "whoopee socks." Realize what you are there for. Should you start to see yourself as different, as "Adult Student," you will become confused and confuse those around you. Life will be miserable. In school, remember, you are *not* the boss. Treat your professors as your elders, although often you'll be tempted to punish them as your children. Hold off or you're headed for trouble. Whenever I got *hot* inside I had to remember where I was. I cooled off, quickly.

"Staying power," that's a job. We learn all about it in the theatrical world. "Stamina." You will feel many times that you're running out of it. Get a refill, take a deep breath, and march on to victory. Giving the professor the "Missouri look" ("show me") won't help. Keep in mind, you are the "payee"; don't waste your time or money on rebellion.

Everyone knows it is not easy to break old habits. Your way of doing things seldom, if ever, will work. What to do? *Do it their way.* If you buck the system, they'll get back at you: unfriendly criticism on your papers or exams.

Today's teaching styles are out of sync with what we remember from twenty or thirty years ago. You'll start to feel, "They know it all, they think I know nothing." Rest assured: you *read, spell,* and *write* better than the young ones. The computer does exist — but so does your brain, trust me. And professors will often praise your ability.

"Hanging in there" is advice I cannot stress enough. I followed it myself. There has to be a longing inside your bosom to be or to do something *for yourself*. To return to "Act I" of your life. My philosophy is: confront life, be a child again. You may find the child within yourself in those classrooms. And you'll be an inspiration to others your age to continue — or start — their education. You may not become "head of the class," but you'll be respected.

# "Apples"

People say to me, "How wonderful you went to college. How could you do it? Where did you get the courage?" Well, folks, all I can say is, "Thank God I did go; and who knows, there is always more to learn and experience, so I might just go for the collegiate bit again." It's a special experience, a chance to grow up again.

Kids used to be teased about bringing an apple to the teacher, accused of "seeking favors." My dear readers, it has been a joy to find out that teachers give apples too, not just good grades. Long after graduating, I've had letters from some expressing their feelings about having had me as a student. It gives me a glow. A teacher, who has taught so many, has taken time to say, "You stayed in our thoughts — your efforts, ability, consciousness about what you were there for, compassion toward others." What a treasure that is to receive.

Once Father Donald Freeze, the provost,

told me, "Pearl, from my office window I could overlook the campus. I'd see you many times passing back and forth diligently. I heard students talking about you. You are loved." What an apple! *That one I ate.*

Yes, I have very fond memories. Filling my scrapbook are some wonderful letters that I shall treasure always. I can't resist sharing a few snippets:

Dear Pearl,

I remember vividly the first important lesson you gave me. "Professor," you said, "you got to learn to mix your students up; keep them off guard. Sometimes be stern, sometimes meet them with kindness. Then they'll always listen." I understood, and began to give more of myself, to meet your love of learning with my own love of the classics.

. . . I see you are much blessed because you always honor learning as the key to the human heart. The wisest teacher of all, Socrates himself, was trained by Diotima to understand love. I'll never match him, but I count myself lucky to have been blessed by my own Diotima. Thank you, Pearl, for so much.

Love,
(*signed*) VICKI

Victoria Pedrick
Associate Professor of Classics

September 25, 1988

Dear Pearl:
Nothing had prepared me for meeting you. And to tell the truth I knew very little about you and your career. Words and my legs were failing me. Were really Pearl Bellson and Pearl Bailey one and the same? I discovered they were. I also discovered that you wanted to be treated as any student and intended to do the work. You were keen to participate and were doing the readings.

. . . Both of us were interested in the human. Both of us are looking for the human wherever it is and in all its forms across cultures and particularly in Arabic and Islamic culture, you in the present, I in the Middle Ages. Both of us give a place to God without whom the human cannot be fully understood. And both of us are professional but our professionalism is there to enhance the human not to supplant it. I felt suddenly that friendship, affectionate interest and capacity to laugh together were possible. I also discovered that for you formal education was something very serious but also that you were giving education in the art of human living while talking with the other students and with me. You opened up about your life and your expectations and shared some of your experiences with the other students and with me. I learned about Louie and met him and some of your friends and you tasted my chocolate mousse. We were real people meeting each other. . . .

Yours,
(*signed*) THÉRÈSE
Thérèse-Anne Druart
(School of Philosophy)

Dear Pearl,

How delighted I was to receive your letter of Sept. 6 and how pleased that you continued to be my friend! . . .

. . . in the two ethics classes of mine in which you were a student, you supplied the experience of life, as Aristotle says, is often lacking in the young and immature. You also gave us a living example of a life that is being well lived, which is something that young students are in great need of.

. . . Happy to be your friend and
as always,

95

*(signed)* ROCCO
(Rocco Porreco, Professor of Ethics)

Dear Pearl,

. . . You don't know how I miss you at times. Not only for your eye, your biblical knowledge, but your natural sense of humour. No one can take himself too seriously in your presence. If we could only put you on a computer disk . . . or maybe we can begin a graduate program in Art History and you can then begin a graduate degree.

> With fond regards,
> CARA FERGUSON O'MEARA
> Associate Professor of Fine Arts

More than "Apples of Wisdom," my peers gave me "Apples of Love."

Bless my soul, once in 1988 as Louie and I and E.B. walked the streets of New York while I was working at the United Nations, we bumped into one of my prodigal children — Nat Hyman, the successful Wall Streeter, who now has four jewelry stores on Worth Avenue (the "Rodeo Drive" of Florida). We still keep in touch.

On another occasion E.B. was in a small Chinese restaurant and heard a commanding voice announcing, "Mr. Greenberg, table for two, please." Later, after hearing the other man's voice from a nearby booth, E.B. approached. "Avrom, what are you doing here? Your Aunt Pearl is going to wipe you out." That scared the *now* big-time lawyer. He met Louie, E.B., and me two days later, gave us a splendid meal (at a posh restaurant), and we relived our GU days. We had another meal together to finish the saga, this time at Abe's Steak House on Third Avenue. The place rocked with our happy spirits. This happened around Christmas, so we had to buy our darling a gift.

The day after we'd seen Avrom, Louie went over to John's Greek restaurant to get me a sandwich and coffee. While he was gone the phone rang and the scream that came over the phone when I picked it up frightened me. I thought, "What has happened to Louie?" *Nothing.* It was my Kyra screaming, "Aunt Pearl, I've found you." "Found me," I pounced on her, "I've been writing you and not receiving answers." She begged to come upstairs in the hotel. "But I'm not dressed," I said. "I don't care, Aunt Pearl, I've got to hug you." And she did. I sat on a chair in the hall awaiting her; she leaped out of the elevator and plopped herself on my lap. We were a charming, crazy pair. Kyra Sedgewick and I had met on the television special *Cindy Eller,* a takeoff on Cinderella, that aired as an ABC Afterschool Special. Instead of the fairy godmother, I played a bag woman, for which I later received an Emmy. It was directed by a great actress, Lee Grant (we did *The Landlord* together for the late Hal Ashby), and it was produced by her husband, Joe Feury. Most of the young people in that film went on to higher things. Anyhow, Kyra (now an even finer actress) had married actor Kevin Bacon. "And guess what, Aunt Pearl?" she squealed, "I'm pregnant." So what am I now, *Aunt-Grandma Pearl?* Oh! my children.

Then there's Philip, to whom I gave a clock in Greek class. Dear Philip *never, ever* made it to class on time; well, that is, until *the clock.* Professor Pedrick stressed to us starting class on time, with no exceptions; to Philip she stressed it just enough times to finally tell him, "Okay, Philip, once more and you're out of this class." I knew she really was fond of him and wanted him to do his best. That brought on *the clock.* He made it on time. We met again in our senior year in an art class — and he was still on time. Philip is now in the dry cleaning business and has invented some new kind of venetian blind. He is very consistent with letters informing me of all his activities.

My Michelle now assists in some capacity

on the Ted Koppel production staff and is still going to law school.

I just got a card from my Cathy, who is now in medical school. She informed me: "Aunt Pearl, I just helped deliver six babies." Gracious, I wonder if it was all at once!

I love receiving these "Apples." And whatever my children write in the future, I shall eat them with great joy. So many wonderful young people have been a part of my life, as I have been a part of theirs.

I save the best "Apple" for last.

These "recollections of Pearl Bailey" are written by a fellow student and my *very dear, special* friend, John. I could not have recounted this myself — but you deserve to know, anyway.

The very first time I encountered Pearl, "Aunt Pearl," as I would later come to know her, I lent her money. She probably has forgotten this. It was the beginning of a new semester at Georgetown. Pearl was new to campus, so it was a novelty, at first, to see her. We were on line together at the bookstore and she had purchased some books. At the cashier she realized that she didn't have her checkbook with her and she didn't have enough cash with her. I felt embarrassed for her, so I offered to pay for her books, about $30, and she took my name and address and sent me a check a few days later. I remember thinking it a great story, that I had lent Pearl Bailey money to buy her books. I also empathized with her, as would anyone who has ever waited in line at a university bookstore during the first week of classes. I remember having photo-copied the check before I cashed it, just to keep as a memento. Years later, looking through some papers from college, I came across a copy of that check, which I had for-gotten. Only with ten years of hindsight did the symbolism of our first meeting come through to me: I had been able to help out Pearl Bailey, and she'd always been there to help out me. In unique ways, we've always been there for each other.

Other than this first encounter, I really didn't have contact with Pearl until the Spring of 1979, when we took an Art His-tory class together. I recall that first class meeting to which I had arrived late. The classroom was packed — standing room only — since it was a very popular class with an excellent professor. I looked around the room for a seat, but there were none to be had. The only seat left in the entire room was next to Pearl Bailey, and she had her books on it. I thought that I could not be so bold as to ask her to move her books and sit next to her, so I just sat on the floor at the front of the room. As soon as I had, she called me over, removed her books from the desk, and asked me to sit next to her. When the class was over she asked for my name and phone number in order to get notes from class, in case she missed one. I remember lending her my notes on occasion and getting back my notebook with all these little inscriptions written in the margins. Just Pearl's musings on the subject matter. I kept that notebook, thinking how unique my college years had been, with Pearl Bailey's scribbling throughout my notes. I'll never forget the image of Pearl waiting for me in front of the library, in the winter, with a knit hat, a warm fur coat, and my notebook under her arm.

I can clearly recall when it was that Pearl became "Aunt Pearl" to me. We were sitting at her kitchen table at her small, but homey, apartment at the Watergate, and there was a pot of home-made chicken soup simmering on the stove. Our art history books were spread out all over the place and Pearl took my arm, looked me straight in the eyes and said: "Now honey, outside of here, I'm Pearl Bailey, the entertainer, but inside here, when we're together, I'm your 'Aunt Pearl.' " I never forgot that.

My advice to anyone wanting to be friends with Pearl is simple: speak from your heart. She doesn't tolerate baloney, and she can read right through you in a second. I can see how perhaps there were many students and professors that were intimidated by Pearl, but if so, it was only a manifestation of their own insecurities and fears.

Through the years, Pearl has remained a true, dear friend. Letters, postcards, telegrams, and phonecalls followed me from her, from all over the world. She invested in my business back in '85, and today she's one of my closest supporters and friends in my battle against AIDS. She speaks and loves directly from the heart, and she's all any friend could ever be. We learned alot from each other at Georgetown, and that mutual learning, love and support has grown over the years.

Last month, in a phone conversation, Pearl said to me, "John, how blessed I am to know you." I was touched. And you know, I've always felt that way, too, about my darling "Aunt Pearl."

# *The Arizona Girl Comes Through*

On May 23, 1985, Louie told me that Assistant Dean Carey had called and asked that I come to school Saturday, the twenty-fourth, to Healy Hall. The dean had never called me at home before. Oh, my lord! Was I not going to graduate? "Oh!" Louie said, "Dean Carey said wear a dress." A dress? Heavens, not my pants; something must be terribly wrong.

"Louie," I asked, "do you know what she wants?" "It's a secret," he said.

At 1 P.M., dressed in my nice frock, with Louie and E.B. in their Sunday best, we headed for Healy Hall. There were parents all over campus, coming to see the "grand finale," the payoff of their investment. After shuffling slowly up crowded stairs we entered the hall. It was packed. The faculty members sat on stage. I still didn't know why I was there.

Dean Davis began speaking. This cere-

103

mony, whatever it was, had started. I didn't bother to read the program, I was too busy looking around. Students were straining at the leash wondering who won what. What were they talking about? As the winners marched to the platform, the audience went wild; the parents wept. "And now, ladies and gentlemen, a lady came here from Arizona, and worked . . . " Dean Davis went on, "and her name is Pearl Bailey." I thought, "How nice." Louie said, "Honey, get up there, that's you." "That's who?" "You, honey." "Wow!"

It was the "Dean's Award," given to me by my peers. You've never lived until you see a sixty-seven-year-old-woman fumble her way up *three tiny stairs* to a stage and grin like a Cheshire cat. Yes, friends, it's worth it.

Throughout the week before graduation, Louie, E.B., and I walked the Georgetown campus, watching them build the huge platform in front of the Healy building that was going to be used for seating. Sometimes we'd sit on a bench and watch from the distance, trying to focus in on Pearl, the graduate, walking up the stairs to receive her diploma. Pat Ewing, our basketball hero, who was graduating with me, came by one day and we took photos. He is so tall (over seven feet), which made us look so small. But we all had the same wide grin.

It's hard to describe the feelings that come with knowing *finally* it is happening. The years have paid off (about seven for me) and you're getting that diploma. Feelings are high all over the campus for those of us who are leaving; and those who remain know, "Soon my turn will come."

I thought about leaving my friends and classmates Michelle, Billy, Kathy, Philip, Nat. There would be no more cooking and sharing "chicken soup" with Avrom and dear Paul. No more living with the people at Guest Quarters (which, by now, was home to me), with all their kindnesses. No more walking "Charlie" the dog out in the yard where on the coldest, rainiest, snowiest days he took the *most* time to perform his act. I remember how he loved to sit (and could he!) and watch people pass, while I shivered. He was my relief between studies. In fact, he was more than that: Charlie had to listen to some of my "papers" when no one else was available. *When* and *if* he stayed awake, I gave him a "goody." When he went to sleep I decided I'd better re-work the paper.

May 25, 1985, arrived bathed in sunshine. It was eighty degrees. Guests came from California, Pennsylvania, New York, and D.C. Families intermingled with people they had never met, taking pictures. A brunch was planned at Mr. Marshall Coyne's beautiful Madison Hotel. The lawn emptied, everyone was screaming for taxis, it was bedlam *and hot*.

During the graduation ceremonies, my sisters Virgie and Eura (Mama, Papa, and brother Willie were in heaven) all sat in their seats cheering for me, I know. Mr. Parvin (whom I call a second father and my favorite boss), Phyllis (his wife), George and Helen Neams, E.B., Dodi, Michelle, Cathy, Lois, Michael, Tony Fantozzi, Stan and Margie, Gary, Remo and his Marge, Artie, the Cunninghams, my professors Soudée, Druart, Assistant Dean Carey; we were all kids that day.

All this time I never took off my cap, with its tassel dangling in my face. Louie held my diploma. That night I think I slept with my cap on. I got gorgeous, unexpected graduation gifts; it was a treasure chest in that room. My "heart treasures," I call them.

Two people stunned me that day. Mrs. Sally Lefkowitz, wife of the deceased chairman of William Morris, a dear lady who has been and is ailing, had gotten permission to come from her doctor (*I'm sure he fought that battle*). The gifts were passed around, then suddenly, Sally, sitting in a far corner, arose, and said in

106

that strong voice, "Pearl, I have established a fifty-thousand-dollar scholarship — Nat and Sally Lefkowitz, in the name of Pearl Bailey. It is to go to any school of religion you choose." My degree was in theology. That dear lady had never given me a hint as to what she was planning. "This money," she said, "is not refundable." *Bless you, Sally.* As of the present time there have been three scholarships awarded to deserving students.

Then a man of fifty, handsome, tall, and very serious though he often hides his emotions (I know he's warm), came and stood behind my chair. He attracted attention by his composure. "This lady I'm standing behind is my 'stepmother,' so being older than her and Louie's children Tony and DeeDee, I shall represent three children." I thank that human being so much. Noticing that DeeDee and Tony were not there, he perceptively pushed his fingers into my shoulders as if to stop me from saying anything, or to strengthen me. I obeyed his wish. Thank you, Boogie (his nickname), for mashing down a "hurt." He said, "Louie accepted me as a father would and I love him." Then without any fanfare he produced a square red box.

"Open this," he said. *"Now!"* he ordered. I untied the string; inside were all new dollar bills. "Count them," he said. I did. There were ten stacks of one hundred dollars each: a thousand dollars in each stack. In almost a whisper, he said, *"Bread cast upon the waters."* Everyone felt a lump.

Tony Fantozzi (whom I call son also) later said, "Pearl, how did you mix people of all ages, nationalities, and professions? No one there knew each other and yet we all melted into one. Nobody had really been formally introduced." Very seldom do I have an affair that does not end up a "love fest"; I try to treat people all the same way. "Tony," I said softly, "have you ever read, or do you fully understand, how things acted out in love produce more in love?"

Nothing has escaped my mind about that day; each detail lives fully within my soul. Everyone was filled emotionally. The day ended as it had begun so beautifully in the morning. It was the climax of a week that I'll never forget.

And I thought, no more going by Neam's market with my weekly grocery list, or by Canon's Fish Store. Louie or E.B. did most of the other shopping at Safeway, across the street from the hotel. No more sitting, every weekend, surrounded by library books, never leaving the room until Monday; nor seeing my dear teachers or Father Healy, a man of deep devotion, who made numerous trips all over the country for our school.

No more watching the dogs romp all over the lawn, playing with the kids. The first year we must have had at least twenty-five; some even wandered into classrooms and sat. Many times I would have gladly given them my spot.

No more of my childhood. It would be all gone on May 25, 1985, and I was sad.

It's been almost four years since "the big day." I invited President Healy to share his thoughts for this book. His reply, dated February 1989, made me relive my college days all over again. This is what he wrote:

Every student brings a special gift to a university, helping to form the composite character of the institution. The individuality of each young and supple mind brings to the whole of the university community a richness that transcends the limitations of the written word and enhances the restrictive learning process that is the classroom experience. The richness that is the offering of the student is what helps us educators make our houses of learning better with every year. From my angle, it was evident from day one that a woman named Pearl Bailey had much to give the Georgetown community — and give she did.

When Pearl Bailey first made her way to

Georgetown over a decade ago, she made a pact both with her teachers and herself: she resolved to give her all. And so, like her fellow classmates, Pearl attended lectures, prepared assignments and commiserated with colleagues. Pearl proved in short order that she was a serious student. Pearl asked the tough questions, the ones that don't come with textbook answers, the kind of questions people ask when they're trying to do more than "make sense" of this life. Rather, these questions ask how can I continue to grow as a person who can never stop learning, how can I give of myself to others?

I've no doubt that Pearl added a special luster to the classroom scene. Professors and fellow classmates alike remember her as a wonderful asset to the educational process. And when she danced her way across these grounds, she moved with vibrancy and pride — she was a part of the Georgetown family. In such small and tender moments, the waves of excitement and countless smiles told me there was something special happening here. And whenever this grande dame returns to this place, the laughter, the love, the joy, the richness of her presence pervade these grounds.

Indeed, Georgetown is richer for the

many gifts of Pearl Bailey. We are proud to number Pearl among our alumni — and as a special friend!

Sincerely,

TIMOTHY S. HEALY, S.J.

# *Tying the Knot*

It was time to go back to the family. The family that I had never mentally left. I began thinking back to all we'd done together while the children were growing. I had given my all, climbed mountains with them, seen Disneyland until they knew every ride, gone into dinosaur caves, shook hands with almost every one of the wonderful Indian persons we'd met along Route 66; gone to their festival in August at Gallup, New Mexico. We had visited countries all over the world, heard lectures by famous people, seen the greats of *singing* (Ella, Frank, Sarah, Peggy, Warfield, Leontyne), *dancing* (Alvin Ailey, Arthur Mitchell, and ballet stars), *comedy* (Milton Berle, Danny Thomas, the fantastic Jonathan Winters, Skelton, Hope, Jan Murray), *acting* (Cliff Robertson, Dietrich, James Earl Jones, Yul Brynner), *entertainment* (Sammy Davis, Jr., the rare talent, Newley, Wayne Newton). You name 'em, they seen 'em. There was the Ringling Bros. Circus, Holiday on Ice, the

112

Ice Capades, the Dodgers, Mets, and Red-skins — you name 'em, they seen 'em."

"What," I asked myself, "was missing?" We needed to sit down, reevaluate, count our blessings, and pray. By now they had grown up, and had lost some insight into our common foundation. Their heads had gotten like cement; money and fame had taken over. "Heh! Let's swing. It's out there for us. You and Dad had it and got it. We want to do our thing. We remember all of your basic teachings. We know how to take care like you told us; we're grownup."

Yes, children, you had grown up, but you'd begun to go through some of the madness of the world today. You had grown *out* of what Louie and I had laid down. But I knew it was all still there; only your practice of it seemed to us to be slipping away. Somehow it looked like the ship of life was sailing and you were going to miss it. You forgot to buy the right ticket; without it you can't get aboard. Let's reevaluate ourselves.

I think not only of my family — but *all* families. Why can't we bring back the work habits, study habits, cleanliness habits, respect for others, the how-fast-can-you-run, how-high-do-you-think-you-can-go habit? Why can't we get the God habit on again as families and go on? Why can't we pull it all together and "go for it"? If we don't, there'll be *nobody home.*

# TWO

There's Nobody Home
*Dedicated to My Family
— and Yours*

# Getting It Together

"Honour thy father and mother . . . that it may be well with thee, and thou mayest live long on the earth." (Eph. 6:2–3)

"Children, obey your parents in the Lord: for this is right. . . . And, ye fathers, provoke not your children to wrath: but bring them up in the nurture and admonition of the Lord." (Eph. 6:1, 4)

Here it all is, as clear as can be, yet we remain confused. Why can't we follow these commandments of promise and save ourselves? I think we are cleverly avoiding the exercise of what we know can, will, and must work. Parental authority has seemingly gone down the drain. We parents no longer seem to have control of the home. Is it because we no longer have control of ourselves? Do we fear our offspring? What's wrong with our attitudes, our thinking? The listening and hearing ears of parents and children have gone deaf. Are we afraid of losing each other? Or hating each other? How will we know the an-

swers when we don't even *touch* each other —
except when absolutely necessary?

All of us are asking, "To whom shall we
turn?" We cannot run to our next-door neighbor because we would only bump into ourselves. It is a constant threat. Where are we
all headed? What are we seeking? The truth
about ourselves is lying on top of the "table
of life," yet we do not care to eat from it. If
we hurry and taste of that meal, we'll know
it is a dish full of our own negligence.

Watching my family through the years, I've
seen some good, some bad, some indiffer-
ence; but I know we've grown. Whenever
there is a strange silence from my children, I
know they've lost step or wavered from the
line of training that my husband and I instilled in them; their foundation is starting to
crack. But because of their training they usually make a "U-turn" and come back home.
So far, they have always found their way
back, through whatever methods. I found a
touching poem in a newspaper once which
said it all:

> On the darkest days
> When I can't seem
> To find my way
> I still have hope.
> It's something

that I always look for,
like the homing pigeon
looks for home.
Even if it's hard to see
   I'll find it.
Like the pigeon
flying through the storm,
   I know it's there.
For I can deal
with dark despair
only for so long,
Then my spirit searches
for the silver lining.
It may be just
a tiny shred of sunlight,
but knowing that there is one
keeps me strong.
And hope is all I ever need
To find my way back home.
RAE TURNBULLS<br>Las Vegas Review Journal

Every family is made up of some who want to pull, some who want to push; these tensions interrupt the "connections" of love. Suddenly you find your young are searching for Lord knows what. Giving in to pressure from outside sources is often bad. We hear promises everywhere: "Follow me and get success quickly, get rich, be powerful, be 'Somebody.' " This dragnet sucks up our children.

I see an America today filled with young people seeking "instant fame," whether in theater, sports, or business. They have no time for that "waiting/working for" period; it must happen for them *fast, now, big.* There is this madness over the land about being "number one." Our darlings have been so brainwashed, they really think they're a failure if they are "number two." What a pity. Why can't they — or we, for that matter — glory in having *tried;* why can't the goal be to *succeed at trying?*

A great artist, the late Miss Sophie Tucker, gave me some words of advice years ago: "It ain't how good you are, it's how long can you last." Recently a dear and courageous lady, who is desperately ill, raised her head from her pillow weakly and said to me, "Pearl, do you remember the Sophie Tucker line you told me?" "Yes, Liz," I replied. "Well, darling," she said faintly, "I'd like to add a piece. *You've got to be good to last.*" Here is a lady who literally has what most of us crave: *money, fame, land* — all but health. Still, thank God, she knows, "You have to be good in life, at what you do, to last." This lady lasted as one of the top "horse women" in the world, until the end. She was Mrs. Liz Whitney Tippett, my "sister."

# Sharing and Communicating

Families must learn to be inclusive, to share. Not to feel "If I've got it made, the hell with everybody else." If you think you are surviving, wait until loneliness for "the others" grabs hold of you; wait until you long for *someone, anyone,* to walk through the door, to touch your life. I know what that feels like from the time I was away at Georgetown, missing my children.

If we make peace with our families and ourselves, we can take that peace and spread it around so other families can learn from us. This is the way to become a community. If we could get that going, maybe it would spread across the nation — and strengthen us. I believe *the nation starts in the home;* that the family is the "feeder" our nation is seeking. The process begins with communication.

How often do we pretend to communicate with others or listen as though we're hanging on to their every word? We think we fool them until they suddenly ask, "What do you think?" *What a helluva feeling!* We weren't tuned in. We were never really listening. So our answer is, "About what?" Our minds have drifted so far from the issue, perhaps to some personal problem. We're not *tuned in to life.*

When this happens at home, wouldn't it be nice simply to say to our mate or children, "Dear, I have something else on my mind at the moment; if it can wait, I'll listen later; but if it's urgent I'll listen now." Instead, we often just ignore each other.

Have you ever looked up and seen the eyes of the person you're trying to communicate with and know *you've lost* them? When that happens to me, I simply stop my conversation and wait. But by the time the other person apologizes and encourages me to go on, I've either forgotten the subject matter or don't care to try again. I'd rather go tell it to the mountain. Obviously, good communication depends on listening *and* hearing.

It amazes me how some people are capable of remembering so much. People often say to me, "You have an extraordinary memory." Maybe so, maybe not. But I can tell you, this memory got a workout back in my youth. Papa and Mama would say many things to us at once; and as small children do, we would forget half of what they told us as soon as it passed their lips. However, when they mentioned weeks ahead that we were going someplace on such-and-such day, or if Mama said, "You're going to get new shoes [or a dress]," *that was well remembered by me.* What had been said was what I *wanted* to hear. My interest had been aroused. In our house one's interest could be-and was — aroused in many ways.

Mama had never bothered to put a clock in our room — and I have to smile when I use the words *"our room."* Many children today are so blessed when they can refer to "my room." How many of us can recall sharing beds, cots, with sisters or brothers? Today a child balks at the thought of not having his/her own private room, bath, TV, VCR, or whatever. I pray for them. The parent of today breaks his/her back to provide children with those "necessities" (usually unearned) while they cry "I'm broke" to friends.

There may have been no clock in the room when I was small, but today I'm sure there are three clocks in every room. Louie is a clock fanatic. It's cute (but boring) to hear him ask while we're still in bed, "Honey, what time is it?" "Louie," I answer, "I'm asleep, I don't know."

But the little Baileys managed with no

clock. For our regular excursions between Philadelphia and Washington, D.C., we were up and ready at 5 A.M. — for the train leaving at 7 A.M. The night before, we had to take off our socks and panties, which was a chore, scrub them, and hang them to dry. We had to clean the room; everything was meticulously done. The reason we didn't need a clock to wake us up was, as Mama would say, "Interest." My theory is that, like small children, we all conveniently remember what we want to and *forget* what we choose.

Years ago we lived in a house in California that had a small dutch window area. From there, we could see across the length of the house. While cooking breakfast, I'd watch the children on their way to the kitchen. My questions flew fast. "Did you brush your teeth? Comb your hair? Bathe? Change your underclothes?"

Louie would say, "Honey, you just asked them about eight things, how can they remember all of them?" "Louie," I would answer, "I don't expect them to; today they may do three, tomorrow four — who knows — one day they may listen and hear, and do *all*." Strategy used toward good purposes works. The main thing was, I kept them thinking all the way in. It was gratifying to see them make a quick turnabout and go back to perform the forgotten tasks. They would return terribly pleased with themselves. Of course, Mom got *no credit* for thinking these things out.

# *Family,*
# *the Vanishing Breed*

I think one reason for family trouble today is our *noninvolvement* with each other. We too often fail to observe what is going on around us in the home, to be involved (not meddlesome) in a loving way.

It used to be, does Mom have a pain? Is Dad tired? What's bothering sister, brother, husband, wife? Are we *all* okay? Now, it's an "I'm-fine-and-to-hell-with-everyone-else" attitude. Shame on us. Husbands and wives, ask yourselves, "When did we last go out on a date alone? When did we share a day with each one of the children to learn about that child's interests?" The so-called "me" generation is — or should be — dead. "Why did my husband/wife/children leave this morning without that usual hug or kiss?" "It doesn't matter," you say. "Oh yes it does," I say. It shows there is a *caring* going on, which will bring unity.

Instead of working on these things, we

126

allow ourselves to stay constantly angry, our moods all bottled up inside. When the inevitable explosion comes, there is bedlam. We holler at each other, "Nobody told me dinner was at six; nobody told me to wash the car, clean my room, do the laundry. Nobody mentioned the affair at school." A complete breakdown in communication, an entire household thriving on selfishness. I lived that once a long time ago, and it was miserable for all concerned. *What we thought they wanted was not what they wanted.* Louie and I couldn't handle this "modern" (do your thing) philosophy. I was hurt and angry. My family doctor, Robert Rood, said to me once, "What makes you think you can't be angry, lady?" Well, Doc, I went home and I got angry — real *angry*.

The others just selfishly go about what they are involved in and forget to tell you. They are pleased with it; so . . . It's something we've all experienced. I had a beautiful comeback: "Why don't we simply put up a tent, a table with a crystal ball on it, and tell fortunes? That way we could see where we're coming from and possibly going." Finally, we cleared the air (and my brain), although communication still does break down. And then I hear, "Mom, it's tent time."

In my house, whenever we realized how silly we had acted — and how thoughtless of

127

each other we had become — we'd do something nice together. Rather than dismissing our problem, we'd discuss it. I can say now in all honesty that we should have done it more often.

We parents sometimes make the horrible mistake of vying for the favor of the children, shying away from being an aggressor or oppressor because we know that only makes things worse. Now I look back at some of my "losses" and see "victory," because my children learned a lot. I know because they've *told* me and *shown* me. I was never going for the win, I was going only for truth. At least now we know each other.

In Laguna Beach, California, one night while we lay in bed listening to the surf of the mighty Pacific do its work — in-out, in-out — my thoughts wandered to the *give* and *take* of life —

> I hear your awesome power
> As it rolls in
> I feel it in the pit of my stomach
> And I know it's you
> You — God.

— and I knew we must open the doors of our household and let Him in.

A child aroused and encouraged early in life

will respond to the good vibes in the home and grow into an "interested-in-life" adult. It's fascinating to watch a baby trying to walk. Groping for something he wants. His mishaps do not deter him from reaching the "cookie jar." Bumping along, he whines, cries, nearly gives up. He looks around for help; when none is forthcoming, he continues on his way. Who said the road was smooth? Even in our everyday pursuits, we fall into potholes; but if we're like that baby, we plod on to reach our "cookie jar."

Why is it, in dealing with family problems, we feel that blame has to be placed on someone? We lay mistakes at someone else's doorstep. It's too difficult to point to ourselves. It took me years to realize that *I allowed you to do this to me, I allowed myself to accept it.* I had to learn "compromise," by coming together with my family.

I've seen personal relationships in which we almost crucify each other, driving our pain into others' hearts. We push the hurts in wherever we find soft spots, when the other is not aware, thus splintering love. Why do we continue to force ourselves into these miserable corners? We act coldly and boldly. Maybe because we're afraid to look into each other's eyes and say, "I'm wrong, let's try again."

# To Children/Adults/Us

The more we entangle ourselves in trivial things, the more we turn and twist to avoid God's gift of love, the weaker we become. The game of life is like baseball; as Yogi Berra said, "It's not over, till it's over." The score is not final until we have lived a full life. I think we can take the full measure of this statement into our bosom because growing up is measured in the same way as a baseball game. It's good to tell our children, "Of course you'll strike out, but heh! isn't it nice when you get those wonderful opportunities to run to home base, and can tell those you love, 'I made it, safely.'" I love to see young people smile; when they do, we parents do too, and it makes us all a happy team. Love coming around full circle.

The important thing is to bring our ideas and thoughts into the open — and know the thoughts of our children, too. I remember the time my DeeDee was to play in *Sweet Charity* at school. While the rehearsals went on and on at school, her chores were being left undone at home. We made a deal. "You can be in the play," I said, "but that means you will have to either get up earlier and do your chores, or get them done when you come home after rehearsal." It appeared that both ways seemed too difficult. One day about 6 P.M., in a heavy rainstorm, I drove down to school and said to the teacher, "DeeDee will have to give up the part because it is not going well at home; surely there must be some way to compromise." This lady looked at me like I had just been born and said, "These things take time and energy, and must be executed right." She paused; it was a few minutes' pause, as the students gathered around us to watch and listen to this Sarah Bernhardt. "*I* teach drama." I said, "You teach it, and I *execute* it. Home, DeeDee." She worked out a method. I wouldn't exactly say she was delighted with her mother; but, honey, they must learn they can't "win 'em all."

Of course, having two parents in show business, DeeDee could have listened to at least one of us on "makeup." You haven't lived until you see a teenager coming home every afternoon looking as if Ringling Brothers had called her for a clown part. Globs and globs of makeup. Listen to Mother's views? *No way*. Then came those lovely pimples. Today, this

131

gorgeous girl wears such a tiny bit of stuff on her face. And she calls me: "Mom, what do you suggest about 'so and so,' 'this or that'?" Gee, it feels good! These are the things that make trial and effort worthwhile.

Louie and I often think of how Tony might have been a great baseball player. This young son of ours can paint, play drums, sculpt, etc. His father, originator of the double bass drum, and a "master" of his instrument, had offered him the instrument and the lessons. But no! Not Tony. Neither Louie nor I would ever push or even encourage either of our children to go into the theater, although it is a noble profession. But my point is they had the opportunities that few young people who want to go in the profession have because they had parents who were out there. Tony kept looking for "his thing" to do in this world. He was taught to maintain a sense of values and gratitude for those who loved him. "Tony," I'd say, "your mistake is letting your values lie dormant, or become warped by taking the wrong turns at the wrong corners." I've said the same thing to my daughter, and all the young ones who have come into my clutches.

To parents I simply say, "Don't feel bad if your children don't care to follow your profession." Let them jump around a bit in different things; they eventually find their way. What

132

you and I as parents must pray is that they *do* pick a decent job and stay out of harm's way. Too many young ones today use the excuse that they are under peer pressure. They say, "The kids at school think I should be like you." That's sad. Or when they go wrong, they try the same excuse in a different way, blaming their parents: "Well, I tried to do and be like you, and it got so tough, that's why I took drugs, alcohol," etc. No, dears, I say, you became weak, and wanted it all too soon. My message to every young person out there is: "Be yourself; and use, protect, and glorify whatever profession you choose to the best of your ability." I think that's what most parents are looking for for their children. I know it would make Louie and me proud to say, "This is our son and daughter; they have done their best." The feelings we have for each other are stronger than any that try to pull us apart.

# Learning and Exercising Respect

It's time to raise the curtain of darkness that has been descending on our households and make it light again. Night has been creeping up on our children and has darkened their path. Parents keep sitting on the shores of uncertainty watching their babies drift away; we ourselves, in fact, drift too. If we all simply walk on hoping we will eventually "discover ourselves," we're making a mistake. The time is now to restore in every household a sense of respect for authority — based on love.

I think of little ones wading on the beach; unless parents show concern and keep an eye on them, some big wave might come and engulf them before we touch hands. I think it's no different with our teens, who, if we're not paying attention, will be sucked out by the strong tides of wrong thinking, bad company. Where is that "haven" we once had to offer? That security? That peace? That shore to return to? Are we parents sitting on our private beaches, or have we drifted out so deeply that the waters of "too much looking the other way" have covered us?

Letting the children flounder without a system or any order is dangerous; a no-win situation. Louie and I found that out when order began to get kicked around in the Bellson household. We had to work harder. Can we — or will we — once again nurse our young with tenderness? Years ago, we nursed them physically, held them to our breast; now that they are teenagers, or almost grown, we put them quickly from our breast to pursue our own youth again. Granted they leave home; but we can't take away the invitation "Come lay your head upon my bosom." I leave that door wide open. It's a good feeling for parent and child.

It's wonderful, even for an older child, when Mom and Dad reach out and say, "Come give me a hug." He or she will blush and say, "Oh, Mom! Oh, Dad!" then melt into a parent's arms. It feels as warm as it did when they were small. It might take two or three *beckonings*, but it's worth it.

To anyone who feels that today children are getting in their elders' way, I say *let them*. Maybe then we will stumble over them. Glory be! They do exist. It is sad to see parental patience wearing thin; we want others to do our work: the *relatives*, the *neighbors*, the *baby-sitter*.

We say, "What a blessing to have someone to help me raise my children." But, darlings, we don't even know they are our children after a while. All of our rules and regulations go straight out the window. Our television bill goes sky high; the child starts to tell *us* how the sitter or Grandma or the lady next door thinks we should act, or lets them act. The little babies who used to eat mashed potatoes, spinach, etc., now refuse anything but potato chips, tacos, and soda pop. If we don't have a responsible person to stay with our children (if we have an outside job, especially), we'll come home to, "The sitter said . . . " or "Jim thinks you should paint the house or get a new TV." Who the hell is Jim? That's the sitter's boyfriend. What is he doing in the house?

I've always found it useful to give the children some chores to do. Keep them busy. Keep yourself busy. Require things of your children, give them responsibility, and you will be amazed at how well they respond. It's a good way to foster respect.

Recently, as I was leaving a building I crossed paths with a small family coming in. The children, on entering, were acting up;

heads turned. They were snapping at their parents, who recognized me. "Who is she? What does she do? Is she somebody?" All in one breath and in unison. I thought, "Hurry, and tell them everybody is somebody so they shut up." All the while these rude, unmannerly children were doing their act, the parents never tampered with them; instead they kept trying to have a conversation with me. Oh, how I longed to own those kids for five seconds, maybe ten! The parents started to explain, "She's a celebrity." "Please don't do that," I asked; "just tell them my name." Unsatisfied, these adorable brats kept squealing.

Suddenly I said, "You either take time to hear what your parents are saying, or I have to move on." One of them turned to me and said, "You be quiet." "Wait a minute, now, you listen to me. Maybe you can talk to your parents like that, but I don't have to accept it, and I won't." They *stared, glared,* and shut their mouths for a while. When they started talking again, it was decently, as one human being to another with respect.

The parents were now seated and the children and I were still standing, laughing and talking. They were completely unaware that their folks had moved on. Frankly, like the Pied Piper I could have marched them right out the door and far away.

When they were delivered to their parents all neatly wrapped in a "package of respect," Mom and Dad beamed. "Look how you changed them," they said. "We wish we could have them behave like this all the time." I said, "You're not going to be that lucky; take this in small doses." We exchanged addresses and I left. I could see them huddling together telling their parents all about this lady (who had evidently met their needs). As I reached the door, I saw a woman sitting nearby crying. "Why are you sad?" I asked. She said, "I watched that whole scene with you and those children and I don't know many people who take the patience to do what you just did." "Lady," I answered, "I have no idea what prompts me to behave like that; I only know if we don't take time and patience to help the children, God help *us.*"

Affection . . . Attention . . . Love . . . Respect. Not easy. Through the years my tiny friends and I have corresponded. To all of them I am "Aunt Pearl." We do need to take time for our children. Michel Quoist wrote a piece that has become my constant traveling companion. I read it at my brother's funeral.

# I HAVE PLENTY OF TIME

I went out Lord.
Men were coming and going,
Walking and Running.
Everything was rushing; cars, trucks,
    the street —
the whole town.
They were rushing after time,
        To gain time.
Goodbye, Sir, excuse me, I haven't time.
I'll come back, I can't wait, I haven't time.
I must end this letter — I haven't time
I can't think, I can't read, I'm swamped,
    I haven't time.
I'd like to pray, but I haven't time.
You understand Lord, they simply
    haven't the time
The child is playing, he hasn't time
    right now — Later on.
The student has his homework to do,
    he hasn't time — Later on.
The student has his courses and so
    much work — Later on.
The young married man has his house;
    he has to fix it up.
        He hasn't the time — Later on.
They are dying, they have no —
Too late. They have no more time!
And so all men run after time . . .

★

. . . time is a gift that you give us,
    But a perishable gift,
A gift that does not keep
    Lord I have time
    I have plenty of time,
    All the time you gave me,
    The years of my life,
    The days of my years,
    The hours of my days,
    They are all mine,
Mine to fill, quietly, calmly
    But to fill completely, up to the
        brim.

# Responsibility

Longing for a method to establish harmony in families, I found the largest word in my small vocabulary, *"Responsibility."* It is defined as "the condition, quality, fact, or instance of being responsible, answerable, accountable, or liable, as for a person, trust, office, or debt."

It is mind boggling how we complicate things, how difficult we find it to get things going. We are all so full of excuses as to the reason *nothing* will work. It *can* and *will* work if we truly take the responsibility of trying, without griping, complaining, or giving in to despair.

We have let so many of our little birds "fly the coop" that now the path of togetherness looks hopeless. It is not. Recently someone very dear to me came to Disneyland to hear Louie's band. Her child, whom I once held in my arms, so tiny and lovable, had flown the nest. As we sat there listening to the band, a tall, good-looking girl loomed in front of me.

141

"Hi, Aunt Pearl." Well, many young ones say that to me, so I smiled, and I said, "Hi, darling." "Aunt Pearl," she said again, "I'm Andi." I almost fell over. This gorgeous girl, I hadn't seen in years, had come out to see Uncle Louie and Aunt Pearl. She wanted to get me popcorn, coffee, etc., etc. I saw how she caressed her mother, and I mean without pretension. It was as if she were saying, "I'm so glad to be with people I love, and remember, if only for this night." I knew what it meant to her mother (who tried, unsuccessfully, to hide her pride); I knew what it meant to me. The mother bird keeps the nest warm for the return; don't worry, the babies feel it.

In our travels Louie and I have often questioned, "Who is responsible for the chaos prevailing over our land?" I think the answer is: "All of us." Communities are becoming unraveled because of a lack of responsibility, to ourselves and our families. We're sitting back, observing each other, and letting chances pass by. We eternally ask questions to which we already know the answers; but we do this because we keep waiting for the answers that we *want* to hear, that will suit our particular needs. In this case, we're acting not like adults, but children. It may signal the time to either loosen or tighten the reigns of authority. We might need to be more forgiving, understanding, forgetting.

I say these things freely because of the experience with my own lost and found sheep. Louie and I rejoice that we've been through the same mill, and ground the same axes, that so many other parents have. In working on the *how* and *why*, we draw closer to conclusions. We feel so good when we can relate to the children — and they to us — on an equal basis.

The "birds" leave the nest so early, often before their wings are strong. Getting a job is their big deal (thank God for that ambition); picking friends to *their* taste (many times not to ours); what the heck, Mom and Dad have picked a couple of "doozies" as friends. The "flying birds" succeed with some things. But they also run into obstacles that make them long for their easy beds again. So they'll fly back home for a "fresh can of worms" to get fat on before taking off again. That's just what my Tony did.

# The Bellson Household

If only we could deal with the moods and emotions within the household, we might be on our way to pulling it all together.

As I write this, I have some regrets and almost want to punish myself for not applying certain actions and thoughts years ago — starting with Tony, the elder of our two children.

Words. Oh, does he have a way with words. He could con himself out of a "snake hole." He'd have such a story to tell the cobras that they'd rear up their heads and do any dance he would demand — even rock and roll!

Then, as now, Tony gets himself into the biggest messes. Always inside of him has been the feeling (why? don't ask me), "The world owes me a living. If not the world, somebody." And I think he wanted everyone in the world to pay him off — one by one.

On his thirty-third birthday I told him, "Tony, I'm not even going to ask what have you done for others? It would be a mistake; I already know. *Nothing.* Because you've done nothing for yourself."

Inside of this handsome, healthy human being is a very gifted, kind, loving, humorous, generous, and caring man. Well-traveled and educated. Someday (I think it's coming soon), all the shoulders of the false friends will fade away; he'll see that they are just "skeletons of truth," and he will come forth as a shining example of how God can draw it all out.

If he can, then he will be an asset to the warm, loving father who cares desperately and wants to see only the best in his children. It is painful for Louie to reprimand the children; he speaks to them in loving, musical tones. Every now and then when the going gets tough he hits that "big bass drum" of authority — and they know. Oops! This guy can be tough as well as tender. DeeDee has the qualities to go forth; she's very ambitious, thrifty (Lawdy! she can save a buck), stubborn (she can come charging down the hill), talented, and clever.

When you as parent see these qualities emerge (almost always later on), you start to feel confident. DeeDee and Tony are full of love, and still full of being children. They know that the "big bass drum" is there as well as the "ewe," standing on the hill — watching, waiting, and praying for them.

Sometimes our reins were tight, sometimes loose, but the cart was never too heavy to pull. Up the hill — or down; like a seesaw. That's life. That's us, the Bellsons. And we're proud of our "old-fashioned home training." One day, going through my mail, I came across this letter:

Dear Mr. and Mrs. L. Bellson:

As one parent to another, I like to get and give credit where credit is due.

I worked on the Panasonic Video starring DeeDee on Sept. 10th. It was a visual bit.

I thought you'd like to know that she is a very dear, sweet, young lady. She is cooperative, and responsive. Always with a smile.

As soon as a celebrity's kid messes up, the news blows it up. But the good kids don't make good copy.

Thought you might appreciate having it.

Sincerely,

(signed) DOLLY HUNTER

# There's Nobody Home

From what I see, most American families have a weird notion about what "togetherness" really is. We have separate schedules, separate interests; we travel (together) in separate cars — and we even eat at separate tables. It's bad enough when we can't be together during the day; but why can't we enjoy recreation together once in a while?

I was so filled with this terrible "apartness" in America that I had to write a poem. I think it expresses it all:

### THERE'S NOBODY HOME

There's nobody home
Upstairs or downstairs.
Mom is out of work, looking,
John is in or out of school
Who knows, who cares.
Mary is — now let me see.
Oh, dear! It's time for the family
 get-together

To eat, to share time together.
Where shall we go? Fast food, slow food
Who cares — just — just — let's eat.
Who's gonna cook? Cook? Cook?
Have you lost your minds? Not me.
Daughter asks, "How do you cook?"
Son says, "I know, but I'm not going to."
Okay! to punish us all — out we go
At least we'll be together — that's it
   — together
     You in your car
     Me in my car
     Us in their car
     Mom drives too fast
     Dad too slow
Well, we'll meet there, anyhow; I may
   jog.
     We're here — same booth or separate?
     No! let's eat together
Conversation! My mouth is full, I'll
   choke
     I must run — where?
     Home — so we can be together.
     I forgot to tell you, I've got a date.
     Goodness! the game is tonight
     Yeah! I've got to watch "Dallas."
     He shoots him tonight, wouldn't
       miss that.
     Thought you were going to the
       hairdresser, honey?

No! I told you — "Dallas" tonight.
"Aliens," tonight honey, here or
  Tina's house?
  See you when I get home
  Bring me a snack — Never mind,
    I'll take a tray
    To my room
Isn't it nice we're so together.
Oops! time for bed, turn off the lights
Where's Sarah? At Tina's
Where's Jimmy? Into his thing,
    in his room.
By the way, do you think they're
    into drugs?
Who knows? Watch their eyes.
You want one more drag, before sleep?
By the way, why are you asking me
  about the kids?
Because they're yours — oh! well —
  Ours.
    You see them more than I do.
I think Sara's boyfriend either sells or
  uses.
    At least I heard he did.
Did you notice white powder in
  Jimmy's room?
    Maybe he borrowed my "talc" again.
We'll check them out. Gimme
  another drag.
Why don't they just smoke like we do?

Or have a couple of martinis?
Too simple, huh? Crazy kids.
Yeah! but they are really nice. Cute.
  Intelligent.
Oh! Crap — you forgot the bathroom
  light.
The kids will turn it off — Do they
  have a key?
      They always have a key
      If not to this house — to someone's.
Good night, dear — Oh! how did the
  game end?
Like "Dallas," I guess — more next week.
It's all so nice all of us — together
      A real family
Not like those weirdos next door
      They're strange
      Terrible kids
      Winos or something
I can't sleep — I'm going in the kitchen
      And turn on the late news
By then the kids should be home
If they're not staying over somewhere.
      Enjoy your sleep, honey
      See you in the morning
      If I don't leave
        Before you
      I'm with you
        In spirit
        Together

So there we are, wherever "there" is. What a pity. I am frequently asked to speak on campuses; when I get into problems within "family," sooner or later I'm hammering on about *drugs*. Because I believe so strongly that drugs sit on our doorsteps, very few households can escape its effects.

"Cocaine" is the highlight of modern society. One dare not have a party or an innocent gathering without it. A friend once said to me, "Pearl, the real drag is you can't put your finger on those who do not use it." Young people are selling it to old ones and vice versa; cars are whisking up the street with the stereo blasting and the driver is "stoned"; you get on an elevator and pray you get off, especially if you're wearing anything valuable. When you walk down the street you keep looking backward, forward, all around, because you know they're out there seeking money for drugs. America, how long are we going to take this?

It seems no one in the family is immune. A sister or brother can get hooked, then involve the other. Drugs have no respect for relationship; even parents themselves may "do" alcohol or drugs with their kids just to show them they are "with it." Most surprising is that even professionals — people we trust — can be into drugs. The doctor, dentist, lawyer, teacher, banker, celebrity, athlete — just about every profession.

I had a frightening experience a while back. A dentist treating me, said: "I know you have lots of pain; I'm not going to use the Novocain, I'm going to try something new that I've been using. It works beautifully, you'll feel nothing." He was right. *I didn't.* After performing the surgery, he said, "I'll leave this here in case you feel pain." (This took place in our home, by the way.) In the bedroom alone — all of a sudden I had *pain.* Ah! The stuff in the box. I took a bit on my finger, as he suggested, and rubbed it on the affected area. My heart started to flutter. The next thing my husband and children saw was Mama reeling into the kitchen, mumbling incoherently. Someone asked, "What did he give you?" (No one had wanted to stay and watch the surgery.) I showed them the box when I calmed down. "Oh, my Lord! That's *cocaine.*" Need I tell you, it was flushed down the drain; and the man was really told off. In fact, I threatened to expose him. The big danger was that, with my heart problem, taking this stuff could have ended my days. Later, we heard the dentist was out of business, hung up to dry. What a pity.

Users, then, come in all sizes and all ages. When it touches our lives, our family, the grief for those we love is unbearable. Lives are locked in closets (from the inside), so no family or friend can enter. We ponder what will happen if we can't help them. We ponder, too, what could happen should they ever be institutionalized or jailed. Horror stories, we hear.

These are heartrending moments for a family. I take every opportunity I can when traveling and speaking to make a plea to "Friends and Countrymen" to look at the handwriting on the wall. Those of us who are still safe *must* save the others.

## It's All Show Biz — Family Biz

Once I was ill and could not make an appearance. Someone sent me an irate telegram: "Your action is outrageous" and then went on about what he thought constituted a great star. Oh, he was livid! The telegram sent no shivers of joy through me; and though I was quite sick, I wired this person back. However, I can't print that response here. Anyway, at this time the saying "The show must go on" had to be put to the test. And I found out the *show will go on,* whether you are there or not. I have also come to see how the same applies to the family. We go on without our family life intact; we go on even with troubles.

For us all may I present a message of hope: Parents, bosses, let us try being for a moment the person who gives our children, our employees, a great enough part to warrant them needing an "understudy." To aspiring youngsters — say perhaps you will not get "on stage," but knowing what is expected of you should the chance come keeps you on your toes, alert, eager, and prepared. That experience is one of the most exciting you'll ever have. In 1946 while working in New York City on the East Side at the Blue Angel, my day came — not as an understudy, but to fill a spot. The ladder of professional success is to be climbed slowly. Life requires a great deal of understudying. I've written this poem just for you:

## DEAR GLORIOUS UNDERSTUDIES

You have stood in the darkness so long —
    you think
Not being able to claim the light of your
    own self.
Do you not feel any rays of love
        From the sun of your parental souls?
Is the heat so intense it sears your innards
        As well as your outer soul
*Against us* — Do you think we have for-
    gotten the pain?
Is the pain of us being ourselves
Who once too stood in shadows
And worked hard to eliminate shadows
    — too much for you to believe?
We too sat in the enclosure of the "womb
    of seeking"

Wanting to be sought after.
All this we did — before they let us out.
We stayed inside the womb, that secure
   warmth
      Not knowing what awaited us.
We felt secure in that lining of the womb
   — that encasement
      Never knowing what awaited us.
"It owes me a debt," you said.
Do you, my dears, want it fast? Do you
   want it slowly?
Will you make use of it? Will you discard
   it forever?
If so — may I ask — Will you love it
   then?
      If ever?
Will you hate it? It — Daring you to be
   patient and wait.
You want to get out from that "cave of
   protectiveness."
Is it going to be so good, being free;
Cutting the string so the opening will be
   tied again.
      Leaving you out in the free air
      So you will not be trapped, stopped
      In your search — ever
Clean, clear, free — How nice
I am now my own — my air — my wind
The womb longs to hold, enfold you
   again

To shield you from the pains of the
world.
The womb has opened before, dumped
before
And waited for the returning pain.
You've been tearing and ripping to get on
with it.
Waiting to be yourself — I, too, waited.
Never feeling or seeing
the bleeding.
Do you feel like crawling back in, to die,
to relive.
The "womb of love" longed for you
many times
I, too, was once enclosed
I, too, pained as you
To have a beginning
We all do.
Pained womb, pained heart
Once out, secure in growth, you'll be
able to tell your story to others
And watch them rejoice, or weep.

This is the saga of coming out in the world,
friends.

# Bending a Little

Papa and Mama taught us early in life to "bend a little." We carried images in our heads of ourselves breaking in half. Their statement was, "Stand like an oak and bend like a willow." Their reasoning was to teach us the art of "compromise." We try to live that in our marriage, family, and work. The more we practice "standing and bending," the easier life becomes; rough moments become smoother. I remember all you said, Mama and Papa. But I confess, many times I slipped — knowingly, unknowingly. Pray God for forgiveness. Am I alone in guilt? If so, then here I stand. But I hope it's on the path of openness.

Pearl (the "poet" again) calls

## COMPROMISE

A stooping, a bending a bit
A pulling, a bit of action
A cutting, editing of self

158

A pruning; knowing what to take out
A closing up, what to leave in
A caring; love is the essence
A waiting, tears of joy and pain
It's all so complicated — simple
Blind we are all — Blind
   Clarity will return —
   With Compromise.

# Love —
## A Serving, a Returning

Living every day to its fullest is like a tennis match. I practice it on stage and at home. "Serving" and "returning." Watching the ball come over the net, positioning myself to get it back, calls for a wariness; a swiftness to react to what is really happening. Who said we must "do all things equally"? Things should be done to the best of our abilities. Circumstances themselves will teach us what to do and possibly what not to do. My theory is, "Work for another as if you are working for yourself." Hit that ball over the net as if the receiver is yourself.

A *honest serve* brings an *honest return*. If it doesn't, fear not, because the person who doesn't give back in truth has lost a great chance to experience "love returned." Remember that life pays its debts, sometimes more, sometimes less. Don't bother to rest on the laurels of what your gain or loss will be. The wreath has thorns in it and you might bleed. It takes a steady head to hold a crown. However, *if* and *when* you have done your best, you can be assured of a good, unmeasured return.

Louie and I often stressed this to our brood. We would say, whatever your "dream job" is, first get a *rent-paying job* while going after your "real" goal. "Don't seek promoters, for if you should rise above the crowd the promoters will seek you." But above all, "Don't rush." I'd remind them only God holds the stop watch on living and dying, so enjoy. In God's time, all happens. He also gives us that inner strength we need in time of pain or loss — and the understanding to face our problems along the way.

The brilliant educator and teacher Marva Collins, who founded Westside Preparatory School in Chicago, Illinois, in 1975, has nurtured and cherished so many children under her wings (including three of her own). She has taken children under her tutelage to exceptional heights. Once she wrote me: "God gives me a strong back to endure the pace of what is expected of me here and to be reminded that we eat an elephant one bite at a time. I like me, I like what I have done, and if this is my last day on earth I will never have to say, 'God I wish I had done more.'"

# Teamwork

Papa and Mama gave us a lesson to live with. "When are you really sure of what you will never do," they'd ask, "or what you can't do?" Scales are not balanced until the right measurements are in place. We've often heard that boys lean more to the mother, girls to the father, and vice versa. I think there's a lot of truth in this. I've heard many girls complain, "I don't get along with my mom. She's too tough. She doesn't understand me; my dad does." Nothing is more infuriating than when the daughter and mother are going at it, and the dad steps in. He'll say to the wife, "Honey, why don't you try to get along with her, understand her?" The wife could strangle her husband for that. There he stands (she feels), reprimanding her in front of the child, as if *she* (the mother) is a child. Now the battle turns between the husband and wife, as the daughter saunters out, head held up, the "victor," it seems.

Once daughter finds a boyfriend, however

— especially one she can twist around her finger — Papa is out. Now it's Mama who's the "highlight of her life." And when she experiences "love problems," she pleads: "Mom, what's wrong with men?" Honey, now that you have one — you figure it out.

I feel strongly that raising children is both mates' mutual responsibility. Taking sides is not love. Children should know they cannot drive a wedge between their parents. I have no regrets over sore knees, aching back, and empty purse because I took the children places. Neither does Louie, who always did the same.

# Authority, Please

Sitting under a tree at a golf course, I once questioned, "Why do we contest authority?" "What gives others the privilege to order or decide for us?" We would do well to use authority first on ourselves.

As I watched the golfers, teeing up, defying that ball, I laughed. This little round, white ball had grown men under its spell saying to them, "Unless you whack me correctly, I'm going no place. *You* are the one who can set me off on the right track." When the golfer misses, he swears, fumes, talks to himself, the ball, stick, tee, ground. Everything is caught in the net of his anger. His authority has been challenged.

This golfer was ordered or directed to do something a certain way. With misguided thoughts he strayed from his orders. If he had obeyed, he would have hit the ball. Instead, doing his own thing, his own way, he lost direction. Once more he tried it, lined up the club head behind the ball, tenderly but firmly grasped his club, made a beautiful swing, and off the ball sailed. His smile was broader than his swing. Executing his authority correctly, he had succeeded.

Behavior patterns set in childhood will carry over into adulthood.

I learned this firsthand. I watched closely my elders' training methods. And I wound up repeating things on my children that bugged me when I was growing up. It's no wonder the children now would have the same reaction. The *ideals* taught me were right; but the *method*, as I see it now, might not have been. Teachings had been passed from generation to generation, nothing had varied. Parents in my age group can see their mistakes now; they see the flaws in some of that upbringing and seek their children's blessings. We can learn from others' past mistakes — and our own.

When we as parents gloat over our "power," we misuse authority and our children will rebel. They will feel their physical and moral strength are being sapped. In the Bellson home during moments like this, when Pearl went a bit haywire *(and I did, sometimes)*, Louie was a "knight in shining armor." He was the defender who would have a talk with the small ones. He'd allow them usually to go back to what they were doing while the "wicked witch" watched. He and his smiling elves just ignored me for a while and enjoyed each other. It didn't take me long to see what I had done. I learned what happens when we stifle a child's free thinking by exercising more power than a given situation calls for. If we don't admit — and correct — our mistakes, the child suffers unnecessarily. He begins to think, "When I'm older, I will no longer take orders from anyone; I will exercise the freedom of myself, living fully as I choose." If the pressure on him has been too heavy, he will fill up with hatred — for all authority.

I'm the first to admit how difficult it can be — knowing the difference between *too much* and *too little* discipline. And how important it is that fathers and mothers not let their own personal problems govern their behavior toward the children.

Religiously speaking, I choose to think that God is the supreme voice of authority; the voice from which we all seek direction. He has given us the permission to exercise self, to act upon our choices. Words that deal with "love of family" can be carried over into "Love of God":

For I am sure that neither death, nor life, nor angels, nor principalities, nor powers, nor things present, nor things to come, nor height, nor depth, nor anything else in all creation will be able to separate us from the love of God.

(Rom. 8:38–39)

# Helping Hands

One day, riding along on Amtrak, I received a powerful message. Since I am not a tunesmith and don't write music, I didn't jot down the words and music that now flowed like the passing scenery. I was thinking how others are capable of helping us; and how most of the time we take advantage of kindness. We become beggars. Our friends continue to reach out and help, figuring things are beyond our control. We may not realize that our friend has needs, too. If the good friend continues to help the "constant griper," there's bound to be trouble. Why are some people eternally miserable, thinking everyone else's problems are less important than theirs? The words of the song inspired by my thoughts, copied and arranged later by Louie, have touched many hearts and minds.

### "NOBODY CAN DO IT FOR YOU, BUT YOU"

Nobody can do it for you, but you
Nobody can make all your dreams come
    true,
You think that you're making it
        Simply by faking it
        But that will never do.
The dreams you dream they all belong to
    you
        (Then you'll say quietly)
Nobody can do it for me, but me
Wake up and face that reality
You think you're all alone
When you're out there on your own
But nobody can do it for you but you
No! No! No! No!
        Nobody Can Do It for You, But You.

At my graduation from Georgetown University the song came back to me as I stood on the podium, and so I sang it. Everyone thought it had been written for that moment. The message fit all of us departing students, so I'm proud of that.

We must all think positive thoughts about our lives and transmit those thoughts to others — beginning with family, but extending beyond. This is a real and open world — let's live in it that way. Even the best of friends disagree. But we've got to put things in their

169

proper perspective, use our common sense more, and stop blaming the world for ourselves. Most of all, as I'm always "preaching," let's be *honest*. Catch the disease of mistrust in each other before it runs rampant.

Parents in show business, I assure you, have trouble with their children as much as any parents. We can tell you some wild tales. Our children are cast in the "limelight" of our lives, unfortunately, and many cannot handle it. A lot dig their own holes to stand in. In loving them, understanding them, the juices of love flow freely. My son Tony will never realize how much I learned from him — good and bad things. *He gave me more insight into how to deal with children than anyone; for that I thank and love him.*

We must recognize the ability we have to harm, wreck, or ruin each other's lives. Every day is a lesson in relieving tensions, increasing our substance. Everything we *do* is a test, involving necessary risks.

If we keep communicating with God, though, we will be able to link ourselves to peoples' needs. "They" become "us"; "theirs" becomes "ours." Then "ours" becomes "His." A natural and free gift, a partnership, that has great payoffs for *family*.

As we grow older — and more tired — we

feel a need to tie things together. I've had people tell me, "Pearl, you must understand that the children are going through stages." I reply, "So are we elders going through stages, and it's not easy."

My sister-in-law, Lucille, once remarked to me: "You're busier than all of us, yet you keep going. All I do is complain." It's not easy for me, Lucille; but I was taught there is always more out there. More work to be done. I think Mama and Papa were really teaching the Bailey children to "clean up our act."

# Letters Shared with My Love

My love, Louie, writes love letters. He started when we met; and every now and then after thirty-six years, I find one on the pillow. I rediscovered a couple while working on this book:

In the beginning God created the earth. In your beginning He created a human being who could spread Peace and Love. One who could help others find the way. God gave you the ability and strength to cope with all individuals. Your task has always been to solve the puzzle and make things right. Only the chosen few can do this. Your work is never done because you *care* and many people *depend* on your guidance. May your light always shine in the darkness of many unfortunate people's dreams. You help others to find joy in helping themselves and others. Peace and love are a beautiful twosome shared only by those who live it. You Live It.

From LUIGI 6/7/87

## A BIRTHDAY LETTER: 3/29/83

Javile, you are the essence of God's creations. You come from the earth, reach for the sky and point the sun on everyone's face. In the quiet of night you're like the moon with a watchful eye. When trouble comes, your great strength turns a tornado to a warm summer wind — your path has been marked since you were born. You are to lead, to give of every fibre in your body and know that you are a disciple of God. Your goal is to create Love and Happiness and in your darkest hours you will shine like the real Pearl you are.

More love now than ever.

(signed) LUIGI

## LETTER TO MY LOVE — (Oh yes!
### I answer)
### "We made our bed — 2 special people"

5:29 P.M. — Louie abroad — Riding in car to meet him in Chicago — Feb. 8

173

Oh, Louie! I am so full of love for you today — All day. You are far away, in Frankfurt, Germany, but you have never been so close.

All day I loved you so that a sense of play acting guilt came over me. What I played at — If Louie and I were not married and not even having met — worked together — then it would have happened as it did — And has.

I played at — *what if we had both been married, could we have been spared that unfortunate, helpless thing of falling in love — and hurting others?* Again, again, I know God is good — *because our love is guiltless* — He, God, allowed us to be free to love — free to enrich that love even more — Forever is today — Tomorrow is forever, is now.

Why today do I love you more than any other day? Perhaps I feel your foreverness. Feel mine, Louie, Feel mine.

Love,
(*signed*) JAVILE

After thirty-six years, it's still glorious to read a love letter from my mate. Louie, I'm glad I met you — you are "the loving," "the toucher" in the family, *quietly*. I'm the "loving force of 'let's get it done' "; not so quietly.

174

The two of us have different ways: he the *quiet* toucher, lover; me the *not-so-quiet* lover, the forceful do-er. Our children have been able to live with that; not always peacefully, but hopeful that we could always work it out. How nice if children would write love letters and put them on their parents' pillows and vice versa. Some can't express themselves verbally — so write it; tell each other: "we are family."

Our children are already old; they are now thirty-four and twenty-eight. The things we advised them about have already happened, been experienced, believed. Daily we listen to the news, watch happenings in the street, abhor what we see and hear, and pray our children's children will not become a part of it. We pray daily for all children to escape it.

I am reminded of a poem that all parents and children *should* and *can* relate to. Written by one of the greatest poets ever, Langston Hughes. It touches me deeply with its quiet power, its encouragement. It really speaks about all of us.

## MOTHER TO SON

Well Son, I'll tell you
Life for me ain't been no crystal stair

It's had tacks in it and splinters
And boards torn up,
And places with no carpets on the
    floor —
Bare.
But all the time, I'se been a-climbin on,
And reaching Landins,
And turnin corners
And sometimes goin in the dark
Where there ain't been no light
So, Boy don't you turn back.
Don't you set down on the steps
Cause you find it's kinder hard
Don't you fall now —
For I'se still goin, Honey,
I'se still climbin
And Life for me ain't been no
    Crystal Stairs

# THREE

## Reflections at Seventy
*Pearl's Gems*

# The UN:
## An Experience of Love and Duty

Sitting in the United Nations General Assembly can make one start to feel a lack of religiousness. It almost seems impossible to hold on to that undying faith that God can and does heal people's souls, ease their pain. We tend to forget that He alone cures all ills, stops all quarrels; but we must cease name-calling and hate-mongering. We need a great deal of spiritual guidance in that hall; everywhere in that building needs touching by Him, for we have said to the world, "We are here to exercise the peace you seek, so it will rub off on the rest of the world."

So many times, sitting alone in my delegate's seat, I get a feeling that He will come sauntering in, looking at all of us, reading our minds. I pray that He will stop by the aggressor's chair and say in a quiet voice, "Stop it this instant; obey my rules, stop all your ranting and raving because I will not allow you to disturb the peace of the world that man should

179

seek. You are here to help mankind, not to destroy each other."

As I watch for Him daily I can see people of all countries; some smile, others just stare or keep a blah expression on their faces as if to say, "Let's get on with the agony." I assure you that except in the delegate lounge where they're smoking, sipping their cappuccino, etc., or when they're on lunch break chatting away, or at one of the *far too many nightly* receptions, there is no laughter in the United Nations. Bargaining and cajoling are very much in style; name-calling is also in season. How does one make a speech using words such as "murderers"? The first time I went to the UN was in 1975, under Ambassador Moynihan of New York. I returned in 1976, under Governor Scranton of Pennsylvania. At the time the biggest issue was Zionism as a form of racism. Boy! Did they call one another names such as you hear in school yards, or on street corners. All I could think to myself was, "And these are the men who decide the fate of the world."

The Israeli ambassador was Chaim Herzog. This man has to be one of the most brilliant speakers I have ever heard; and he is one to be heard. Sadly enough, when the issues got hot and heavy, about seventy-seven countries really lit into the Zionism issue. The United

States was in the thick of the fray; then came Herzog's time to speak.

There was loud shuffling in that hall, as chairs were pushed back and men walked. Yes, about seventy-seven nations walked out simultaneously. At first it shocked me because I thought, "What the hell, if someone is going to talk about you, then why not sit and listen?" Instead they went out to lean on the railing by the side balcony to talk, disturbing the atmosphere within the hall. And these are grown men, mind you.

During this particular period the Palestinian Terzi (spokesman for the PLO) was allowed to sit alone in a box on the fringe of the hall and *listen*. Many times I'd see Terzi and Herzog pass each other in the hall going to lunch or elsewhere. Neither one spoke, of course. Here were two highly intelligent men, the whole world awaiting their next move so we could get on with some more of the business of world peace, passing each other without uttering a word. How, please tell me, can men make any sense if they don't communicate? It's *impossible*. Both were capable, I know, of sitting down over a cup of coffee, *battling it out* or *shaking hands*. That didn't happen; so more hatred was flamed over the Assembly hall.

How in the name of the Lord (both Israeli

and Palestinian say they believe in Him — "Yahweh" for one; "Allah" for the other) can they pass by each other? How will they ever resolve their differences, find that necessary peace, if they never stop and talk or at least make eye contact.

Once while awaiting the elevator I saw Terzi and Herzog coming from different directions. Being just about midway between them, I spoke to both and they simultaneously answered me. It must have scared the hell out of them, how close they had come to making the mistake of talking to each other. That's when all of this business really hit me.

My first run-in with a country was under Moynihan. I had a feeling that as soon as I entered someone was going to make a remark related to my show business career. It happened with Cuba on about my third day. Anib Alacorn, tough as nails, made a long speech on the Puerto Rico item (statehood with us vs. independence) and made a remark relating to the United States having someone who could sing their statements, etc. etc. Well, sir! Ambassador Moynihan went red and started scribbling his "right of reply" speech hastily. I asked (I wasn't quite as red), "Sir, can I read it?" "You sure can, Pearl," he said. Without realizing, I took off for the podium minus Moynihan's notes. I went into into a calm,

182

deliberate speech — the kind that *only* a woman could deliver. My fingers, I'm sure, were weaving patterns in the air as I spoke; that speech was run off (and copies distributed) for about two days. In fact it was said that "It was the only time that someone had spoken 'off the cuff' there." Every man and woman, however brilliant, reads from prepared papers.

Years later, I had still another encounter with the Cuban delegation. And, again, it began with a paper on the Puerto Rico issue. I read the U.S. statement of our opinion. The original Cuban speaker then shifted to a young lady who read a scathing reply — adding things about Broadway, commercials, and the like. Everyone in the hall understood it was intended for me. I turned in my seat and almost trembled at the stupidity of what was said. Our delegation was livid. But I got back at them. For the second time in the UN, I spoke without a prepared text.

*Statement by the Honorable Pearl Bailey, United States Adviser to the United Nations Third Special Session of the General Assembly Devoted to Disarmament, in Plenary, in Right of Reply to Cuba, June 3, 1988.*

Mr. President, my delegation understood

that the purpose of this special session was to explore various arms control and disarmament issues in an effort to reach agreement to help set the agenda for the multilateral consideration of these issues. However, the Vice President of Cuba has introduced hostility and confrontation into this session.

He has made personal attacks against the President of the United States. He has stated that Puerto Rico is a United States colony and he has accused the United States of being responsible for most of the regional conflicts in the world.

His direct personal attack on a head of state of a member of the United Nations is a violation of the traditions of this body.

My delegation rejects the falsehood spread by Cuba that Puerto Rico is a colony of the United States. The United Nations by a resolution of the General Assembly adopted in 1953 decided that Puerto Rico had achieved self-determination. In that respect I note that the people of Puerto Rico will again elect their governor and legislature in free elections this November. When will Cuba hold free elections with a genuine choice among candidates? The world has been waiting since January 2, 1959.

It is particularly curious to hear Cuba express such fulsome support for peace and disarmament. Cuba maintains the largest military establishment in Latin America and is a major exporter of mercenaries and arms. It is Cuba which is embarked upon expansionist policies in Latin America and Africa. We hope that this body will not be subjected to further extraneous remarks during its important deliberations.

Thank you, Mr. President.

*Extended Right of Reply Statement by the Honorable Pearl Bailey to Cuba. June 3, 1988.*

Mr. President, and all distinguished people here, there are no such words as "behind the boards" of Broadway; they are "on" them. I think that when we reach the point in any lifetime that we have to resort to mentioning people's professions, I would mention all of my professions but it would be a pity — we would be here all night because I am more than Broadway. You are not attacking my country now, you have now made a personal attack which I will not accept in this hall. Broadway, TV, we all have to eat. Now many, many years ago I was here and I spoke to the Cuban Representative about the same subject matter — Puerto Rico. Unfortunately, he pulled the same trick, he went up to that podium

185

and brought up Broadway or whatever it is. Beware I am not going to stand up and sing the "Star-Spangled Banner," you can bet on that. I never mix my profession with this, this is my country, your country, or all our countries, and I'm here for strictly business. We have all gotten older. What a pity we don't all get wiser. Trust in manners and talking about matters in the wrong way, simply defeats the purpose of what this is about. The boards of Broadway, the TV halls, and all of this have long been forgotten whenever I sit in this seat. I am here for my business and the love of the entire world because I love God, I love truth, and I want to see peace on this earth. There is no money that can buy that for me. I thank the Representative of Cuba, and I will send you a résumé of all my professions. Thank you.

In response to this, I received the following note from President Reagan: [*see page 187*]

That again called for a whole lot of printouts. It's sickening that human beings make such sordid attacks. All the dignity goes out of our halls at times like this.

In between these two Cuban encounters came one that I wish had not involved me at all. It was an official paper I read to Zimbabwe

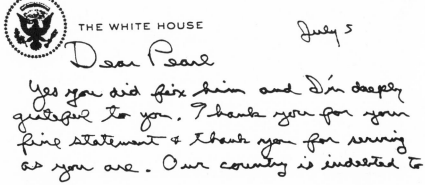

THE WHITE HOUSE

July 5

Dear Pearl

Yes you did fix him and I'm deeply grateful to you. Thank you for your fine statement & thank you for serving as you are. Our country is indebted to you.

Nancy sends her love & so do I.

Warmest Regard
Ronald Reagan

in answer to an opinion on Namibia. The press was quick to jump on it and pass it around the world; but as it turned out, the friendship between our countries has been preserved. For a long time the Zimbabwe ambassador, a smart man and eloquent speaker, sat directly behind us. I had never seen much of a smile from him. The young people from that delegation would sneak me smiles and I'd return them. The paper I read was from my country and did not necessarily reflect my opinion; everyone in that room must and should realize that policymakers set the policy.

I really liked my friends from Zimbabwe; one of them asked for my crochet cap and I gave it. Actually most people in the UN like each other; it's just weird how we have to behave there. Many times I wish for a reversal of seats, so the policymakers from all the countries would be forced to sit there and get the reactions that their policies receive in that hall. Many feel pain. As you pass some delegates on the way to the lounge or the ladies' or men's room, or even in the dining room, you look at them as a friend would, as if to say "I'm sorry." What a pity.

One day a strange thing happened. By nature I don't stay upset with people and find it distasteful for friends to look into each other's eyes and not speak. Turning sideways in my chair one day, I looked at the ambassador from Zimbabwe, he returned my gaze, and I said, "Why don't you smile at me, ambassador?" He looked at me for a moment, intently, then smiled. We both did. He got up to deliver his speech on the podium, and without stopping, he dropped a copy right in front of me. I said to Ambassador Herbert Okun, "Did you see that?" He said, "Yes, I did. Wonder why he did it." I thought to myself, "It's a symbol of friendship that all mankind needs."

As I think of it now, there was a fourth encounter — a happy and amusing one. I met up again with that tough rascal Ambassador Anib Alacorn. President Ortega of Nicaragua was getting ready to speak (our delegation had walked out on him once), when I left the Assembly hall for another meeting. Who should be coming out of the hall with a long black Cuban cigar, but Alacorn.

I said, "What are you doing here?" Ever since our first encounter he had been fascinated with this odd (I think he thought I was odd) woman, and fairly teased me in a cute way, always *without* speaking. He answered, "Why are you leaving? Don't you want to hear him [Ortega] speak?" I replied, "I see you're leaving too; don't *you* want to hear him either?" He howled. "I heard you are now a minister," I said. He beamed. I wouldn't be surprised if he didn't end up as head of the Cuban government.

Yes, it's a love/hate relationship that is spelled out in the United Nations. If we could only channel all of this in a positive way, we could get the universe to live in peace. If used correctly, the United Nations could be the *most constructive* force of man we have; if not, we can destroy ourselves. Let me explain a bit more about the working plans of the UN General Assembly.

If a resolution were proposed on "snow," it would be read even if the sun had been shining for six months. How else could one be seen marching down the aisle, wearing one's best suit or dress, to deliver that *powerful* and *long* speech. Though some speeches last only fifteen minutes or so (rare), others can last an hour or more. The listeners have a choice: *Listen, Chatter, Look* (or be) *Interested,* or — as often happens — *Sleep.* If you choose the last, be careful because the TV cameras for upstairs monitoring keep focused on the Plenary at all times. Embarrassing if caught.

Once the oratory is finished, it's back to your seat, then wait for all your friend-nations to line up in the aisles to shake your hand (the enemies don't move). By then, the next speaker is already droning on. Who is going to miss his/her golden opportunity? *No one.* The same words are repeated and interpreted over and over again. Originality is out. Believe me, no one throws caution to the wind and speaks out. There is no Lincoln vs. Douglas style in the UN forum. I should add that there are many "cheek to cheek" kisses here. I will not get into whether they are sincere or not. *It is done, period.*

Sometimes, especially in the opening session weeks between September and early November, there are heads of state in attendance — Presidents, Foreign Ministers, Prime Ministers, coming and going. Black limousines arrive; and the security forces of host and visiting countries pour in. The hall is packed.

Normally, except for voting times on important resolutions, the hall is half filled and visitors (who should come more often to see the General Assembly and learn) are absent.

The "Biggies" speak and then retire to a special section where practically everyone lines up to shake the hand of the "potentate" or whomever. He in turn is surrounded by his ministers, wife, others. Pictures are taken by the roped-off press. You are thought to be someone important yourself if the "Biggie" takes your hand and makes a fuss over you (usually done if you've been to their country). You strut back into the hall a bit grander. Some then reach out to "touch the hand" that "touched the hand."

Once in 1988 Prince Bandar Bin Sultan, the ambassador from D.C., and Prince Saud El-Faysal Al-Saud of Saudi Arabia came during "Biggie Time." Alternate delegate Noel Grass (my friend) and I sat on the side right across from the Saudi delegation. Both princes are handsome, and we girls said, "Look, two Tom Sellecks." Noel said, "Pearl, do you know them?" I said I knew the one from Washington. He had done much good work donating moneys to children's causes; the other, a nephew of King Fahd, I'd met on his 1987 visit. "Yipes, here they come," I said. There by the railing these gorgeous two men spoke with me. Noel fainted, I think (smiles).

I remember in 1987, after Prince Saud El-Faysal had spoken, most of the nations went outside to talk with him or shake his hand. The line had been so long that as I arrived the party was leaving. Prince Bandar Bin Sultan spoke and they proceeded up the walk. As I turned to reenter the hall, Prince Saud El-Faysal stood in my path. "Prince Bandar Bin Sultan gets to meet all the pretty ladies; I don't," he said. Someone had said something to him, heaven knows what, and he had come all the way back to tell me that. Honey, I fainted. Well, one has to enjoy a few smiles to make up for the tears.

After all the ceremony, you either return to your seat; go into the delegates' lounge to chat, sip coffee, and inhale a roomful of cigarette smoke; or go to your office at the mission to read through the mail. Delegates (of important countries) receive numerous invitations. One thing is certain: The hall is again half empty, unless the next speaker is another "Biggie."

When I say "numerous invitations," I mean it. Most mission ambassadors, deputies, committee heads, and delegates are swamped with from two to five invites a night at different embassies. How these dear people make it the next day is beyond me. They *look and are* exhausted the next day. I remember well one time when Governor Scranton said, "There are just too many parties and I don't want my staff exhausted." They say these after-business meetings are helpful for establishing diplomatic relations, making new friends, even picking up pieces of gossip here and there. All I know is, you're standing on your feet (there are not *that* many sit-down meetings) and I got tired of looking at "the painted brown turkey," little pieces of bread with caviar or salmon spread on them, ham, meatballs with toothpicks stuck in them, Perrier water, and booze (for those who wanted it). I got tired of the whispers, too. I suppose these events relaxed a lot of people but I'm sure many wanted to go home, kick off their shoes, and eat a good hot meal. Yet I must admit it is almost impossible for boredom to settle in when such high drama is being played. Shakespeare really laid it on: "All the world's a stage, the men and women merely players."

The first President of the UNGA (United Nations General Assembly) I met was the man who is now not allowed in our country — Kurt Waldheim. This tall, long-nosed, small-eyed, austere-looking man presided over the Assembly for ten years. He sat there like a military figure; as it was later proven, he was a military figure in the German Army. The issue of our keeping him out of our country involves *where,* *how,* and *if* he figured in the Holocaust.

I once had asked Governor Scranton if it was okay for me to crochet, hands under the desk but not looking down, and he said it was all right. Mrs. Eleanor Roosevelt, the great lady, used to knit and I'm sure while doing that she not only heard every word, she wove some beautiful patterns. (In 1987, I continued my "operation crochet" and furnished many in the mission, overseas, and on the home front with warmth for the winter.) At the end of the session in December 1976, there was a big "handshaking" deal and there in line stood Waldheim. "Sir," I said, "you always watched me so directly from our podium, I could feel you studying me. Do you know what I was busy doing?" "Yes," he answered. "My mother used to do it. You were crocheting." Heavens to Betsy, they not only have cameras in there; they have good curious human eyes.

My favorite moments were always with Ambassador Baroody of Saudi Arabia, the first Arabic member of the United Nations. His table was the first one inside the doorway of the dining room (small enough for two, maybe four opened). This man loved poetry and music and was a true diplomat. When he

194

spoke from the podium, he truly was seeking a way of peace.

One day as I passed his table he asked me to sit with him and have a steak. This soon became such a ritual that a person in our mission (now deceased) once called me aside and said, "I would be careful sitting all the time with Baroody; you must keep in mind he is a shrewd man and may be picking your brain." "Thank you," I answered, "I can handle myself." This man continued, "But you're not a foreign service person and may not understand how he is going about it." "Thank you again, sir," I said, "but I can well understand what he's talking about as our conversation from beginning to end is about 'the Lord.' " *That did it.* The ambassador and I continued our luncheons. He'd include my husband Louie when he came to visit, and even had Louie write music to some of his poetry. Diplomat to the end, Baroody went to the podium and read his closing statement for the final session. It included me, "Pearl Bailey is the freshest breeze that has blown through here." Thank you, my dear friend, and farewell.

What bothers me and others is the lack of interest displayed when nations speak about what some deem "small issues." What is nothing to one might mean a great deal to another. A couple in our group one day wanted to know why I felt so strongly, as General Vernon Walters did, about our six seats being filled at all times. Whether anyone else was there or not we were supposed to sit and hear all the issues. Empty seats bugged me because coming from the theatrical profession nothing is more painful than looking at empty seats or, as is said in night clubs, "snow tables" (blinding white tablecloths with nothing on them).

In one such case each country was discussing the idea of loaning their artifacts to another country to be shown in museums (thus earning money). Speech after speech went on about that. Egypt had Tutankhamen, Greece was talking about the "Elgin Marbles," and so on.

"So what," someone asked, "is so important about marbles?" "Well, honey, for one thing these are not 'aggies' we're talking about. Suppose you go to Greece on one of your grand diplomatic missions to borrow some ships; when you arrive at the President's palace there is a long line of diplomats ahead of you. A man comes down the line inquiring of everyone his purpose in meeting with the President. 'Well,' you explain, 'one thing is about ships; the other may seem unimportant at this time but I wanted to express my interest in the 'Elgin Marbles.' The magic word. Out of the line and into the President's presence you are ushered to talk about a subject dear to him, 'the marbles of Greece.' The ships may now be automatically granted. That's 'love diplomacy' and it can work. More of it should be practiced."

I think what I said went right over my friend's head. He was one of two Foreign Service graduates at the session. I did not despair about my two young friends because they will learn that we have got to sort and sift out things in love, taste life before we swallow it, smell life so we can get its true fragrance. In this manner, we will be able to absorb the fullness of life; reality will come into focus and peace in this world can be achieved. Let's remove our blinders; let us seek quality of life, not so much quantity. Feeling poetic one day, I put my feelings on paper:

Where is the light at the end of the
    tunnel?
Is it out? Is it dim? Did it exist?
Are the keepers of the light alive? Dead?
I think we'd better go back from whence
    we came
It's dark, that light is gone
We're trapped in our own darkness
There is light — so the digging must
    begin.

We in our mission run across many who are forever griping and telling us off about what they feel we Americans owe to the rest of the world. As if no other country in the world exists. They speak of how rich we are, how beautiful our homes (have they seen the ghettoes?), our lackadaisical style of living. So we owe, owe, owe — the debt of taking care of everyone. Ironically, many of these gripers are from very wealthy countries.

Foreign people who come to our shores are amazed at our technology; we visit their homelands and we're amazed at the splendors of their *ages*. Every man is rich in the sense of having something to give the other — things not measured in dollars and cents.

America has many problems just as other countries have; we make terrible mistakes. However, being the only real democracy left, people tend to think about us in a strictly material sense. After they come here to live, they miss many of their homeland values and expect us to rectify that in some way or other. And so, we become the scapegoat of every country that is hurting. Heh! We pain, too.

I tend to think that we are spreading the wrong kind of thinking to the world. We need to exert more emphasis on "spiritual values" and stop shoving ahead with "material values." Put back on the true face of America we

198

used to wear and then perhaps we can teach these people who come to our shores *how* America really became the place they thought it was.

A New York taxi driver really bugged me one day going to work. I said, "We worked hard in this new country just as you did in your old country. You should see where we were a hundred years ago, then you'd know how far we've progressed." He then proceeded to tell me what he had expected when he arrived, and what he had left in his glorious country to come to us. By now he had me really angry with him so I said, "If you're so damn unhappy, then why don't you go back home. I'm sure we love you but I'm not too sure we'll miss you." One long glaring look in his front mirror, our eyes met, and he drove me to work. Maybe he wasn't happy, but I was. *One for America.*

I cannot write about the UN without acknowledging my colleagues. I remember in particular (1987–88) our UN Chief, General Vernon Walters (he speaks eight languages and understands them all; loves chocolate cakes — I mean the *whole* chocolate cake; loves to travel; and loves people, including his Sergeant Pearl, who loves him too). . . . Ambassador Herbert Okun (the diligent redhead who comes daily to the big building to do battle) . . . Ambassador Patricia Byrne, one of the hardworking women of the world . . . Dear Ambassador Lester Korn and my "sister," his wife Carolbeth . . . A very dedicated "brother" of mine, Ambassador Hugh Montgomery, a bundle of brains with a fantastic sense of humor, and his Anna Marie . . . Rose, the secretary people pray for . . . Cameron Humes, one of the most honest men I've ever met . . . Bob Rosenstock, a brilliant lawyer whom I met when I first started at the UN in 1975 . . . My "son" Joe Merante, who even went to Switzerland with me on the World Health Organization for AIDS affair and gave me the pleasure of buying him a *bright red sweater* and socks. (I had never seen "the boy" in anything but a suit, knotted tie, and shined shoes. I can't wait to see him show up one day at the morning meeting in the sweater. That would send him to a new country for sure!) . . .

There are so many I spent a large and important part of my life with.

Probably no one could be more dedicated to the UN work I did than my devoted husband Louie and my road manager, E.B. The hours were long, and Louie patiently waited for many dinners. Whenever he was out of town, E.B. escorted me to "handshaking" affairs.

We've been to many delegates' lounges and missions (including the Soviet). One thing for sure, no one stays long at these affairs, it's in one door, shake a hand or two, and out the other.

On one occasion Louie had a big moment that gained us many new friends. Secretary of State Shultz gave a luncheon for the Caribbean countries at the River Front Restaurant and invited me. As I passed him and General Walters in the receiving line the Secretary said, "Pearl, do you know any Latin American songs?" "No, sir," I replied, "but I know a few Arabic ones." General Walters named one or two he thought I might know. I did; but I told him, "No one would understand me at all."

I had been escorted to the restaurant by Ambassador Lester Korn. My stomach was actually turning. I was getting sick at the thought of entertaining. Show people can seldom go out "to relax" without being asked to entertain. But each one likes to have the tools of their trade (proper dress or suit, musicians, arrangements, etc.). It's what makes the whole thing work for the performer. Lester kept boosting my morale; I just kept getting nauseous. He couldn't understand how this woman so used to performing could feel this way. "Well, here I go again for my country," I thought.

Then I had an idea. Louie had just come in from Chicago and was at the hotel writing some music. I excused myself and went to the front of the restaurant where Shultz and Walters were greeting more guests. Secretary Shultz said, "Pearl, are you leaving?" "Oh no, sir, I just got an idea." I called our hotel; the operator seemed to take a hundred years to answer. "Louie, honey, please grab a pair of drumsticks and come to the rescue." I explained the situation, then returned to the party. Ambassador Korn was seated at the little bar. I beckoned the bartender and told him what I needed: an empty cocktail shaker, an empty bottle, a saucepan from the kitchen, and a bar stool; that would take care of everything. Ambassador Korn looked at the wild "drum set" I had put together.

We went to our respective tables and Korn let the Secretary know something would be forthcoming because I had sent for Louie. When he arrived I thought, "Lawdy, Louie forgot the sticks" (of course he can do as well as the best with knives, spoons, or forks); it turned out he had them, tucked up his sleeve.

After the speeches from the host and visitors, Secretary Shultz said, "Folks, you think you had your dessert but now you're going to have your real dessert." He introduced me and I did a bit of humor (all but the truth) about our recent (August 1988) trip to the Persian Gulf; then I introduced Louie. I went into "Hello, Dolly"; up and down the long room I traveled, then bowed to Louie's artistry.

The master drummer worked his skills with the simple tools at hand; everyone watched as if he were a wizard. When he finished we did a combined finale; the room was screaming. Our country took a deep bow — and made some new friends.

Secretary Shultz got up and said, "You all thought General Walters was the boss at the UN; actually, it's Pearl." General Walters came back with, "Pearl, you're good but Louie is good, too." Louie gave the drumsticks to the Secretary and he started beating on chairs and tables. They all went wild. What a beautiful feeling to see these men let their hair down and be just plain folks.

When you enter the "big room" at the UN the first sight of humanity overwhelms you. You feel a great deal of pride and dignity; I suppose it's the feeling of being a part of the entire world. A delegate struts to his seat and becomes a "thinker for the world." Sometimes when you look around you say to yourself, "Each person sitting here feels the same — important, needed, helpless (sometimes), but chosen. "Chosen" because someone has to nominate, recommend, and confirm (as our Senate does) each delegate to the United Nations General Assembly.

The chief of protocol, Aly Teymour, an Egyptian, has been my friend since 1975. He gets the opportunity to escort all the "Biggies" to the rostrum and he does it with a touch of class. Mr. Teymour also takes the heads of state and VIPs to the "handshaking" bit after their speeches. Dignity is his name.

At the top of it all sits Secretary-General Pérez de Cuéllar, a quiet man whom I read loves music; next to him sits President Dante M. Caputo of Argentina; with them is a man that I know was actually *born* for the job—may he sit there forever — Ambassador Verner Reed. He is under-secretary-general.

I don't think there is anyone in that assembly who doesn't like Ambassador Reed. He is certainly as well liked as the other gentlemen. I speak of him more because I have had more contact with him than with the other two men. After meeting his dear wife Mimi, I knew why he survived. She's a down-to-earth, classy lady.

Ambassador Reed, from the very beginning, would refer to me in the General Assembly as a "national treasure." I never understood why. One thing I do know: he worked diligently every day. He'd look down from that tall perch where the three men sit, clasp his long elegant hands together, and give me a "hello bow" every now and then. I knew he was saying, "Glad to see you keeping a vigil, Pearl; keep it up." He made me feel proud to do my job. Thanks to America for giving us a Verner Reed, a dedicated man of distinction.

Well, I've now reached the end of my 1988 term at the United Nations and I feel sad. With all its hang-ups, it does have great points. Some wars have ceased, some minds have opened, and I've met some wonderful men and women from all over the world — people who will be friends for many years. Dignitaries from Cameroon, Algeria, Tanzania, Oman, Kuwait, Bahrain, Nigeria, Egypt, Jordan, Greece, the United Arab Emirates, Israel, Pakistan, China, the United Kingdom, Saudi Arabia, Haiti, Turkey, Uruguay. The list grows long. There are many I call "friends" who are not mentioned because I don't think the U.S. is "in touch" with them.

Someday we will all touch. No matter how big or small the circumstances, I know that this body of men and women will find a way to the *peace* we all seek. I have done nothing in my life that I am prouder and happier about. A part of my life is in those seats of our delegation, a lot of my heart is in that hall. Should I be called upon again to serve, I shall, willingly.

# The Persian Story

The Shah is dead. I remember the first time I met him. It was in Muir Woods outside of San Francisco. Louie and I were walking in the splendid quiet and beauty of this paradise. We saw a group of men almost closing in on another man — a small, but seemingly important man. They kept looking around apprehensively. One man approached us, smiled, and said, "Hi, Pearl. Would you like to meet the Shah of Iran?" Indeed. We went over and the men introduced us. I faced the most intense eyes I've ever looked into. He smiled faintly. We had a short conversation and we parted.

Now we were facing this same man again. The Shah of Iran, Mohammed Pahlavi. He was sitting on the Peacock Throne. Louie and I were guided into his presence by Amir Abbas Hoveida, the Prime Minister. He was, I think, one of the first men executed in the revolution of 1978–79. The room we entered could perhaps be duplicated by a Hollywood expert. There were approximately sixteen Roman-style columns of cut glass, the ceiling was mirrored, polished floors glistened around huge silk Persian rugs. Chandeliers, which *dared not move*, hung high in the room. The doors through which we had entered were carved of the finest wood. "This cannot be real," I thought. But it was. We stood transfixed, waiting to be told our next move.

Smack in front of us stood "the Man," looking tinier, but mightier, than he had in the woods. Here was a monarch. I had seen those eyes in the woods. Now I noticed the high forehead, tanned-looking skin, a large, prominent nose, and thin lips. His hair was as black as his eyes. The ears were large; however, no features stood out as much as "those eyes." They didn't turn you loose for a moment. You were literally drawn into this man. The eyes said, "I can be a lover or a beast"; the world had heard he was both. I think he chose what he wanted to be, depending on the need.

This was the "Shahanshah of Iran," ruler supreme. This was Tehran, Iran, seat of the Persian dynasty. Iran was the controller of the Persian Gulf, which basically is the entrance into the Middle Eastern world. One of the most important waterways in the world, it is guarded fiercely by all concerned. To the

United States of America it is terribly vital. So we kept close ties with Iran. We got closer.

The Shah beckoned us to be seated on a small divan. Across from this divan were two single exquisite chairs; spaced between these seats were two more chairs. They had higher backs than the others and were even more exquisite. He occupied the chair next to our divan. I'm sure Her Majesty occupied the other.

Those black eyes entertained us for a while. Could it be that he was wondering, "Do this man and woman remember me from Muir Woods?" Now, as I write, I wonder whether recalling our meeting, we would have referred to it? Would this ruler want to relate to the "Shah in the woods"? Who knew what would have satisfied those strange eyes?

He spoke: "Some say I'm a mystic." *Pause.* I said, "Some say the same about me." What an opener. It was weird.

"Sir," I asked, "what kind of glass is that? Is it cut glass?" "No," he said, "that is thick mirror glass which has been carved so that it appears to be and reflects even more than crystal." Each niche looked two to four inches deep. Never had we seen such a sight. So this *was* the storybook opulence that one heard and read about.

He spaced his words, asking us nothing

Onstage in the 1960s, Las Vegas Convention Center.

With son Tony and daughter DeeDee, late 1950s.

Husband Louie and Charlie at home, February 1985.

Louie, Virgie (sister), DeeDee, Phyllis (good friend), and Eura (sister), Washington, D.C., October 1988.

"The Graduate," 1985.

*To Pearl — with great affection & respect*

*G. Bush*

With George Bush.

USO tour, Persian Gulf.

With His Majesty King Hussein and Her Majesty
Queen Noor at Georgetown. (Looking on, rear
left, is Fedwah Salah, wife of Jordan's Ambassador
Abdullah Salah.)

With Her Majesty Empress Farah Pahlavi (wife of
the Shah of Iran).

about our trip, nor telling us much about his land or people. Only those eyes burned with the fervor of a powerful magi. The feeling was, "He was there, *but* he was not."

After another long pause he spoke softly. I'm sure that same soft voice could have filled that whole palace in anger. "You know your country is going through things now that we went through centuries ago. You are a new country, we are very old." What he *said* and *did* next I shall never forget. It was strange. He said, "It would be a shame" — then he slowly turned his head and looked away from us — "no, it would be a pity if it did not fulfill its destiny."

The three of us just sat saying nothing for a while. I had the feeling, "Speak when you're spoken to." The meeting was friendly, but stiff. A few more words passed, then he arose and walked us to the big door. When we reached the doors where a guard stood rigid, the soft voice spoke again, "Have you seen the jewels? We have the greatest jewels in the world. The Queen of England was here and Her Majesty was awed by their splendor."

Louie and I have had the opportunity many times to see the jewels in the Tower of London. These stones are world-renowned. The Star of Africa, the coronation crown, etc., etc. "You mean, Your Majesty, they are finer than the ones in the Tower?" He looked at me for a long time, as if to ask, "Is that a question or a doubt?" I wondered, "Dared I to question this man whose eyes bore right through me?" For a moment, there was a sly smile at this innocent, funny lady. "Yes," he answered, "she was awed."

"Sir," I dared again to satisfy my brain, "you are saying that the jewels in the Tower are to your jewels as — as" — I tried to think of a comparison. It came, I started again. "You mean that the Tower of London jewels are to *your* jewels like a filling station is to an oil well." The man almost lost his composure. He concealed a cunning smile and said softly, "That's exactly what I mean." One small wave of my fingers, and we departed company. But we were to meet once more.

These jewels are under a bank building which opens at 3 P.M., when special people of the world (visitors, dignitaries) are permitted to view them. Should the relationship between our countries ever come back to normal, and if the jewels are still there, please go see them.

This visit was in 1973. We had been introduced to the Middle East by then Secretary of State William Rogers at a State Department affair for ambassadors from all over the world. During the course of the evening (and before we did the show), Secretary Rogers said, "Pearl, I want you to meet the new young ambassador from Iran." He stood shyly looking over the room. This was Ambassador Ardeshir Zahedi. He was approximately forty or forty-five years old. I reached for his hand and we walked to a quieter outer room to talk. Though he had not mastered English, we managed. I asked, "Are you from near the biblical region of Mesopotamia?" He looked at me as if he thought I read fortunes.

Ambassador Zahedi was tall (about six foot six and a half inches), with large black inquisitive eyes, and a prominent nose. His hair, although he was young, was thinning in the front. As he spoke, he gazed intently as if anticipating your next question to him. The Middle Eastern people *read eyes, not lips,* as we in the Western world do. Maybe we'd better start getting into the "eye scene." That's the best way to read a man's soul. After talking to Zahedi, I went off to change for the show.

A week or so later, one of my agents and a dear friend, Tony Fantozzi, who can really drawl out words, phoned me. "Pearl, I've got some kind of nut here; you're not going to believe this. This cat asked if you would go to dinner with the Shah of Iran?" "Tony, have you lost your mind?" I asked. "These people

211

have been looking for you," he said. "They say that you, Louie, plus anyone else you want can go. Your fares, hotel, everything will all be *first class*." Tony continued, "I can't pronounce this guy's name." "Spell it, Tony, or better still, give me the phone number and I'll call."

The voice was very soft when it came over the phone. As I was piecing Tony's information together, he kept saying, "True, true, true." So it was *true*. Louie and I talked it over and decided to "go to dinner" in Tehran, Iran. I had made one ultimatum about our going. I told the ambassador, "I realize your people are very wealthy but we cannot accept such an invitation without doing some good. Possibly you can arrange for us to do a concert, sponsored by your people, for the benefit of the handicapped of your choosing." He thought that was a good idea. So along we went — Louie, Dodi, E.B., Remo Palmier (our guitarist), and Milt Hinton (bassist). We were all out of our skulls with excitement.

Off we flew (I was a "bird" then, now I'm an "Amtraker") to this distant land. First class. All the way. Were we scared? Heck, no!

It was a very long flight, over twenty hours with time changes. We had to be an interesting group landing at Tehran Airport. Milt, with his big bass fiddle case, Remo, with his guitar case, and Louie, with ten pieces of equipment. We were only there for about three days. It caused quite a stir.

We had entered the mysterious Middle Eastern world; different, far different from ours. The clothes, food, living quarters (of course there were modern hotels, too); the mules, donkeys, open sewers; the contrast was so great. It was an exotic world. When you spoke, the people smiled, and returned your nod.

We stayed at the Palace Hotel (the first to be burned down when the revolution came). The Bayats, who owned it, were lovely people. There was Perinouche (the mother) and Minouche (the daughter, who now calls me Auntie; she was a stunner). The father, whom we did not meet, was consul to Germany.

We had barely put our bags down and started to unpack when the message came. "You will be meeting *him* [the Shah] at 4 P.M." What? Oh, my goodness! Steaming out clothes, trying to figure out what was proper. Dodi helped me decide on a long, black, high-necked evening gown. It had beads of (fake) gold and silver. It was lovely. I also wore a turban. Louie wore a nice dark suit. Off we went and had that *first* meeting.

After our first meeting, we left and were led by Prime Minister Hoveida down two short carpeted (hell, everything was Persian car-peted) sets of stairs into a small room. Soon a group of men came in, one by one, while Prime Minister Hoveida stood there smiling. Each carried a load. One had piles of some of the greatest books of the past, bound beauti-fully. The paper in the books was like silk; there was one on the history of their empire, another about the jewels, and writings of Omar Khayyám. Another gentleman carried tins of the great Persian pistachio nuts for which they are world-famous, a third and fourth brought a rug and flung it on the floor. It had been wrapped in a large blue satin piece of material. Louie and I often laugh and say, "Boy, what kind of house did these people think we had?" These were treasures of the past, present, and future. They're now stored away, all except the *books*. Being a reader since I was three years of age, I touch the books every now and then like a small hun-gry-for-knowledge child. I sit on the floor, slowly turning the pages of time.

How could we sleep after the first day? What would the day of the concert bring? We found out that the Persians never stop once they start. In fact *now* it seems to be the same way, unfortunately. Lucky for us, at the time, it was good.

On the second night Rudaki Hall (their

concert hall) was packed to capacity. Remember at this time the Iranian audience was not naive about American music. Many were rich and had traveled; records and cassettes were available all over Tehran. The benefit was for the School of the Blind under Her Majesty's sponsorship.

No sooner were we finished, than the summons came: "Quick, quick! Upstairs to meet Her Majesty." "Wait till we dry off, honey," I said. "No, no! Come, Come!" Everyone in these countries runs.

We climbed the long stairs to the mezzanine. I was sweating and breathless. There awaiting us was a tall strikingly handsome woman, about five foot eight, henna-colored hair and those same eyes — only hers were "laughing eyes." She looked exquisite, in a stunning dress. Elegant earrings hung from her ears; a string of pearls adorned her neck. Beckoning me to join her on the small divan, she took my hand. I was meeting Empress Farah. This lady has to be one of the most unpretentious women in the world.

A tray the size of a small coffee table was brought in piled high with all kinds of fruit, nuts, and dates. Boy, this was fairyland! We have read of the fabulous feasts the kings of yore had; this was it.

Her Majesty was quite the opposite of her

husband; no wonder he loved her. A couple of times she grasped my hand to make a point; her warmth pervaded her whole being. It was a long visit, with lots of laughter. The Empress was inquisitive about us and how we were enjoying our visit. Finally, bidding us farewell, she reminded us to try and see the "jewels" (not stressing their awesomeness as her husband had. Most of the world thinks that Iran's wealth is based all on oil. It's the jewels that establish much of its wealth.) We were also invited to return to Iran at any time, "First class all the way." The next day we saw the famous jewels.

We entered a large, well-guarded, underground bank building. There were a few important-looking people there waiting. Our escorts swept us by them and we entered right on time — 3 P.M. Here sat the famous chair, the Peacock Throne. It is a high-backed chair, with a very wide seat. I don't think there is any stone in God's kingdom which isn't encrusted in this chair. Emeralds, rubies, pearls, diamonds, turquoise, sapphires — nothing was missing. It is indescribable. Then there's a globe of the world, also encrusted with the stones.

Crowns of captured kings; the crowns of Darius and Cyrus; swords from beaten tribes; when the Persians were on the move they took

216

it all. I wonder since the reign of the Ayatollah Khomeini what happened to that treasure. Seed pearls, large pearls sitting on wet cloths, spilled out of treasure chests such as the pirates used. One small match box (similar to those we used to pay a penny for) was made entirely of emeralds. The man told us that they took inventory only about every ten years, and although no one spoke of the value of things, he said, "That box is worth between — at the last evaluation — ten and sixteen million dollars." And it was the smallest piece in there!

We left the bank and went to the palace (everybody had a palace, it seemed) of the Shah's older brother. A prince. He was a quiet, pleasant man, taller than the Shah, with a very warm attitude. Then we met the children of Her Majesty; there are four: two boys and two girls. His Excellency Prince Reza (who has now been declared, by the old regime, the new Shah) is the eldest. With all the turmoil in his country today, it will be many days, I think, before he mounts the throne. It would really be a miracle.

Reza was about fourteen when we met. A pilot, a drummer, a prince. He owned a single bass set from England, and when he heard Louie, he wanted the double bass set. He literally flipped out. On one of our frequent

217

later visits his mother and I sat on the floor listening to him and Louie banging away. Her Majesty was tickled pink at this exciting drummer. Reza and Louie had a few sessions, and Louie left a set there for him. In his apartment (small palace), he had an upstairs room filled with nothing but his instruments (both drum sets) and a wall of tapes. No music store in America could have had more tapes. As he played, Louie and he were totally unaware of Her Majesty and me. They were lost and we were wishing we could get lost.

To move around in Tehran takes sheer courage. We had three cars, bodyguards (I'm sure they were not just drivers, I could see the bulge under the coats), and all one could do was hang on. It seems everyone drives a Mercedes in the Middle East, and no one drives under seventy miles an hour.

The streets are very wide, there are no marked lanes. Folks drive wherever there is a space. We are beginning to drive the same way now in the States, unfortunately. If someone struck another car, and became immobilized, he simply left his car where it was and I suppose went and bought another. After all, at that time in Iran, what was money? It seemed *everybody had it*. One day a guy trying to cross the street landed right on the hood of the car we were in (luckily we were "crawling" at about thirty miles an hour). He bounced off, laughed like hell, and went on across the street. I tell you these Persians were flying high.

They raced each other, darting in and out of traffic. The more we hollered and cringed, the funnier they thought it was. It was worse than drag racing. And the horns were *deafening*. Iran was in a hurry. Little did it perceive the fast road it was taking would lead to such a disaster. Everything to them was "peaches and cream." They were the "masters of the Persian Gulf," thus "the rulers of the Middle East."

We went en masse into the souvenir store. The drivers went too. As soon as we made our purchases, the escorts waved their hands, and we paid nothing. We were guests of Their Majesties. When we caught on to what was happening, we asked them to let us go in on our own. We paid. Getting home was welcome; during the drive we were too nervous to appreciate the souvenirs.

Another memory is the blind children at the home for which we did the benefit. We watched them as they ran their little fingers over a square of braille pattern, then relayed it down the long line of approximately nine girls, until they had executed the pattern. At one command all of them pulled down a long pole. That meant they had completed a square and would start on another. So much of this sounds like fairyland. *It was.*

Our second visit to Iran was via Jordan. There is another wonderful world which I shall tell in another story. Before visiting these lands, we had to learn a lot about "protocol." And we did; however, many times in the excitement of all this newfangled stuff, we forgot what we learned. Luckily we were among people who did not take it as seriously as many heads of state do in the Western world.

Our son Tony made this trip with us; and à la Tony he purposely forgot, or didn't remember, to do as he was told — such as packing the right things. At Rudaki Hall, after the concert, I, as usual, called everyone out to take a bow (that included E.B., Dodi, and Tony — all of whom had helped). In the box sat Her Majesty, Empress Farah; Queen Alia, a beauty, for whom we had performed only two days earlier in Jordan and who had flown up; Her Excellency Princess Ashraf, the Shah's twin sister; and several princes and princesses.

What did Tony wear to take his bow? The planned tuxedo? No! He had on the tuxedo coat and a pair of jazzy black satin bell-bottom pants (they looked like pajamas). It was "the fad," he said. Really, if I had owned one of those encrusted swords I would have left a stone or two in his behind. It was too late. There he stood, looking up at the royal box, *grinning*. They cracked up. My face must have shown the shock, which made them laugh even harder. Added to that, his collar was opened (he had been sitting, sleeping downstairs, or socializing with the crew and left his bow tie off.) Oh, my *Redeemer*. "Your Majesty," I said, "this is my son and he didn't listen to me." That's all I could think to say or do. The royal box roared.

They presented me with six dozen roses. I held them in front of Tony. Now the royal box was hysterical. It wasn't funny to Louie and me at all. I suppose, being a mother, the Empress could see her own children pulling the same trick. Later on, a young big shot departed with Tony (I suppose to meet some pretty girls), and we didn't see him until the bags were downstairs in the hotel and we were ready to leave. He had been swinging in Tehran. Dear, dear Tony. As I think of it now a few years in Iran might have cured him forever of goofing off.

I mentioned "protocol." Well, imagine that night when E.B., who did the introductions, really got screwed up. A man came running (as usual) backstage to tell us about all the

"Biggies" we had there. Panic set in. I was no help.

I know when speaking to royalty individually, it's *Your* Majesty; speaking *about* them together it's *Their* Majesties; speaking *of* them *singularly* it's *His* or *Her;* and so on. It got real mixed up, because, added to all that were the princes (a few) and princesses. So what to say? E.B. said it and again the royal box roared. "Your Majesty" (then he realized Her Majesty Queen Alia was there) — he stuttered "Your Majesties, Their Majesties" — now he was completely confused, *"Princessessess"* — yes! the long-endings — and *"Princesssss."* Oh! That place was in an uproar and E.B. was sweating. But did he give up? No! He waded through, came off, and almost needed a sheet to wipe the perspiration away. Louie, the fellows in the band, and I went on stage and the whole place, including us, needed about ten minutes to stop laughing. Poor E.B., I'm sure he'll long remember that. One thing for sure: He did his gig, under fire.

We wound up at Her Excellency Princess Ashraf's home. What an experience. All those who had been in the royal box, plus friends, were assembled; suddenly the room stopped. I mean stopped. Standing in the doorway, resplendent in his white uniform, was the Shah. Eyes were riveted on the doorway. I don't think anyone knew he was coming, not even his wife. As usual, he stood motionless for a moment letting us "drink him in"; it seemed like ten years. Then he moved slowly into the room and approached his wife; and then he addressed me. All looked amazed that he did that. Frankly, I had no idea *what* he said, I too was awed.

Having dinner at Princess Ashraf's house was an experience. The funniest thing is that this was my second time in Tehran. What the hell, I thought, dinner was why we went the *first time*. The table seating is different from ours. I like it. Instead of the host sitting at what we call "the head of the table," they seat the host in the middle. (Recently I went to Geneva, Switzerland, and Dr. Hiroshi Nakajima, head of the World Health Organization, arranged the same seating.) It affords the host a better look at the guests and gives a more intimate feeling. Louie was seated next to a beauty; those women are gorgeous. She watched Louie (with his dazzling smile). *I watched her* — royalty or not. I was seated at the top of the table.

The Shah made conversation, glancing every now and then with those dark eyes to study me. Wonder if he was doing his mysticism bit. Was he reading me? Well, I was reading him. All he could have read in my face was "What the hell am I doing here? Is this for real?" This was *Ali Baba and the Forty Thieves*. Open sesame, close sesame.

Dinner over, they relaxed a bit and then the princess asked us to entertain. Louie, Joe Harnell (my pianist), Remo (my guitarist), and I started without E.B.'s stuttering introduction. This was more relaxed. I'm sure E.B. felt no pain at not having to repeat those names. The "Biggies" sat on the floor, leaning on huge embroidered pillows. Talk about luxury up to your elbows. Everyone stood, all except the "mighty threesome." His Majesty sat in the middle of those two gorgeous ladies, Her Majesty Queen Alia of Jordan and Her Majesty Empress Farah. I kept thinking, "Don't they ever blink?" They study you as if looking into a crystal ball. They try to see your soul. You feel admiration, love, curiosity, and the wisdom of the ages in all those eyes. Who would know that in a few years, some of these eyes would be closed in death, some would be filled with great hatred for us, and some would have disappeared to other countries. Fate plays odd games.

Not having ever attended the show, the Shah had no idea what we did — although our kind of Western entertainment was not new to him. He had been a world traveler since his early youth and had seen it all. Louie was very interesting to him (he leaned forward — yes, he really leaned forward!). During one song I went closer and touched the Shah's hand. I always do that in shows. The whole room looked to see his reaction. His hand remained still, his eyes moved toward mine and warmed. *Good heavens, I had struck a match.*

The next number was one I had done the night before at the theater, and Her Majesty wept. "As Long As He Needs Me." The reason I know she cried was the princess told me "she cupped her face in her hands and wept." Also, when we went upstairs that night as we did before, she was not there. Later, she walked in and said, "I'm sorry to be late, but I had to *make new my eyes*" (they used eyeliner a lot).

After the show, I flopped down on a gorgeous throw rug, over the big beauty already on the floor. I said, "I'm on a magic carpet and probably will fly home." Why did I say that? They gave me the rug. The Shah bid us farewell; still the attention holder. And the dancing began in earnest.

"Come out into this small room, please," a man requested. The musicians and I went into a small antechamber. For what we had no idea. The Empress and princess had excused themselves earlier and now we saw them descending a spiral staircase. They were giggling like school girls. Behind them marched men with boxes. The boxes were placed upon the sofa. A rug was thrown across the back of it.

The Princess passed out gifts to the guys, while Her Majesty beamed. My turn came. The goodies flowed. The Empress presented my gifts. It was overwhelming.

In between visits to Iran we became very friendly with Ambassador Zahedi. He was also the ex-son-in-law of the Shah; his father was the general who helped restore the Shah to the throne. Ardeshir by now was the toast of Washington. His parties were the talk of the town. Ardeshir and his entourage would sweep into places and heads would turn at the entrance of this imposing figure. The ladies all vied for his attention; they did not hide their intentions. Zahedi *was* Washington; the Iranian embassy was *the* place to be.

The Iranians owned two buildings on Massachusetts Avenue; one was the embassy, the other was the grand residence of the ambassador. *Special guests* were invited to both. The entrance to the embassy was staggering; up a long flight of Persian rug-covered stairs into a huge outer hall, then into a large room. As you passed through that you entered an even larger room with a circular pool in the middle;

a fountain spouted water over floating petals. These rooms held over two hundred or more people. Fabulous paintings hung everywhere. *The world we had seen in Iran was being quietly transported to Washington.*

Around the fountain area, at affairs, wide boards about three or four feet would be placed. Keep in mind this is an enormous room. Covering these boards were white linen or silk tablecloths. Whatever, they were the best. Male servants (and they were servants in every sense of the word) did all the work. No females flitted in and out of this operation. The buffet setup could not be matched in our part of the world at that time. Huge crab legs, caviar (the finest in the world perhaps, though the Russians lay claim to that honor also). All kinds of meats and poultry; every delicacy known and unknown to us. Rare champagnes, wines, whiskies — you name it, they had it. Extending off this room many times they had tents put in the outside area. I tell you, they did a number on giving parties; they were actually too overwhelming. I think more people came just to look than anything else.

Once a very grande dame sat next to me at a dinner heaping caviar on her plate as if it were navy or lima beans. "Oh," she cooed to me, looking down her long pointed, painted nose, "I just love caviar." Her dinner-sized plate was stacked. She kept adding to it — the eggs, lemon, capers, etc., etc., missing nothing. As she talked, she piled it on. Fascinated by her actions I had not put much on my plate. "Don't you like it? You don't know what you're missing. [I thought if I didn't know, she was not going to leave enough for me to find out.] Aren't you going to have any?" I was *thinking*, "Lady, give me the spoon," but I *said*, "Yes darling, I am going to have some, but a dinner plateful would be a bit *much* for me." What the hell, it went right over her head, as she took another large spoonful.

Every bigwig, government VIP, and social-ite was represented. Many deals were *pushed*, and *shoved* too. If Ardeshir had an invite list of fifty or a hundred, each one of them brought along friends (uninvited). Feeling close to Ardeshir by now, I said, "Ardeshir, why don't you keep all of these freeloaders, gossips, etc., out of your home? You are so taken with all of this adoration. Remember, you are a 'nomad in a tent'; *now you're a king;* lose your oil and riches, and you'll be a 'nomad in a tent' again." Those eyes listened, he became a bit more cautious. It wasn't the true friends that I was warning him about, it was the drifters into his domain. More than that it was the dissension which was creeping in among some of his relatives who had come to America with him. Above all, it was his staff.

His staff always warmed at our presence. I think they felt we didn't look upon them as "slaves in pantaloons," expecting them to run around to do our bidding, to bow low to our mighty presence. The staff worked many, many hours. At the parties some grumbled, "It is now late, and we are not allowed to eat until it's all over." Believe me, it didn't end soon. Anywhere from midnight to 2 A.M. would be early.

At the height of Ardeshir's popularity he would ask special people to cross the small street to his residence and continue to serve, eat, and dance the night away. We made a couple, then gave up. These folks were not to be believed.

Now, don't think that this man *was* or is a "playboy" without brains. This man, Ardeshir, has to be a fantastic human being. He *charmed, frightened,* and *awed* you. He never seemed uncertain about what moves to make; nor was he fooled by friends. Athough the Persians got caught in the middle, he was aware of the trap at the end but it was too late to squirm out. Following the orders of his Shah was his cause; he did it well. In America, he was "the court." I don't think, in my time, I've met a man nicer, shrewder, and more loyal to his

229

cause. Still, there was never any doubt in my mind that this could be a cruel, demanding human; *again for the cause*. The reign of the "Persian Empire in America" suddenly took a "winding path to destruction" and the "conquest" was over. One day it might arise again on Massachusetts Avenue, much wiser because of the past.

The handwriting was on the wall; the moving finger had writ. After doing a gig at the Washington Monument a few of us were asked to the embassy. The garden was stunning, twilight came, and a girl was swimming alone in the olympic-size pool. I'd never been out there.

Nasser, Ardeshir's cousin, had come. He came to America to work with the ambassador, but nearing the end, it had become a bit too much for him, too. *Too busy*. Nasser took charge of the passport division. Louie, E.B., and I became very close to him; a nice guy. Later, after the revolution had started, Nasser told Louie and me a story over a chicken soup dinner. He had called and I inquired as to his status (working, living quarters, etc., etc.). "Lulu [a nickname]," he said, "I'm with friends, but I have no job, frankly. People close have been feeding me, my wife left with my son." He was a broken-in-spirit man. We sat on the sofa at Guest Quarters after a happy dinner and Nasser said, "Lulu, life is so funny. All those parties, all the big shots in industry offered me a job to please come work for them." (Keep in mind, Nasser also had money and *influence*.) "They literally begged me to leave the embassy to work with them. Now they don't even answer my call, nor can I get a job." "The hell with them, Nasser," I said. "Just keep looking for the job and know that Louie and I are around." There were two big frozen roast chickens in my freezer. "Take these 'cotton-pickin' birds home, roast 'em, forget the past, and go for the future." He laughed his ass off and left, content that he at least had three friends — Louie, E.B., and me.

This particular night was strange at the residence because I saw an "omen." "Look, Ardeshir." I pointed upward and spoke softly. As we sat at a small dining table, I said, "Look up at that tree." Hanging down was a stiff piece of hemp, or whatever, from a tall tree. At the end of this rope was a "hardened circle," as if someone had starched it. *A vicious circle.* His eyes instantly grew large. He studied it. He called Nasser, who was inside, and spoke in Farsi. He did not want to call others' attention to it. Then he turned to me and said, "Over there is my bedroom window." Strange; then it was Ardeshir and the circle that had to do battle. *"Cut it down, Nasser, cut it down early in the morning."* They were both frightened. The handwriting was there.

Our last trip to Iran was queer. Usually there was no sweat, everything was in order, someone to meet us, cars waiting. We noticed the guards, instead of being at military attention, were leaning against the walls, guns propped loosely beside them, smoking, and perfectly at ease. A lovely lady from the palace kept looking around apprehensively. We could not find Louie's drum set. Ten missing pieces in marked steel cases.

Time passed, the lady was making demands. No one appeared to be listening to her. That was not normal; she was a representative of the Empress. Nobody seemed to give a damn. They laughed when she spoke. Finally, she and Louie asked us to go on to the hotel. Hours later, the drums were found; a case of mixed-up cases. Numbers did not match what was on the slip, plus they were at the farthest point on the loading dock. It was a game being played.

Dr. J. C. Folsom, a brilliant man, from the ICD (International Center for the Disabled) in New York, had responded to a call I made. "Doc, how about coming along with us to

Tehran, bringing some of your company's and your expertise?" More than that happened. Doc got permission from ICD to *have* and leave a Micro-TOWER (Testing, Orientation, and Work Evaluation in Rehabilitation). This was really a wonderful thing and I knew it would be pleasing to our host. After all the excitement about us bringing this machine, the next day after our arrival it proved hard for Doc to fulfill his appointment with the Minister of Health; to get inside the hospitals or any place which had been set up for him to visit. I began to wonder, what's happening to those doors that used to literally fly open at the snap of a finger?

The hall where we played the big benefit show the next night was not entirely filled, although the house had been sold out. There were many VIP seats empty; and Her Majesty Empress Farah was not there. Earlier in the day, we had a beautiful visit with her in the palace library; it was a glorious time, swapping stories. Boy! She could laugh.

After the show, again it was "go up" to be received by His Excellency Prince Reza. He was then only about seventeen. My feet were killing me, the pain had passed all boundaries. I mean they had reached the "impossible period." Waiting for the prince, my pain increased. I reminded the guys of the "protocol" bit, although this was just a boy greeting us. All was going well except the "agony of dee-feet." I asked, "Your Excellency, my feet hurt so bad, may I sit down?" He broke up laughing and said, "Why sure." Usually one is supposed to stand in the presence of royalty until told to be seated.

Reza leaned over to speak to a man, and sent him out of the room. The man returned with a rug and again "a flinging over the divan." I think they love to awe you with that gesture. Well, honey, it works. No need to tell you, this rug was another story. You probably think I don't have anything but Persian throw rugs in our house. Ha! Ha! You should see all my hook rugs.

We left Iran in 1978. The Shah and his family also left later in the wake of horrible experiences. I do not understand what happened there. We had met, loved, and been loved by the people of Iran. In streets, hospitals, homes for the handicapped, and palaces. What had happened to this country? *Too far, too fast.* We had seen the beginning of the end; in Tehran and America.

The "Keepers of the Gulf" were through. The once-beloved Shah was hanged in effigy. Their Empress with her brood of four left with her husband. The modernization of a country halted. Many Persians said, "We want our insides back." Some said, "Stay with our ancient religion and times." It was a tug-of-war between the past and the present. *Only the future* will tell. These people, once warm and real, became confused. The main thing I pray is that the Iranians cease destroying each other.

Approximately two years later, with permission from President and Mrs. Sadat, we were permitted to go to the palace of ex-King Farouk to see the Empress. Her husband was now dead. Egypt had opened its doors to her — a woman and her children without a country.

We drove up this mile-long tree-lined road. Looming in front of us was an enormous palace. The home of Farouk, where he had presided. Some men came running to the car, helped us out, and led us inside. We entered an unpretentious room, with a large sofa and about four chairs. There was also a large oval coffee table on which was a big tray filled with fruits and dates. Small cups had been put out for coffee or tea. The door opened.

There she stood in a simple beige silk dress, hair pulled back in a bun, Her Majesty Empress Farah of Iran. *"Farah."* Her smile warmed the chilly room. Although it was warm outside, it was cold inside, probably because it was so empty. Just men plainly dressed, no coats, the children, and Farah.

She said, "A few guests come, but in general, we don't have people coming and going." Our afternoon brought nice memories. I caught a wistfulness in her face as she sat, clasping her hands. Time came for us to leave; none of us seemingly wanted to leave her alone. As a woman, I felt she wanted to release something privately. All said farewell. Louie lingered, but then caught my eyes and left too.

Farah said, "Lulu, where did all the friends go?" "Nowhere, Farah," I answered her. *Nowhere, because they were never there.* Did I see a tear? Yes. "Let it out, Farah," I said. "Even an Empress has a right to cry." *She did. Very softly;* for a brief moment. We parted: Her Majesty Empress Farah and "Lulu."

When we got to the cars, a screaming, laughing threesome came running over. "Lulu! Lulu!" It was her children. We hugged, and talked there for about twenty minutes. Prince Reza was out of the country.

Farah calls every now and then; I hear, "Hi, Lulu, this is Farah." We talk. Then she's gone until the next time like a mystery. In Chicago, on one New Year's Eve came, "Happy New Year, Lulu." Then gone again.

The last time was in the afternoon at our

home. I was cooking cabbage. The phone rang. My cabbage needed water to keep from burning. The phone or my cabbage? I ran around the small partition. Thank God, I made the choice of the phone. It was Farah. No holiday, no birthday, just, "Lulu, I thought about you." "I'm cooking cabbage," I said. What a wild thing to say to an Empress! She laughed. Wished for my cabbage. I excused myself, turned the fire off, and continued to chat with my sister Farah. Perhaps someday everything will return to normal and Farah and I can eat cabbage together.

# The Egyptian Episode

The full moon seemed to take us by the hand and guide us up the dark road. The stars watched as we slowly made our way to the summit. We were not prepared for what awaited us. It had been decided by our coordinators (who were preparing for our show) it would be best if we did the lighting and sound check at night so as to get the full effect. We got more than the full effect, *we got a shock.*

As we reached the summit we could see a huge, triangular object sitting to our left. Good Lord! It was Cheops, the grandfather pyramid. I turned my back and leaned against the car, looking away from it. The sight was too much. "Honey," Louie said, "turn around, this is what you want to see." I couldn't. After a time, but not then.

My strength returned, it was still there. I thought, for a brief moment, I had imagined seeing the pyramid. Standing majestically, mightily against the skyline it was mesmerizing. You don't move, you're not frightened;

you just stand there, *helpless*. All of us appeared to be so small, the structure diminished us. Here was something created by man (not machine). Many backs had been broken, men had died putting this immense object together. Every stone is equally placed. "Who, if anyone, measured them?" I wondered. "They had been floated down the Nile thousands of years ago," a guide said.

"Oh my goodness," one of the group shouted, "look over here." We glanced to the right and again — complete awe. My knees almost crumpled. Looking straight ahead, wide-eyed, was the Sphinx; with the body of a lion and the head of a woman. The nose was chipped from time and weather. We felt so insignificant.

The drifting sand piles itself against the base of the huge and long body of the Sphinx. It's a ten-minute walk from where we were; the sand makes the walk slow, it's so heavy. Why did this thing have the body of a lion and the head of a woman? Could it be meant as a symbol of the thinking power of woman over man; the strength of man's body being the force of woman's mind? What is it saying to the world? Only the human who created it knew.

"You're not through yet, lady," the guide said. "Look!" I obeyed him. In the not-too-

239

far distance stood two more peaks. What could they be? Ah! The Father and Son pyramids. *Three wonders.* I thought of the Hebrew *Life — L'chaim.*

What was so awesome about this was the dark night. Eerie is the word to describe it. I think the moon and stars were enjoying our emotions. These were no New York skyscrapers, these were true masterpieces of time.

Work had to be done, so the crew started. I yelled, "I saw something move." I sure did. Camel riders were coming over to watch the strangers. Now I'm a zoo lover, but the animals are always penned in. Here was Pearl looking straight up into the eyes of camels and grinning men. "Want a ride, lady?" *"Thank you, no,"* I said politely. E.B. promised he would on the next trip to Egypt; he fulfilled his desire and almost collapsed from fear.

While the crew worked upstairs, the head man took me down winding stairs (like an underground tunnel) to show me the dressing rooms. They looked as though they had been used as dungeons in times long ago; however, they were clean and well lit.

When we got on the stage we felt dwarfed again. It was wider and longer than any stage I'd seen (stone, of course) and what would have been a curtain was a thirty-foot-tall stone wall about three feet thick. Everything around us was gigantic. In front of the stage was a huge orchestra pit (big enough to pass elephants through); men were setting up chairs for the thousands of people who were coming. This was our first journey to Egypt and the people were seeing their first American show since *Porgy and Bess* (so we were told).

E.B., our road manager, was in a dither. We needed *red, yellow, and blue* lights. I was helping in my halting Arabic and pointing to clothing that was blue, the moon for yellow, a match tip for red. We got it done.

The following night was beautiful, with a full moon. What an experience. Our efforts had paid off; we had found an appreciative, warm audience. Madame Jehan Sadat and many dignitaries of the governnment were present. I mounted the two small stairs to the back wall, touched it lovingly, and began to sing their national anthem in Arabic. The silence was deafening; then when I finished, the applause erupted from the thousands. We all then sang it together; and some wept.

Madame Sadat had arranged an after-show reception smack-dab in the middle of the desert. She looked lovely in her silk dress; this is a strong, stunning woman, a Deborrah Kerr look-alike.

Early the next morning there was a tap on

241

the door. "A gift from Madame Sadat for you." A round disk with *Myshallah* (Walk with God) spelled out in diamonds was put around my neck. I continue to try and walk with Him.

At the university, they honored me with a degree that was signed by President Anwar Sadat; then next day we took off for Wafa Wa Amal (Faith and Hope) on the outskirts of Cairo. Madame Sadat founded this village for the handicapped — lame, deaf, blind. Within this village small houses were being built so that the disabled could live as families. What a great idea. At that time the area was under full construction. Twelve homes were already built and about to be occupied when we were there.

The last time we visited, the village had been completed and homes entirely filled. They have a unique idea where every house has *five* to *nine* children; a mother and aunt stay in each. These children may or may not belong to these two women; but they have two in case one has to go out. The children are never left alone.

The children are taught well and are very adept at doing everything. Singing, dancing, crafts, music, reading. It's good to see. I told Jehan, "This sort of thing should be established all over the world." Jehan and I are sisters now and see each other every now and then in America. We place our hands on each other's shoulders, look eye to eye; our eyes grow misty, we hug tightly — all in silence. *We remember.*

Yes, *we remember, the first visit* of President Anwar Sadat to America when we met. Sadat had become a symbol of Egyptian unity and was leading his country calmly and intelligently into a strong world position after the downfall of ex-President Nasser. President Ford had invited Louie and me to the state dinner.

President Sadat had a dark, lean face which gave off a look of religiosity. I sat next to him with great pride. President Ford and his Betty (another sister) always had me sit with them. Sadat spoke softly, he was very aware and observant of all that was happening around him. When he laughed there was a nice softness about his face. A tall man, he cut quite a figure.

We had our second meeting across the street from the White House; he had told me about his knowledge of our trips to Egypt. It was a large dinner attended by top dignitaries from both countries. I had gone to Egypt by courtesy of Ambassador and Mrs. Ashraf Ghorbal (the sweetheart of the diplomatic corps). No one was more loved than these two people and their children.

As we passed him in the receiving line after dinner, Sadat reached out, laughing happily, and embraced me. Ashraf, Jehan, all the line really were impressed. I didn't know that hug could — was to be — so *final*. That was August 8, 1981.

On October 6, 1981, on a reviewing stand now occupied by President Mubarak of Egypt, President Anwar Sadat was brutally assassinated. *We felt the bullets over here* in America. We had lost a friend. I know I did.

As in the case of some other leaders I've met, it seems that they get on a roll; modernizing and steering their countries toward some of the ideas they have seen in other countries. But others in their country lean to the years of the past, and in the resentment of change, they revolt.

Anwar Sadat did something so decent it should be well remembered. When the Shah of Iran (a man on the run) and his family were about their last place, he sheltered them, gave them the right to bury him, and sheltered his family in the palace of Farouk. This was truly an example of man's humanity to man; it was love. That was Sadat.

I can't leave the Egyptian Episode without recalling a harrowing — but humorous —

incident: One day Helen Eilts (wife of our U.S. ambassador to Egypt) and I were speeding along in the embassy car in Cairo, Egypt, after having had a pleasant and exhilarating visit with the handicapped and others at Mrs. Sadat's Wafa Wa Amal. Behind us in a van were Louie and E.B. Ahead of us was a maze of overcrowded buses with people hanging on the outside and goats tied on behind. Dense smoke was emitting from the buses' diesel engines; it filled the air. Helen and I continued our chatting in between her telling the driver in Arabic, *"Slower, Slower." Everyone speeds and drives eratically in the Middle East. No lanes.* Sometimes you can stop only by banging into someone or something.

Then our attention was drawn to two mules coming from opposite sides of the wide street. Each was being pounded by a man with a rod to keep them moving; their backs were piled high with goods. They were slow-moving and I could tell we were headed right toward this fiasco. The driver seemed to be immune to our impending disaster. *"Slow! Slow!"* Helen screamed at the man. We were getting closer, so were the mules. You don't hit mules and walk away easily. Closing in behind us was the van. The mules were almost touching, it seemed. Swish! Our car went right between them. Helen and I awaited the sound of the van crashing. We had barely made it and we knew how close the van was. We held our breath. There was no sound. Peering cautiously back, we saw the van. Safe.

Not thinking of protocol, the proper words, good taste, or anything I said, "Thank God, Helen, for 'fast cars' and 'slow asses.'"

# *He Sits by the River of Jordan*

Your throne is made of marble, may it never break; your crown is like the mountain standing . . .

And so the words are sung in Arabic in the Hashemite Kingdom of Jordan. Here rules His Majesty King Hussein with his queen Her Majesty Queen Noor (born an American).

When I saw him walk into the large room where Louie and I had sat with the late Queen Alia and felt the warmth of his smile, I knew not only had I met a King, I had met a friend. It has remained so for sixteen years.

When the review of the troops was held, the grandstand was packed with members of King Hussein's court. E.B. and I sat there with them; later we sped through the night in a motorcade (doing at least seventy-five miles an hour), horns blowing, no moon. It was dark and we were moving. I was thrilled; these people really knew who was coming down the street. The King.

247

When His Majesty gave me the Hussein Ben-Ali (never given to *any woman*), magic began. That medal represents the Arabs' freedom from the Turks. Lawrence of Arabia fought in that one. Wearing that calls for respect in the Arabic lands. It's the "Biggie."

If someone had told me that someday I'd be watching a King sitting with a baby on his knee eating strawberry jam from a jar, and loving it, or a Queen enjoying a taste of apple butter from the United States, I wouldn't have believed it.

Not in my lifetime did I think I'd be sitting on an old-fashioned porch swing with a King; he wore no shoes, his pants were rolled just above his ankles (my feet were bare too, and I had on a simple cotton dress). We just sat there, and he was talking. He had seen his grandfather, His Majesty King Abdullah, assassinated as he stood by his side. He had flown to pick up the body of his late wife, Her Majesty Queen Alia, whom I had the pleasure of knowing and loving.

How did we know when he sent us off on trips during our visits that we'd see some of the wonders of time; such as Wada Musa (the water of Moses). That rock is the one struck on God's command by Moses to quench the thirst of the children of Israel. The water still trickles from that rock. All in the party drank of it.

At the Jordan River, where it narrows at the Peace Bridge, there we looked across at the Israelis behind sand bags; they looked at the Jordanians. Everyone on both sides has guns. The mountain with the Israeli flag stands watching. All of us baptized (or washed ourselves) in the river of Jordan. I remember the three Jordanian soldiers helping me back up the hill. The bulrushes were thick there. I recalled from reading the bible that Moses had been found hidden in the bulrushes . . .

Later, two helicopters deposited us in the desert at the home of the great Bedouin Sheikh Ben-Jazzi (whose grandfather fought alongside Lawrence of Arabia) for dinner. We shared our visit with twelve of his older male cousins; sheikhs of different ages. It was a very simple stucco house. In the small dining room I sat at Ben-Jazzi's right. He taught us to eat as the nomads do. The manservants brought in an enormous tray holding a cooked lamb. They broke the meat into chunks, then rice was put around it, and with a gravy, such as we would call bouillon or *au jus*, it was poured on the rice.

Your meat and rice are rolled into a ball. You eat with one hand (left) behind your back — just chew away. It's a bit different from what we know, rest assured, but suddenly you're eating away.

The sheikh gave me a beautiful short Bedouin dress, embroidered with gold threads, and some silver filigreed boxes. After a warm visit we boarded our helicopters and returned to Amman, Jordan, still not believing what we had experienced. It was like a fable. . . .

We visited the Lost City of Petra, entering through towering mountains which formed a crevice through which we rode over jagged rocks, watching nomads passing us either on foot (how they walked on those rocks is a wonder) or traveling on a mule. (I don't know how the mule made it either.) In this barren place, everything is red; like Oklahoma dirt.

The Romans and Greeks had once invaded this place. They are still trying slowly to unearth parts of it. We picked up stones with faces (eyes, nose, beards, very plain to see), ancient metal that was used as coins, small stone oil pots. These were the relics of the ages.

What had obviously been the palace was touching the sky (or so it seemed). Columns are twelve feet tall and at least ten feet in circumference. (Don't go by my measurements; do yourself the pleasure and go see for yourself.) Faces of men placed side by side, chipped and broken, seemed to represent a Palace of Justice. This was history.

I saw a swarm of "huge birds" on every rock — they turned out to be *people* all dressed in black. They were Bedouins and this place, Petra, was their home. The children clung to my hands, opening small paper bags with dirty brown dried seeds within. Taking one out, a beautiful dark-eyed girl of ten gave me an insight into life. She slowly opened the watermelon seed and produced another small whitish-looking seed. "Eat," she said, "eat." As small an offering as she had, she was sharing. That's love. The Bedouins are said to be the most loyal Arabs. I would see my little friend again in Petra about two years later. I hope to return again someday to this barren, poverty-stricken place and take more than my love. I shall, if they allow me (they're fiercely independent), take some goodies with me to give them.

And Jacob was left alone; and there wrestled a man with him until the breaking of the day.

Gen. 32:24

In the place now called Jerash, we saw the ancient streets made of huge cobblestones; the entire length of the street is flanked by rows of huge columns (about two feet in diameter, and fifteen or twenty feet tall). All of these relics are chipped and worn by time and weather. The souvenir seller has beads of stones, other bits and pieces that have been picked up, and of course the *"Bepsi-Cola."* In Arabic the letter "P" is pronounced as if it were a "B." Everyone loves the *"Bepsi."* I suppose Coke does its share of business, but all we saw was "Bepsi."

There is an amphitheater at Jerash probably built by the Romans. Stone benches encircle the large stone stage, in a semicircle fashion. One can stand in the center, strike a match, and a person seated up top in the last row can hear it. (So I ask why in this modern world do we have to have all these microphones, amps, etc., to drive people mad? The sound is there loud and clear if we listen.)

His Majesty King Hussein Hospital is worthy of its name. The first time I went there, it was not entirely finished but it is now. All of the doctors and nurses know most of their patients by name, which is so beautiful. I have watched so many of the sick and lame children grow up in that hospital. They've acquired many machines from countries all over the world and so they can do marvelous work. Many of the children remember me, calling me by the Arabic nickname for Pearl, "Lulu."

In the Home for the Handicapped, sponsored by Her Majesty the Queen and headed by Her Majesty Princess Sophia, I have become Auntie Lulu to everyone. At Christmastime, after crocheting and needlepointing all year, I faithfully pack all extra thread and add to it denim, gingham, and bolts of material for the children to make clothes and articles to sell so they can maintain their home.

With the King's permission, E.B. and I took the fast ride in a car to Tefila. (Her Majesty Queen Alia had been killed in the plane crash along with four others, including the King's favorite pilot and the Minister of Health.) I felt, out of respect to my darling friend Alia, I would visit the hospital and call on the patients. It was a trip worthwhile.

Whenever we go to Jordan, the night before we leave, His Excellency Prince Ra'ad and Her Excellency Princess Sophia have a splendid gathering at their home. It's a small intimate gathering and the *pièce de résistance* is the presence of the great painter, a powerhouse of a woman, the prince's mother, Her Excellency the Faranissimo. The prince is a cousin of His Majesty King Hussein. We have a big buffet, sit on pillows, and chat away till late hours. Leaving full and happy, we stop to hug and kiss when *voilà!* There stands the piano. Now comes music from the group, Louie keeping time on top of the piano with spoons,

forks, or knives, E.B. joining in with his oper-
atic voice, and me singing my Arabic. This
"bye-bye" time lasts almost an hour, which
might call for another cup of coffee; so on we
go. I tell you, folks, we have beautiful memories of Jordan.

On every Christmas and birthday Louie
and I are still remembered with exquisite gifts
beyond our imagination (and *our* purse).
Their Majesties' children are my nieces and
nephews. His Excellency Prince Hamzah, the
eldest of Noor's children, is my "birthday
nephew" (we share March 29). He is nine
years old.

Her Majesty Queen Noor is a gorgeous
woman, and so kind. To see her face is to
know the love in her heart. I get letters "from
the children" to me, as if they are writing
them. Some have been invitations to come
see them, or to tell me how they love the
games and books I sent. Always they send so
much love.

There are no words I could use to express
my respect for the rulers of the Hashemite
Kingdom of Jordan. I met the King as a
friend; knew the late Queen Alia as a sister;
love Her Majesty Queen Noor, my sister. I
got to meet the Bedouin King through the
blossoming and continuous friendship of
Ambassador Abdullah Salah and his devoted

wife Fedwah. They were the first who said to us, "Come to our wonderful country of Jordan, meet our people, meet our King."

We did. And we're glad.

# Palestinian Misery

I sat on the concrete of the small courtyard with the young child staring into my eyes. I could read her mind, as it begged me to help her. The eyes spoke the pains of that entire yard filled with her family. This child's eyes were a hundred years old; the child was only three.

I was in the Palestinian camp Bakkar, outside of Amman, Jordan, a few years ago, watching humanity learn to live with hate. The temperature was 112 degrees. The family was sitting in the small courtyard (there were four other children), watching the little girl and me. I had been beckoned into the courtyard as E.B. and I walked the dusty streets. Everyone was sitting on the ground except the mother and father, who sat on small stools. I sat on the raised concrete steps, the baby stood. Holding that tiny face between my hands, I read it all; but I did not understand any of it. Who am I to deal with understanding mankind's folly?

The baby's eyes spoke to me of a lost childhood. Even at three, her hair was a stringy, matted brown. A comb had not been used, I'm sure, in a long time; perhaps they didn't have one since all their hair looked the same. I noticed black "polka dots" all over her face. At first I thought they were the "tattoo marks," such as the women of the Middle East use as a feature of makeup. She was certainly too tiny for that, so I peered closer. Those eyes just kept boring into mine; in fact the eyes were all I could make sense of because of the "polka dots." Finally I decided to inspect one of the dots. Lo and behold, it moved! It was a fly. All the polka dots were flies. They were stuck to her face because she had been drinking the customary heavy, syrupy tea. Her face was littered with these nasty things yet she seemed completely unaware of them. It was sickening. The sweetness of this precious face had lured the fly crowd; they had found their flavor and covered her face.

I could find no water available at the moment (there was none in the small tin home; it had to be fetched every day by a member of the family at an allotted time). Suddenly, I raised the hem of my dress, gave it a good lick of my tongue (not the tidiest thing to do), and with that moisture began to try and wipe away the insects. I could not take the sight of the flies on her face. Since I didn't have soap it was a bit difficult. I tried to do it gently so as not to injure that soft face. She never moved and her parents watched my actions, smiling. Picking them off would have really made me ill, so I just kept licking and doing my cleaning.

Finally some clean areas began to appear and the beauty of the child emerged. Her thoughts kept coming through to me, "What is this lady doing to me and why?" All the while this lady's thoughts were, "What has the world done to this child, and why?"

The other children stood silently by watching the process — as if I were an artist creating a masterpiece. As soon as one spot was all clean, I drew her face to mine and kissed her. She did not smile, she just let me continue my work on her, unhampered by any emotion. Lord, it was painful.

Inside the burning hot tin house mattresses were piled high against the wall; these were their beds. The families were given the huts, and no matter whether it was one person or fifteen, that was home for all. The tin house was about the size of a *very large* bathroom, with planks for the floor. This Palestinian camp was home for approximately sixty thousand.

When we left the little family in the yard, smiling and grateful for their clean-faced baby, E.B. and I, plus the man from UNICEF, walked over to the hospital. Only five doctors were there to take care of all of the camp. How those doctors serviced that entire camp was amazing. The hospital space was comparable to a small bungalow in our world. The doctor gave us a Pepsi. "P."

The gentleman from UNICEF, two soldiers from Amman, E.B., and I took a walk through the streets. We saw poverty and unhappiness everywhere. Crowds started to follow us. Folks, it could have felt very uncomfortable within that barbed-wire fence alone with sixty thousand hot, angry, captive people. Yet I felt safe. We didn't speak, I think, because our eyes were so filled with this inhuman mass of suffering people and the reality that a horrible spot like this existed in the world. I felt trapped in their pain. It seemed wrong.

In the marketplace, the "polka dots" appeared again on everything. Meats hanging uncovered, vegetables, half-rotten fruit, not covered with cloth, *but* covered with flies. The purchaser had to wait until they were scraped off — or take them home. The wares were wrapped in dirty newspaper filled with miserable news.

Stagnant pools of water were on the muddied streets, most likely from the residents' huts; there certainly was no drainage system there. Some children played in the filthy streets, falling down, getting even dirtier than before; grown-ups were listlessly walking around, going nowhere. Cigarettes were in abundance; all the men were smoking, furiously. Nervous tension abounded. No one was enjoying the cigarettes. I guess they were trying to burn out their hatred. I suppose they were thinking vengeance.

The Palestinians sit and wait for that vengeance. Unwanted, hungry (for more than just food), unclothed, unkempt, unloved. Black eyes kept boring into ours with a curiosity at our presence. They knew we were Americans but of a different hue from those so frequently seen. Their eyes did not look at us with hatred. The message was, "Take a good look at us, for your people and others *have seen or will see* the likes of us for continuous days and nights. Mutual pain is ours. Welcome to the club, *friend* — and enemy."

The sound of a loud bell marked lunch time. Off we went to the mess hall to see how well the people were fed. The first to be served were the children (there were seven thousand in the camp), then women and men. Of course, the dogs hung around for everyone's leftovers. They had slim pickings, though, because most people ate whatever they got. Everyone was in a hurry. The children were made to line up, many being pushed or shoved into line by men holding billets like our American policemen carry. A tap on the arm or leg with that made one stay in line.

The anxiety was intense, hungry bellies crying out for anything to fill those empty spots. Any semblance of order was lost when they started to let the line move forward to the mess hall, which was filled with about twenty small picnic tables and benches. The whole place was about the size of a small town meeting hall. Bedlam erupted as the line shoved, and soon fights broke out among the children. They were kicking, biting, and bleeding.

Finally some measure of control was regained and they were sent in to eat. It was simple to see why these darling children were behaving in that manner. *They were hungry!* A few whacks on their heads, legs, and butts didn't matter just as long they got inside.

For a while E.B. and I worked with the men at the front door, letting the children in as fast as possible, then watching them swallow the food fast and get rushed out the back door. The tables held about twenty each, so multiply that by about fifteen or twenty and we were letting in about three hundred a feeding; then think about seven thousand children in a camp all awaiting their turn. That's a long wait when you're hungry. In our world two people are furious when they have to wait for the maître d' to seat them in a restaurant. Imagine those kids. Once the door was so jammed that I put my foot across it, while the men kept shoving the children back; some slipped underneath my leg.

I learned three valuable lessons in *love* that day:

A little girl possibly seven or eight — it was hard to tell, since most of these children were malnourished — stepped in front of me. The face was that of an angel; the sadness was that of the world. She stood silently being shoved back and forth, looking at me with those black, pleading eyes. I tried to shove her in, but she held back. What was wrong with her? Everyone dying to get in, and here she was right at the door, refusing. "Go," I said in Arabic, "or you must move." One man at the door gave a rough shove to that frail body which sent her helplessly over to the far fence. "What's wrong with her?" I asked. We soon found out. Hovering near her now were two children (boy and girl about three and four); they were obviously her relatives. At this point I must explain something.

Inside the door to the right sat two large, important-looking men; the authorities. They had to stamp the back of everyone's hand. After the stamping you could move forward where the pita bread was given — either half a ration or whole, depending on the amount of flour the camp received that month. (A ration was ten pounds a month; seven if the money supply from different donating nations faltered in payment to UNICEF.) Though each nation promises to give a portion, such vows are not always fulfilled.

Beckoning to the girl to bring her two small ones over, I grabbed the tiny ones by the hand and shoved them all in. Their hands were stamped; they got their bread and stew on their tin plates and made their way over to a table.

I realized then why the girl didn't go in when she had a chance. After she went in the first time and the little card and hand were stamped, the others could not get in. Her card had been marked for "three." The two little ones would have had no food. She would not go without them. Bless her. I silently thanked God for that lesson.

At the same feeding I learned lesson two. Standing by an open window near the bread dispenser, I suddenly felt a "bee sting." Pow! One, two, three at a time. Where had all these bees come from? I knew they were not flies. Why were they attacking me? There was not enough food for the children, so certainly no leftovers for bugs. Pow! Another one stung me. I grabbed my neck and looked out the window and quickly, as another hit me, I grabbed it. Aha! I've got you, Mr. Nuisance. Then I saw this was no "bee" in my hand. It was a pebble. They were aiming to hurt; they wanted my attention to pass out a piece of bread. Instead of anger, I felt only pity. Pebbles invited pain and secret tears from me.

When we left the place, one of the doctors met us and gave me a bunch of grapes, about twelve in all. In two seconds E.B. and I were surrounded with children begging for a grape. Lesson three. I played a game with them. Using one of their Arabic words, I began clapping my hands — 1-2-3-4-5-6-7-8, etc. *"Wah Ahlam Ah Sah Ahlam,"* — in rhythm; after each I would hand out a grape. It lasted as long as the grapes lasted. Then came a "pow," another pebble. I glared at them for striking me and they became frightened. They backed up, hung their heads, and awaited their punishment. When none came, they crowded around me again and our game resumed. The grapes did not survive as long as I. Pied Piper Pearl and her two or three hundred children went through the streets as if they were made of gold. Grown-ups turned and smiled as we passed by. E.B. and the man from UNICEF trailed along protecting me. That's a laugh. What could we have done among all those bitter people.

It was difficult to leave that day. Had we stayed, I'm sure someone would have loaned us one of the mattresses they had piled high against the wall, given us a piece of their pita bread, or shared a bit of their two spoons of stew, willingly and in love.

As we entered the camp we noticed a huge radar disc across the street. I'm sure it was to monitor the camp. The UNICEF man said, "Look, Pearl, man's intelligence on one side, man's folly on the other." How right he was. That day spent in that Palestinian camp was a lesson in what the world must face and act upon. A lesson that mankind must witness in order to understand. Admittedly there are "camps" on both sides of the Middle East conflict. I can speak only of what I was a part of.

*A Sad Finale*

E.B. and I slowly made our way out of the

camp, climbing a somewhat steep dirt incline. We kept slipping back down on the loose dirt. Inside I started to wonder — are we to leave here or remain with these lost people? We finally made it.

The children were crying and begging, "Please don't leave us." My friends, it was not an easy or forgettable trip.

# A Special Mailgram

President Reagan                    7/9/82
White House
Washington DC 20500

Mr. President:

As a concerned citizen, I feel obliged to contact you concerning our efforts in the Middle East conflict. I have been in that part of the world many times and have some knowledge of the people. I wish my country would send a ship of human needs instead of human souls at the present time to that part of the world. When we see crying babies, unattended women, hungry mouths open, older people needing assistance, handicapped people, then I wonder where the fighting men of our country fit in. If the war stops because an army has intervened, does that stop the hatred and pain? Somehow I feel that love, compassion, and the fulfillment of needs for man to exist in

God's world exceed bullets.

I feel it necessary to request an answer on how you feel about what one says and why we cannot for once try love instead of bullets. This is not an anti-war telegram, this is a cry from one human to another to answer mankind's need for help by doing an act of truth and love. We have much to offer — food, bandages, knowledge, et cetera. Certainly we have not lost all of that, though we are slowly running out of it here.

It is time for man to stretch forth his hand in love to touch, not squeeze the trigger. I have no idea what anyone else will do, but as for myself, I would gladly walk among the people of either side in this Mideast conflict and give comfort to anyone. May I add, I have also been in a refugee camp of 60,000 people, and by the grace of God, emerged. I have sat on the floors, drank the sweet tea, washed babies' faces, et cetera. I am still a firm believer that love can be stronger than military force. This may sound silly in this day and time, but God exists at all times.

For once, let our country surprise the world by doing an act of kindness which can go unquestioned. That part of the world is ready to see Americans as real human beings, not politicians or economists, not favoring this or that race, but truly in favor of survival for all. This should be our purpose at home and abroad.

Whether you read this personally or not, somehow it has to be said, with respect and prayers, that it can be done on some level at least.

Mrs. PEARL BAILEY BELLSON

I sent this wire.

When it was made known that we were going to send Marines into Lebanon because of terrorist actions, my stomach did a "flip-flop." I felt, along with many others perhaps, that it was like pouring gasoline on a burning fire; yet it was obvious we had to do something to protect our citizens and those of our allies. What to do without going to war or subjecting our boys to the kind of treatment practiced by terrorists in that part of the world. Whatever, to me this was not going to be a good move.

As it turned out, almost two hundred and fifty boys died, in bed.

I received this reply, dated September 10, 1982, from the assistant secretary of state:

Dear Mrs. Bellson:

Thank you for your message to President Reagan concerning the crisis in Lebanon. Our immediate aim since the outbreak of hostilities has been to bring about an effective end to the fighting and the tragic loss of life there. As you know, Ambassador Habib has successfully nego-tiated a plan for the evacuation of the PLO from West Beirut, a plan which is being implemented right now.

The United States remains fully committed to the independence, sovereignty, and territorial integrity of Lebanon. Accordingly, we see three basic goals: the creation of conditions for the restoration of a stable Lebanese government and unified Lebanese army; the withdrawal from Lebanon of all foreign Military forces: Israeli, Syrian and the remaining armed PLO; and a secure Lebanese-Israeli border, one which will help assure protection for Israel against attack from Lebanese territory.

We are deeply concerned by the tragic human and material losses the hostilities have inflicted upon the civilian population in Lebanon. The United States has made $15 million available for emergency assistance such as food, medicines, medical care, clothing, and shelter. In addition, the

President approved Congressional authorization of $50 million for the critical major relief and rehabilitation needs of individuals affected by the conflict. In this effort we are cooperating with the Government of Lebanon and with a variety of international and private voluntary organizations, such as the United Nations and the International Committee of the Red Cross.

The tragic situation in Lebanon is part of the larger Arab-Israeli conflict. If there is to be a just and durable Middle East peace, the conflict's underlying causes must be addressed. The United States remains committed to the Camp David framework as the only existing workable basis for a negotiated solution to the conflict. This framework, which calls for Palestinian participation, seeks a resolution which both recognizes the legitimate rights and just requirements of the Palestinian people and ensures the security of Israel. We intend to focus intently on fulfilling the next stage of the Camp David peace process: the establishment of full autonomy for the inhabitants of the West Bank and Gaza.

We will be devoting great attention and energy to these and related issues, and will be directing our efforts toward all

concerned parties. Thank you for taking
the time to share your concerns with us.
Sincerely,
*(signed)* NICHOLAS A. VELIOTES

# Just Thoughts . . .

*"What, me help?"*

I've always considered a "human being" as one who does things that relate to the needs of those we live with in this world. Humans show love, kindness, compassion; but we also have other qualities — those we are not always proud of. In the latter case, a human often behaves like an animal. I had an experience one day, while shopping in a prominent New York store (where I have been a customer for twenty-five years), that made me long for a lick by my cocker spaniel Charlie. He would have shown more "humanness" than what I faced.

After making a purchase on the main floor, I inquired about another article. "Upstairs," the clerk said. The two clerks on the upper floor were completely oblivious to my needs — they told me in effect, "Find it yourself." An attitude not unusual in the world of today's stores. Browsing through the rack, I almost toppled over; my head started to spin, I felt faint. Slowly I stumbled over to the small counter where the two clerks were busy (*both* with the same customer). "Please help me, I'm sick. Do you have a chair or a stool?" No response. It took at least three requests before I got their attention. All the time I was hanging on to the counter. "Sir, could I please have some water quickly, I feel faint." "Water." A *question?* "Yes, please, water." "We don't have any up here, you'll have to go to the basement." "Sir, I can't stand up, could you please ask someone to get me some?" "Well, we're busy at this time, sorry." Not only was I sick, I was stunned. I sat on a small stool that he pushed over with his foot, sweating, getting nauseous. Finally, I had the strength to inquire, "Where did you say I can get water?" "In the basement" was the reply.

Pulling myself together, I stumbled to the elevator; it was empty. I pushed the button for the basement. It was worse down there. They were busy too. I approached the desk, sweating. "Please, I'm ill, may I have water? They told me it was down here." "Go over there, down that way, turn right, it's there."

Fumbling along, turning right, I saw a small office. A couple of people were in the back room. "Sir, ma'am." These humans (?) turned around, looked at me, chest heaving, almost falling down in the doorway, and went right on with whatever they were doing. I couldn't believe this.

Then I spotted a fountain by the wall. I made my way and I drank, a long time. Then I splashed some cold water on my face. No one bothered me. They were busy. It was an extremely hot day; and although I am a desert rat (from southern Arizona), I had walked about twenty-six blocks and had probably become dehydrated by the New York humidity. Now I began to feel better. Almost as human as those other humans. And I was angry.

But the anger didn't last long. I got sad, terribly sad. I went back upstairs to the main floor and I made my way to the front. "Is something wrong, Miss Bailey?" some nice person at the desk asked. "Not really, honey," I replied; but he could see my face. I think he knew. When he persisted in asking what was wrong, all I could say was, *"I don't believe this, I don't believe human beings could refuse to give a person water."* "Who did it, who did it?" That's always the way. Pin the tail on what donkey? There was no way anyone would know because the incident had completely drained me of any feeling for human beings. The manager came over, "Do you want some water, Pearl?" No, nice man, I'll

275

survive. When I look back on it, I don't know what hurt me more: having to beg for water, or my pain for these uncaring, uncivilized people who just didn't give a damn. I left the store.

## *"Loving Beyond Oneself"*

I am opposed to having big charity events at which the man in the street (who indeed may be the recipient of the benefit), if possible, is not invited to take part. Such functions become "for ourselves only" affairs. The sweet taste goes away. All should be included. For example when the man in the street sees that an affair is going to be held and a famous person or celebrity will be the headliner, he wants to come, share, and enjoy. However, the price tag usually keeps him away. Don't say, "But he has no tuxedo." Maybe he'll rent one. If we don't open wide, we become "a crowd of onlookers to self."

I believe we must be able to love ourselves first, before we can deliver love to others; that's being neighborly. If we stay inside our own bag, someone might come along and pull the cord and leave us to suffocate.

But if we come close to another person and see him as he is, look at him, we'll clearly see ourselves. Then our concern becomes, "What is my friend thinking? What is my friend feeling?" We can help another person if we know his "within." Unfortunately, though, so many of us are oblivious to others, we don't know what their pain is. How can a person understand — or relate to — what he has no knowledge of? He can only enjoy his ignorance. The enemy to him is always the "other," never "myself."

How will we deal with the evils of life? Let us pray for *understanding, meeting, and loving.* Let's turn truly to God and ask of Him greater strength and draw upon the will (not will power) to overcome.

In the lobby of the Whitehall Hotel in Chicago, a fine young, handsome actor, Fred Williamson, introduced himself and said, "I'm moving back to Chicago to enjoy my family, and golf. I'm tired of looking over my shoulder." It amused me because I knew where he was moving from — what I call Sodom and Gomorrah (that beautiful land with everything a person could long for — scenery, agriculture, movies, Disneyland; you name it, it's there). Well, we have gone berserk, doing our own thing, etc. I call it "moving God's furniture around in His house." It's happening all over. I lived out in the Valley and I know of what I speak. Suddenly it's like you're out of touch with reality. The sun is shining, surfing is good, beaches are packed. Yes, it's all there — but where? It is getting to the point that many down-to-earth, successful folks want to return to their roots; go out, do the work, and come home, put their feet up by the fireplace, and be *au naturelle*.

## In the "Holy City"

It was dusk in a troubled land. Fear lingers there yet. Ten thousand people came to see our show in the "Valley of Death," in Jerusalem. Each one was thoroughly checked out. Some wore their rifles slung over their shoulders. They sat on the rocks, having come to hear the Jerusalem Symphony and our group. A man had insisted to me he was needed to interpret every sentence of every song. "No way, dear man, these people will understand my heart, they will know the meaning by my soul touching and feeling theirs." And they did.

What a wild thing. We were in the valley where thousands of Jews had once been herded in and slaughtered. I'll always remember that night.

The next day we walked King David Street

278

where Jesus carried his cross. A man from the Arab quarter popped out and said, "What is that on your neck? Take it off." I was wearing my *Myshallah* (Walk with God), given to me in Egypt, and a *chai*, the Hebrew symbol for life, which I had just bought. He was furious. "They don't go together." A silent Louie stood and listened; and when Louie stands silent — watch out. *Don't bother Pearl.* Looking this man unflinchingly in the eye, I said, "They go *together* on my neck; move." On the way back I bought a cross. *They are all man's symbols.* I have "Him" in my whole being. We continued to the Wailing Wall and King David's tomb.

Later we went to Masada, where close to a thousand Jewish people died after a siege by the Romans. *They killed themselves* rather than be taken slaves or slaughtered. Lord, I thought, how inhuman we have been to each other! *I pray we survive ourselves.*

# My Special People

*Liz*

Recently I lost a dear friend, Liz Whitney Tippett, who had it all. A horse farm, cows, acreage (about two thousand), a famous old house where William Penn was born. She was a recognized social beauty. She had it all. I first met this woman while working at Ciro's (the famous night club where all the great movieland people went) in the fifties. For nine nights straight she came with a party of nine and sat at the same table at the edge of the pulled-out stage platform. Her feet could be seen as I reached the edge and I noticed she wore a fascinating sandal (that *would* get my attention since my feet are eternally hurting, it seems). Except for a strap between the big toe and the rest, the foot was bare. Oh, boy! That was for me. I later found out they were Bernardo sandals. I commented on them jokingly; she smiled. I still don't know how, but Liz and I became such devoted friends. Over a period of years sometimes I'd get phone calls, "Pearl, this is your sister Liz. Come to Saratoga, my horses are running." "Come to Kentucky." "Come to the farm in Virginia."

We often sat alone, while her husband, Colonel Clayce Joseph Tippett, Louie, and E.B. wandered around the farm (the colonel recounting to them many Air Force stories). Liz was so sick one particular day, and she kept telling me, "I'm dying." "Oh come on, Liz, you're going to get better!" She'd protest strongly (she was a powerhouse), "No! No! I'm dying." I said, "Liz, God can cure all, please talk to Him, He listens." "Pearl," she said softly (as if she didn't want God to hear her), "I don't know how to pray." "Liz," I comforted her, "neither do I. I just talk to Him all the time, as if He were right beside me." We both spoke to Him. There were men of the cloth who came to her in the short periods she was in the hospital, but I knew she wanted more.

The joy on her face was priceless when I needlepointed a piece with horses for her; eighteen heads on a pillow. Her birthday was the eighteenth of June. She had them place the pillow at the foot of the bed so she could see her animals.

The colonel and Erma (who never left her side) called me before Thanksgiving. "We are losing her. She's not talking anymore, doesn't relate to things," etc. "Erma," I said, "put her ear to the phone." "Liz, Liz, it's Pearl, your sister." I heard little grunts. "Erma," I asked, "do you think she understood?" "Yes, Miss Bailey," this faithful woman said, "because she looked at me and rolled her eyes in a way to tell me she knew." She died in November 1988.

I was unable to make her funeral, or the memorial, as I was leaving the country, so Colonel suggested I write something to be read:

## TO LIZ

I will always have the picture of Liz walking among mankind. Walking with people. Walking among her animals.

Once when we came to visit she was sitting in her chair, not resting, but bemoaning the fate of a calf she could not find. Louie, my husband, E.B., and a friend were hustled off immediately to find the lost calf. The mother, Liz said, was heavy with milk and suffering. Liz could not take that.

When they left she was still unhappy so she arose from her chair and she and I took off down the road in the van to assist in the search. Then we spotted the men.

Instead of waiting in the car, she got out; I followed. Leaning on the fence she directed the search. The mother cow watched us both. I think the mother was saying, "Ah, there's Liz; now my baby will be found."

Soon a cry went up from inside the barn, "We've found the calf." You should have seen her face. As the calf started to suckle at the mother's breast, I think I saw a tear of joy.

We are blessed to have known this rare and wonderful woman. We know her dear husband, the colonel, misses her. We all miss her. The earth she walked will not miss her because she has not left it. Liz was the earth . . .

## Peewee

She was tiny and plump, we called her Pee-Wee or Curly. She spoke broken English, loved to dance, adored children (especially her own), could outwork a dozen people (in the garden, house, anywhere), did all her own cooking, and loved to visit Louie and me in California (she once came for two weeks and stayed three months).

She was both tough and *tender;* she detested not being boss, lazy people, sitting down, sleeping late, hospitals, and the nursing home she lived in in Moline, Illinois.

When we took her back to the nursing home we always got off the train in Galesburg, Illinois. There Louie's brother Frank and his friend Joe would meet us to finish the trip to Moline. The last few years the train ride was painful. PeeWee was slipping away from us. On April 13, 1987, she died.

Sure all the other folks are still in Moline; we still go, but not as often. Every time, now that Amtrak stops at Galesburg, the conductor says to us, "You folks getting off?" We shake our heads. PeeWee was Louie's mama. When she died a big chunk was taken out of us. We'll all put the pieces back together again. Louie hasn't gotten the message yet, though. *No more PeeWee.* Honey, I feel the same way about Philadelphia (where my two sisters are). The train stops there, but I wonder, where is Mama? Where is Willie? Then the train moves on and us with it.

## *About My Love, Mickey*

Mickey Lotz was about fifteen or sixteen years of age when we first met in St. Louis. The place is not quite clear to me, but it is not important because wherever you met Mickey you would have loved him. It was either at a lecture or a show when this darling boy in his wheelchair rolled into my heart to stay. As he sat there looking at me, his tiny, twisted body was lost to me at that moment totally. All I could see were his warm eyes and deep dimples; the dimples were "pits of love." He seemed unaware of his body. He saw himself as perfectly straight and transferred that vision to me. We fell in love.

After corresponding for a long time, we met again in St. Louis. That same warmth was there; he was maturing and giving out even more of himself. Mickey sensed how busy I was by the things I said to him in our correspondence, so he took to cautioning me, "Pearl, I want you to slow down and smell the flowers." He would take a long time to get the words said; however, he succeeded in making himself understood.

On stage and off, people have always heard me complain about my *aching feet*. Mickey, I think, heard it the loudest and began sending me the boxes with three pairs of slipper socks, and a note saying, "Pearl, never let your feet get cold." Today if anyone should unpack my suitcase, they would find foot warmers in pink, blue, and yellow.

Once, during an appearance at the American Theater in St. Louis, while singing a bouncy song, I kept hearing some grunts —

grunts of happiness. The more I bounced, the louder the grunts came. I said to the audience, "What is that sound I'm hearing?" They pointed to the corner of the stage on the right-hand side. There, near the stairs, sat Mickey. The spotlight man swept his light over there and Mickey just beamed, making strange motions. He was trying to imitate my motions, I think.

I walked over, sat on the stairs, and began to sing him a special song. He was King, in his private world of Joy and Pain. I was his Troubadour. After finishing the show and changing, I went out to his bus to say goodbye. As I poked my head in the door of the bus, someone grabbed my neck in a vise. I almost passed out he hugged me so hard. It was Mickey. That little guy was so strong and so in love with me, he almost choked me to death. When I would kiss him, he was ecstatic with joy. It took the bus driver and a couple of helpers to pry us apart. No one was going to pry him apart from his Pearl. That was my Mickey.

Letter to Mickey After His Passing
Mickey, I'm starting to write another book; it would be incomplete without your presence. Your folks wrote me a letter, we correspond as you and I once did,

and filled me in with moments of your life I missed. "Smelling the flowers," has become a part of my life; the scent of your love will forever remain in my nostrils. You, who had so much pain — sought to ease others' pain. That was you, Mickey. Reading this will teach others to "smell the flowers."

## Mike's Death
### (Letter from his parents)

Dear Pearl, Louie, and E.B.:

It is with heavy and yet happy heart that we write to you. Heavy in that we miss Mike so very much and yet knowing that he is now up in heaven smiling down on us. No more cerebral palsy anymore. He has completed God's mission and I know he did it real well.

Mike was in the hospital for twenty-seven days. He had a food tube put in because of his esophagus trouble which was called "Achalasia." He aspirated which caused Pneumonia, then they found out that where they put the tube in, there was a small leak which caused an infection throughout his body. He was so brave through it all. He was the talk of the whole hospital. It really opened some eyes. The doctors and nurses couldn't get over the fact that in spite of his severe handicap, he loved life, and wanted to live. All while he went thru this, Pearl, he was rooting for the Cardinals baseball team. The doctors even gave him a Cardinal baseball shirt. They even had a television going for him while they put a pulmonary catheter in. Mike touched a lot of people up there just like always.

We know he is happy up there now and I want to thank you for helping make him happy while he was down here. Your timing was just perfect. Everytime he would be feeling blue or down, it seems he would get a beloved P.B. Productions envelope in the mail, or a thoughtful gift from his Pearl. He loved every letter, every picture, books that you wrote, everything that you have ever sent him. He valued your friendship so very much. It was better than any medicine for him.

Mike didn't just think of you as a star, he thought of you as a beautiful lady inside and out. Your philosophy of life, your words of wisdom, and your love of life were in his thoughts of you. You have certainly touched his life Pearl, and I know that he is up smiling down on you. We were always amazed how you could find the time, with all you have to do, to be so thoughtful and sharing. You are truly a great lady. Mike thought Lou was great also. Two of a kind.

When we received the rubber tree plant you sent I right away thought of the song, "High Hopes." Pearl, Mike has reached his highest hopes now . . . I want you to know that I will take care of that plant for Mike as good as he would have and we shall never forget you, and Lou, and E.B. and how you've brought a lot of happiness into our little guy's life.

God bless you always and remember, "Don't forget to stop and smell the flowers."

Love and many, many thanks,
(signed) JAYNE and BUD LOTZ

The last time I had seen Mickey was at a theater in the round I played outside of St. Louis. They gave him a seat in the middle of the aisle on the top level; he so enjoyed himself I asked his parents to let him return the next day, and they did. Before ending the show I went up the stairs, the spotlight hit us, and I sang a ballad. *The audience wept. Mickey dimpled. I hurt. His parents smiled.* They knew their child was happy. He never made anyone unhappy with his hurts. He took our pains with him and left us with nothing but beautiful memories.

My feet are warm, Mickey; I smell the flowers; yet a wave just passed and I miss you, Mickey. He passed at age thirty-eight.

## Talk to Me, Sabra, Talk to Me, Michael

They did, and the words were beautiful. They spoke of many things, the weather, the fun that life has afforded them. All the while we listened, laughing, but wondering how much more time did they have to speak of these things. Strangely enough we never thought, "How much more time do we have to listen?" Their concern for humanity was enormous, overwhelming. Sabra and Michael gave me a wealth of understanding. All I wanted was to hear them. Sabra, being the elder of this wonderful twosome, spoke more.

This involves two people that I dearly love. There is no intent on my part to embarrass either one of them. I sat at Sabra's bedside and said, "Lady, you are so magnificent that I'm going to write about you." She laughed, "Really, Pearl," she said, "that's great." "It will be, dear sister, about how grand you are," I said, "and how you love so many."

My other love, Michael, doesn't know Aunt Pearl is going to write about him. He was still warm from the womb when we met. His mother and I met when she was a small girl of eight. She turned twenty-one on the *Queen Mary* going to England with me as my new and first secretary. Years have passed and I couldn't find a better older *daughter*.

Everywhere in the world I long to meet another Michael, another Sabra to show me how to face the trials and tribulations which come every day. Michael's first meeting with cancer was at ten on his birthday; then again at thirteen. And thank God he overcame the meeting at sixteen. What a lousy gift. What a champion he turned out to be, receiving that gift and living *with* and *through* it.

Although Sabra and Michael never met, their lives became entwined. Sabra, the elder lady, and Michael, all of sixteen. They fell in love with each other, although they were total strangers. We, as onlookers, were in love with both of them.

I shall never forget October 2, 1982, when I was sitting on the porch and a breeze whispered, "Pearl, write about Sabra and Mike." Write what? Say what? I knew nothing about cancer; especially being close to it as I now was. The breeze continued, "Write their thoughts, Mike's letters, what you see, and what you feel; the way you met. Maybe when others read about them, it will send a message that will help them live completely while going through the agony and fear of this terrible thing. The faith of others may grow stronger." "All right, Mr. Breeze," I said, "it shall be done."

Michael (who has a great sense of humor) once had written to Sabra, "It seems as though you and I are in the same boat, but I know of no one I'd rather be in the boat with." *Cute.* Gordon (Sabra's husband) came into our lives and we, too (living Michael's experience), all sat in the same boat.

It was June 1981; the Bekins trucks had come and gone, dumping everything. All the furniture was inside, and outside sat about fifteen boxes of household articles. The house we were moving into was so tiny compared with our past home. I just kept saying to the movers, "Put them on the porch." They did. There was a space left for two rockers that Mr. Deyo, the seller, left as gifts for us. We sat peacefully in the hot, scorching 112-degree Arizona sun. We were appropriately dressed. (The warmer you dress there, the cooler you stay; watch the Arabs in the desert.) So there we were, loving that heat.

Our small house sits on the edge of the golf course, surrounded by tall palms, and within full view of beautiful Lake Havasu. The yard has the most fantastic cactus (cabbage, saguaros, elephant leaf, etc., etc.), through the love and labor of Mr. Deyo. They're surrounded by huge rocks on a slope. How this man lugged those rocks into place is beyond me. Our saguaros stand like tall sentinels, in the front and back yards. Our guardsmen. You sit daily and await the sunset. If you see an Arizona sunset and if you don't have religion, you'll *get* it. This is truly paradise.

Louie went inside to get us a cool drink. Being unaccustomed to the house, he pulled the sliding door too hard; we were locked out — *in nature's oven.* At this time there was a house way up the street, whose owners were out of town (they knew about the heat and monsoon weather that often comes in the summer); there were five or six others on hills across from us looking down on the golf course and another small house like ours three lots away.

We pondered our plight. This was new stuff to us. This was not a large city (only seventeen thousand people then) with many neighbors or a telephone booth nearby. We felt like "nomads." Help. Louie proceeded to seek some.

I was beginning to nod when, "What the heck is that? A mirage?" No! They were waving hands. Was I going mad? Alone. No

Louie to make the trip with me? The hands moved again, only this time they were closer. Where in the world was Louie? Glory be! Suddenly two figures were standing before me, smiling at the stone fence. "Hi, neighbor."

The figures had moved slowly across the empty lots because of the hot, large stones and the possibility that a poisonous sidewinder snake might be on his way someplace, or a deadly black diamond-back rattler might be resting in the sun. *They do not like people.* It's mutual. If those people had screamed snake, this city girl, Pearl, would have headed for Philadelphia and parts east. Human snakes, I can handle, but the authentic ones are beyond my scope.

"Are you in trouble?" they inquired. I explained the situation. They offered their cool pool and home as a relief after Louie returned. I pointed to the boxes and explained we must get on with our job as we had no outside help. Louie returned and a lasting friendship began. As I recall now that day Sabra said, "My back is hurting today." How were we to know it would come to hurt even worse?

Gordon was a tall, portly (though now golf-slimmed) figure, good-looking, Louisiana gentleman. Sabra was about five-foot-five or -six, with soft eyes, and a strong face. One look and you felt, "She is a good person."

Sabra was from Mississippi. Clyde, who lived with them, was like a brother to us all. The three of them were prime golfers, Sabra once having been a champion when they lived in Massachusetts. We had clubs but hadn't hit a golf ball in almost a hundred years. That day we promised swimming, golfing, all the good things; we did none. Fate intervened.

On one of our rare home trips, sitting on the porch (actually it's called "patio" in the West), I happened to notice Gordon going around and around in the yard, pausing, standing under a palm, looking toward the lake and then at nothing. "Louie," I called, "come out and look. Gordon is upset about something." Louie said, "Honey, he's probably just enjoying the view." "Oh no," I argued, "I can't buy that. . . . Hi, neighbor," I yelled, "are you okay?" He yelled back, "My wife is sick." He crossed the lots to us.

"You know, Pearl," he said slowly, "Sabra would love it if you came down, but she knows you're busy." Busy? Bet your sweet patootie, we're not *that* busy. No sooner said than done. Sabra was delighted. She was lying down. Her back ached. Our visits became a constant thing, accompanied by my famous "chicken soup," *my eternal cure*. The hurt Gordon and Clyde were beginning to feel soon rubbed off on us; it became more difficult for us to leave home, to leave Sabra.

Many times, working in the yard, we noticed Gordon and Clyde sitting by the pool, sometimes silently, sometimes talking. By now Sabra was bedridden, but occasionally when Gordon (the great chef) made breakfast ( bacon, eggs, grits, biscuits), she'd roll out in a wheelchair and sit with us. Quietly, sometimes she'd give us a wave and go back to bed. She was the gracious Southern hostess.

After a long period away, Louie went down the hill while I began my "chicken soup ritual." Sabra was not improving. Gordon told me her new habit was Pearl's soup at 10 P.M.; that was all she enjoyed. Louie came back. "Sabra looks good and seems really up." Good news. You bet it was. The "Chicken Soup Pearl" was home and ready to help her sister Sabra.

The next day we went down together and she made a grand turn so she could sit on the side of the bed. How many times she'd say, "Wait till I find a good sitting spot. . . . Pearl, look at this — come feel my hair." I didn't have to — it was gorgeous.

Sabra had gone from lots of hair to bald, then to the cutest, mannish, curly gray. It was back — *short, thick, and cute*.

November 6. Sabra and I had our regular

talk on the telephone — it was one of the days I didn't go down the hill to the house. She was so cheerful but at one point I asked, "How about some more reading material?" "Pearl, I don't seem to concentrate anymore these days." For one of those rare moments, she showed despair. "Heh, partner, you're not going to start giving up, are you?" For the *first* time I had heard a note of "enough of this thing." "Oh no," she said. "Listen, Sabra," I cautioned, "you've got your hair back, now you're just getting ready to get this thing together." She stretched out her "carpet of courage" and laughed, "I hope so." "I'll be back tomorrow," I said. The expectation of the visit perked her up. What a lady!

Soon I began to notice an "I'll put on my 'keep-on-trying attitude' " within Sabra. Her stomach was causing her so much pain. You could actually see her agonizing as she tried to cheer us up. Never complaining, she'd make a joke when the pain went too far. Dear Sabra, why did you try so hard to make us smile? We didn't want to really. We didn't know how to weep and hide it from you. "Pearl," she said one day, "I sure wish I could pass gas. This knot in my stomach feels like gas." That was the day the doctor had said, "Things were coming along." Were they?

We phoned each other every day, and in the

evenings Lou went down with the Chicken Soup. He wanted to be with Gordon and Clyde for some minutes of "man-talk, man-feeling."

One day she said, "Come down." I was concerned. Sabra didn't like to be seen lying down, so she always set about getting herself adjusted for anyone visiting. Invariably she would always, for me at least, be sitting on the side of the bed.

We just talked. "Sabra, I'm going to write about you and our friendship. You deserve a book." "Really, Pearl," she laughed, "I'd like that." "You got it, lady. We'll just keep talking. As soon as enough pages are written I'll read them and you'll be the editor." We had a deal. Sabra was going to work. Something to do. Something to live for. No one was surer than Sabra that she was going to make it. There was never a doubt. Of all of us she believed it the most. We desired. She had the faith.

I told her Michael's story. That was a real inspiration. Michael was her phone-mate now. This boy of sixteen who had experienced this thing twice before was now "Mr. Authority" to her. He had taken it upon himself to keep others happy with his, as he says, *joie de vivre* (joy of life).

The two of them chatted about their loss of

hair and its return. Michael and Sabra were enriching everyone they touched. For me it was him screaming across, "Hi, Aunt Pearl," while his mom and I were on the phone and Sabra awaiting my every homecoming to show me her new look of impending baldness. There were some patches. She looked like an elegant Yul Brynner. Michael had been through his bit during school term. He laughed. They teased. He laughed and ignored it. I wouldn't doubt that in the "quietness of their inner space," looking in a small mirror they cried. Either way, none of us will ever know from those two strong humans.

Life turns us around and upside down, many times. In Sabra's friendship I found a wealth of understanding and appreciation of living and dying. Time moved on — another summer and fall; then Christmas. She loved that! Gordon decorated some. The presents delighted her. She sent me a token which obviously meant much to her; I look at it every day.

By now that dreadful disease started to gallop like a fast race horse over her body, digging into the very turf of her soul. It was saddleless, slippery and dripping with the perspiration from her energy, which it was using to win "the race of death." Its only purpose was to reach the finish line — without her. The joy of the horrible horse could be seen in the way it was destroying her fragile body — but she hung on, and kept riding him around and around the raceway like a gifted horsewoman. No giving up easily for her. Gordon and Clyde sat in the grandstand waiting to see their Sabra come walking across the finish line after conquering that horse.

But over and over again she almost slid off as the clever horse jumped the hurdles of death — Sabra somehow stayed in the stirrups. The muddier the track, the greater the challenge. Puddles of hope splashed over as she'd reach one patch after another — holding on as the mud dried on her and caked. She'd scrape it off with more faith and get on with it. All the time we watched and got angrier. We could see that horse, she couldn't. He loomed large; keeping his eyes constantly on us in case we'd try to interfere. He rode on with our love. Every time we entered another "horse of hope" in the race, he'd run faster, kicking up the mud in the newcomer's face. That monster horse wanted the field all to himself. He would laugh, knowing somehow he seldom lost a race. Strangely enough, Sabra fairly glowed, looking cleaner, brighter, and full of more hope. It was so sad some days to watch her thin, emaciated arms straining to pull up on the reins — her slender feet (pretty still) barely able to stay in the stirrups, it pained her bones — her backside was so sore from riding on his strong back — he gave her no cushion. When she'd shift her weight her back pained so. I always looked at her in that fetal position, resting in the womb position — getting ready to settle in the Arms of God.

Gordon, dear Gordon, and Clyde could only stand, look, and ask, "Can we help?" She'd smile, shake her head, and say, "Nope, I'm okay." Dearest friend, I'm glad you were because we were not.

After Christmas we were going to Los Angeles as usual to catch the train east. That morning before leaving we made our trip down the hill; Louie, Gordon, and Clyde sat in the living room talking, I went in the bedroom to Sabra. We took each other's hand, said nothing; we held on to life and let go. She said, "Pearl, ask Gordon to come and turn me toward the window." Now that was not right. She always wanted to be facing the door waving me bye-bye. I said, "I can do it." Sabra smiled, "You can't lift me." Ah friend, *yes* I can, and I *did*. You were a warm baby in my arms. *Now* I know why you wanted to turn (and only now). You knew more than we. You didn't want to see me go, because you knew you would not see me come again.

I called from the hotel around 6 P.M. as the

porter was taking the bags down. "Sabra, don't forget to eat your soup." This soft voice whispered her secret I'd never heard, "I'm so sick, Pearl, forgive me, friend, I can't eat my chicken soup." I felt that was my answer to *how long*. I wanted to cry. I wouldn't let it out, for fear she might hear me. Sabra must not hear — must not know — I had no right to test her, Gordon's, or Clyde's strength. They would need it all for her.

We stopped at Albuquerque, New Mexico, and I asked Louie to call Gordon. There was no answer. "Louie," I softly said, "I've got a feeling. Either Sabra has gone to the hospital or she has gone to God." We reached Chicago and called. She took the long trip.

That monstrous, headstrong horse had thrown our Sabra off, leaving her on the track alone. He had gone back to his stable, satisfied; gone to await his next helpless rider. But somehow I feel one day he's going to take on a rider who is going to stay on his back, *rein him in*, and we'll sit in the grandstand and cheer. All the Sabras of the world will be in the stands with us, cheering.

Sabra left us. Gordon watched and waited two years to feel the truth. His friend Clyde stayed by his side. Gordon still walked in the yard, played golf, cooked the eggs, bacon, grits, and biscuits. No Sabra. They'd pass the house, honk the horns. We talked over the fence. One day Gordon told us, "I think I've found a wonderful person to fill my life." He did add to his life a wonderful, unselfish lady who too had suffered a loss. They golfed together, went to dinner, and finally married. They too are large in our lives. Ruth and Gordon are family.

Throughout this entire story, I deliberately left out a great love of Sabra's. She is about a hundred and seven years old. Every night and day she spent watching, protecting Sabra. She lives still with Gordon and Ruth; well fed — well loved. Sabra never had a better friend than "Miss B.," her schnauzer. She loved her too.

## Michael's Story

Michael is now a superman of twenty-three. *A supermarket man.* Soon he may become the manager of one. An amazing person. He works every day, visits his father, who has now gotten into "that boat Sabra and Mike were in," and offers guidance to all who need it.

Buddy Rich, drummer supreme — the world had given him acclaim since he had been a young boy — was in his final days with "the big boy" in his head. It was inoperable. Buddy was hanging in there.

We were in Atlanta, Georgia, doing a gig at the gorgeous Fox Theater (Anthony Newley, a master, was on the bill). At the end of the show he and I would do a duet, usually one of his songs such as "Who Can I Turn to?" Both of us knew Buddy. Alone in the dressing room one day, something whispered to me, "I want you to sing 'My Buddy.'" Without mentioning his name I did the song, then at the very end reached back to Louie, who gave me a pair of drumsticks. Crossing them I said, "Our Buddy, we miss you." Then I said the name: Buddy Rich. The audience was momentarily quiet, then they applauded the genius and mourned his sickness in love. I talked to Michael.

"Heh, nephew!! Do me a favor." "Anything, Aunt Pearl, anything." "Uncle Louie and I talk to Buddy *every day* [we did] and we told him about you and your courage. Would you like to pay him a visit? You're the man to do it." "Why sure," came his happy answer. Down to UCLA Hospital he went.

Buddy told us one day, "Hey, you guys told me you were sending me a *boy* to talk with me. You sent me a man. He has to be the most amazing kid I've ever met." We told Michael. His face lit up like the sun. Michael had brought some comfort to the great Buddy Rich. *Hot dog*, Aunt Pearl," he said.

This boy did another "wonder work." He had never *met* Sabra and Gordon; he'd only talked to them. We came home and called Gordon as usual. "Guess who is visiting me?" Gordon said, "Michael." I wondered, what was he doing there? Dodi told me later.

He had asked his mother to let him go for a visit if he saved his own bus fare (Havasu is 330 miles from L.A.) and if Gordon approved. Gordon did approve, he did save his money, and came to Havasu to spend a week. What a boy. We returned the day he was leaving. He came up the hill then to see Aunt Pearl and Uncle Louie. Michael was fiercely independent.

Louie often plays Disneyland with his big band and of course the front seat occupant is always Michael. He loves the rides; he loves Uncle Louie. Plus he's a sports fanatic. He wore his cap (all the hair did not grow back). There were a couple of strange dark marks on his head, like the color of lava. I don't know why I think of lava, that hot liquid spit from the earth. Could that spot have been part of that wretched illness spit out of Mike's head and healed? Lord, I prayed, let it be healed.

One opening night at Disneyland, my daughter DeeDee (she and Michael are five years apart) took Mike and her friends to the rides. He said, "First we hear Uncle Louie, then we go." As soon as it was over, they took off — thank heavens. They came back, flustered, full of jokes about Michael and his antics. Dodi, his mama, was so happy that he was enjoying himself. She had been slyly looking around, missing him, wondering about him on the rides. Within me were the same feelings. We both hid them well.

I knew Dodi so well (remember, this was my oldest daughter in a sense). While we were waiting she told too many jokes, laughed too loud, and made trivial conversation. I had twice before lived her pain. Frankly, joining in her emotions, I was a bit silly too.

After they all returned, Mike went to get Aunt Pearl some popcorn and coffee; he was rewarded with the change. Ah! Off to the rides again — alone this time and happy. Dodi watched him go; those large eyes of hers actually prayed. Little did she know I, too, prayed. He tore us apart with his *joie de vivre*.

Often he'd drop us a note, especially after receiving a card or gift from us. Like these:

Dear Aunt Pearl:
I will never forget you because you're a very kind and thoughtful person who I love very much; now enough with the mushy stuff —

. . . "One more thing I would like to say is that you sang as beautiful as you looked as you stood out on the field in your beautiful dress and sang our National Anthem as nobody else could" (9/4/82; Kansas City Royals Game).

. . . "Never stop believing in yourself and things will be easier for you as you go through life."

. . . "I hope to see or talk to you and Uncle Louie soon. Saying for the New Year: "Believe in yourself and you will go far in life." (smile).

Good begets good, as the saying goes. When I went to do my bit with the Kansas City Royals, I talked with Mr. Merle Wood (now one of our dearest friends, he and his Ellen). Merle works for the organization of Mr. Ewing Kaufman. Mr. Kaufman and his Muriel have done so much for so many. (She even designed and decorated the stadium club dining room at Royals Stadium as well as the suite of offices and the interior of their Marion Laboratories, Inc., building.)

Merle was so touched by Michael that his generosity has never stopped — golf clubs, tickets to the KC Royals games in California, medicines. Boy! these Midwestern folks do more than "bar-b-que." *They love hard.*

But no one meeting Michael or Sabra could have done more or can do more (in Michael's case) than love. Nothing has given me more joy than to have the privilege allowed by all involved in these two lives to have lived with and loved these two fabulous people. *More Sabras, more Michaels, more love.* We will always hear you both talking to us.

Again, thanks to Gordon and Dodi for allowing me the privilege to write this. I hope the salt did not cause too much pain in their wounds.

*Rizzo*

Mayor Koch and City Council members were present; firemen and policemen filled the streets; citizens stood behind barricades which had been placed on Fifth Avenue opposite St. Patrick's Cathedral. Some salesmen's faces looked over at the scene from the Saks Fifth Avenue entrances and others watched from the far corner. Later, after coming out of St. Patrick's Cathedral, I saw it all myself.

The cab driver had not been able to turn down at Fifty-seventh and Fifth for some unexplained reason. It was quite windy so we figured maybe some panes of glass had been blown from one of the buildings and this detour was a precaution. Turning right we finally found a way to arrive at Fiftieth Street for the church; only there we could not cross because of the barricade — we were waved around to the Fifty-first Street side. A few snow flurries had started.

The rerouting had made me late. Finally we got to the side entrance on Fifty-first Street. I entered very slowly, not that anyone was in my path; there was something *large* in my view. It was the casket, and I knew what it said to me: Dr. Peter Rizzo.

I had come into New York with E.B. (Louie went to a job) to get Doc to look at my painful shoulder. He was the orthopedic man at the fantastic St. Vincent's Hospital; he knew his business well. Doc and I had met through Dr. William Hitzig, the late eminent heart specialist. Doc — a handsome, warm human being — and his wife and children became my friends. Though medically I didn't see him much, we talked on occasion and exchanged Christmas gifts.

Once when he had a very lucrative Park Avenue office, we talked of other lands where he wanted to go, to stretch his abilities, help children. He went on to become head of orthopedics at St. Vincent's. So here we were to meet on that Monday morning. The previous Friday, upon arrival in New York, E.B. escorted me to the hotel, where I bought the one paper they had left at the concierge's. E.B. hastily departed to make his plane to Los Angeles.

Upstairs, I flopped in my favorite chair. (I can and do sit by windows four to nine days alone in a room, not going out, phoning, or talking to anyone. This causes me, when I do meet friends, to chat on and on. It's the "lonesomeness unleashed to companionship.") Some go to a psychiatrist to lie on a couch; I talk to God and to those who warm me. If one works at the United Nations five days a week and has to listen to sometimes as many as seventy to ninety-two speakers in just a three-day period (it can be thirty or forty a day), something is holding you in that chair. Either it's a love of learning, duty, interest in others, or else your *butt* is *glued* and you can't get up. I sat, listened, and learned. That's what I shared with Dr. Rizzo — a listening, learning friendship. A kindred feeling for humanity. In my soul I'm glad that I try to share myself with others. That's what I was thinking as I turned, got my needlepoint out, and picked up the paper.

The name on the lower part of the front page caught my attention, *Dr. Peter Rizzo*. I thought, "Had helped whom?" He had been involved in helping a lady who had been caught in a dramatic scene of a crane falling on her legs. Doc had been, along with others, the on-the-scene man.

Examining closely, I saw a figure stretched out, a blood-spattered body on a stretcher. What was going on? Snapping the paper back over I read, "Dr. Peter Rizzo shot." A silent hard scream left my stomach; for some time I remember my stomach hurting. Choking, I called the desk for some help — hot coffee — then I went back into a daze. Louie, E.B., no one was there to help me control myself. Had they been there, I realized later, they would have been no help because when we did talk, they too were devastated. E.B. later said, "As I walked to my plane, I bought the paper, saw the scene on the front page, and all the way thought, 'Poor Pearl, has she read the paper?' "

I suppose I did one of the wildest things. Right away I called his office, "How is Doc? What can I do?" The nurse started bawling, "He's gone, Miss Bailey." Oh, my Lord! Was he? "You mean, Lord, I won't see our friend anymore?" The viewing was on Sunday up the street from the hotel. People from everywhere poured in to Campbell's on Madison Avenue; just a steady stream of quiet dignity. Upon entering I had another stunner.

311

A lady named Sally Lefkowitz, whom I mentioned earlier in this book, who has suffered through everything, had called me on that day. When I told her about my doctor, she left her doctor's to meet me inside the funeral home. She didn't even know Dr. Rizzo. And her doctor had told her, "Stay home." Sally was there with Doc and all of us. Madison Avenue that Sunday took on a strange, beautiful dignity. So here was my dear doctor being eulogized at St. Patrick's Cathedral. I'm sure he heard it.

Since the service was already in progress in that packed cathedral, I edged my way along the outer wall, peeping back every now and then, thinking maybe that casket will not be there. It stayed there. Firemen lined the back; policemen were beside them; the news people quietly respected the peace of it all. Services over, the casket came up the aisle. By now I had picked a spot on the end of a row, barely enough space to stand, but a lady allowed me in. The family had wanted me there and I wanted to let them know. *Yes.* I saw the sad group: his father, twin brother (another top doctor), family, his children, nieces and nephews. On the way out his father reached over and touched my hand. I died a little.

The people outside behind the barricades were still there waiting for someone they felt had commanded such respect. Mayor Koch took my hand on the sidewalk to stand beside him and some officials. The silence was deafening in this city. I said to Mayor Koch, "This city has made history; where in these United States have you ever heard of a city being blocked off, people standing, paying tribute to someone who never treated them, with looks on their faces as if they were all wearing halos?" Koch thought a moment and said, "You know, you're right."

"Come to the cemetery, Pearl." I didn't. The press was standing at the curb, interviewing his friend. At the head of the procession was a fire truck. The firemen wanted it to be so. It was a fireman who had shot Dr. Peter Rizzo. Their hearts were broken. "Vic," a newsman from one of networks, walked over to my lonely self — wearing my little black hat, pants (I didn't come to New York knowing I'd be in the cathedral), and coat and asked about Doc. I began to say, I presume, the same things, that others did. "He was kind, he was good, he was . . . " I stopped. "Vic," I said, "something just cleared it all up for me about Doc. Vic, I think we were in the presence of a saint and didn't know it." Folks, I really believe that.

Thinking of Doc, I recalled my first New York doctor, Dr. David Markman. After years of friendship with him and his wife-nurse Betty, Doc Markman lost his mother. He told me how a friend of his was attending her. When his mother passed, he said, in his sadness he started to burn his medical books. "Why, Doc?" I asked. "Pearl, I thought there is nothing in them that I could save my own mother with." It took its toll on him; he survived because he must have realized something in the saying (taught me by a rabbi): "As long as you love the one you lose, you'll never lose the one you love." Doc Markman, survivor of the profession.

Dr. Rizzo's father, over eighty, was a blessing to behold. At Campbell's, he moved around the room quietly; he soothed, greeted, touched everyone. The room was not filled with sobbing people. Everyone had the "peaceful peace" of Doc. Some college kids — friends of the Rizzo children — sat on the sofa near the base of the casket. I joined the children. At the head of the casket was something rare. A beautiful, informal photo of Dr. Peter Rizzo and his dog. I forgot to say, when we left St. Patrick's Cathedral that Monday in February 1986 — it had stopped snowing!

*Footnote of Love: On Willie*

In bed on a December night in 1988, I

received a message to write a section called, "I Remember." On Friday morning I started scratching away on a few isolated childhood memories. One led to another, it seemed. On Saturday came yet another memory: my brother getting me my first haircut.

Sitting on the back porch some days later, I said, "Louie, it's a bit chillier than our usual January so let's go in; I'd better get back to my book and you, your music." Coming inside, I let him read the most recent installment. He loved it, especially the part about Willie, the brother-in-law whom he adored. He had always pained over the fact that "Bill did not get his *just* recognition" in life.

Then I decided to take a brief rest from writing. I still had to sort some Christmas cards and mail. One was from my brother's wife, Pernell. Good Lord! I hadn't heard from them in a year. Eura and Virgie live in Philadelphia, as Willie did, so I'm sure they still keep up with each other. Though I've written, the contact has been lax. We all get busy. I wrote an answer on Pernell's card, which would have to be typed out later. Then I saw a letter sent from my wonderful manager, Stan Irwin, with a note, "Pearl, this is okay to sign." When I looked it over, I noticed he had circled a whole paragraph and written, "It's about time." Time for what? I wondered.

Then I read it — I nearly fainted.

It was a letter asking permission to use the likeness and/or performance of Bill Bailey, in the motion picture *Taps*, which Sammy Davis, Jr., and Gregory Hines were doing. It would be coming out January 29, 1989. Evidently the producers had thought I was Willie's only relative. They wanted, they said, to "Give Bill Bailey the just honors that he was due as the creator of the 'Moonwalk.'" That was exactly what I had written a couple of days before, for inclusion in my book. All I could think was, it had to be God. It was God.

Willie fell on Philadelphia's Market Street — for a few moments unrecognized; and here in Hollywood years later he was being recognized in a motion picture honoring the art of tap all over the world. How? How? You answer it, dear readers, I can't.

Willie, remember what Mama and Papa always taught us, "What God has given, no man can take away." Smile in heaven, Willie, and do your "Moonwalk."

# The Musicians:
## A Rare Breed

When we look at each other, love flows. The sound of one touches the chord of another; it's a spirit within. Young, old, sick, well; brown, black, white, or green; it doesn't matter, they all relate to each other. They are musicians. They have *the* common bond of love: Music.

With them all the senses work in harmony: *smell, taste, hearing, seeing, feeling.* I guess that's what makes them tick. A total use of the five, together; the musician is now functioning as *the whole instrument.* Years ago, Louie asked me to pick up a guy who was coming into the gig in Vegas. His car had stopped and he'd miss the date. *Of course panic set in.* Off I went, about sixty miles, to Baker, and got him (of course he left the car). Louie had said, "He is one of the greatest players," etc., etc. But listening to him night after night left me cold. He was a very strange guy to me. As strange as his tones were.

Sitting on our porch one day in Vegas, this

317

man was griping about different things, like why no one seemed to really be understanding what he was playing. He criticized his horn (no one else dared to), etc. Finally I said, "You know what your trouble is? You grab that horn as if it's a servant to you instead of a friend; you are pumping air into it as if to blow it apart; mainly you seem to be filling it with *hate*. Your horn sounds cold. Why don't you give it the respect it is due, touch it with love. Say to your horn, I love you, let's make beautiful music together. We are one, let's blend." Well, sir, did he look at me — distrustfully and angrily. Remember, I was talking to a musician, treading on dangerous ground. I felt his emotions. He listened, stared at me, said nothing. I excused myself from his presence. He played that night starting off with a blast, then loosening his fingers, relaxing the horn. Then, as though a wand had been waved, the notes started to come out like velvet. He was finally in love and was loved in return. Yes, Louie was right, he was a brilliant musician. *Heart* and *soul*.

People often say to me — particularly women — "I wish my husband looked at me *in bed* like your husband smiles and gazes upon his drums." *Cute*. Watch a player's face — he is a world apart from all others. Look at his fingers — as delicate as a sculptor's. I well

318

remember my pianist of twenty-four years, Lloyd Phillips, one of the greatest accompanists ever, and a beautiful human being. When he was dying, I went to UCLA Hospital to visit. Actually, I felt it was to say good-bye to Lloyd (his wife, Ethelle, was always near). Lloyd held up his hand to me and I smoothed it saying to him, "Lloyd, you have the most beautiful hands in the world." That made him smile. There was not a wrinkle in his knuckles. George Duvivier, the great bassist had the same hands. You were so fascinated by them, you forgot what he was doing. They actually stroked the strings as if stroking the body of a loved one. Duke Ellington wrote "Drum Is a Woman." Perhaps now I can understand what those females mean about "that look" Louie gives his drums.

Love of family is strong with musicians, it's their blanket of warmth *if* and *when* the sounds go cold. Louie is so cute when he comes creeping in when I'm needlepointing, reading, or sitting on the back porch. "Hi, honey." (Pause) "Hi, honey." The poor thing doesn't realize how long he has been in his little domicile on his knees (he writes on his knees). (My *back* would be broken — and forget about the knees!) Half of the time I go in, turn on the lights, and say, "Louie, it's dark in here." "I can see, honey," he replies. Hell,

I can hardly see him. *Charlie, the dog,* goes in to visit him every now and then, finds it dull, and returns to his mistress to report, "That guy in there has no time for me." Charlie sulks, but he waits as I do.

Many musicians who have been at the point of death have been known to say, "If I can't play my instrument then there is nothing to live for." How touching, yet pathetic. What the answer to that is came to me in my reveries.

Something said to me, "You know, Pearl, every man worships God in his own way; some in trees, stones, fire, sun, moon. Men of music fairly worship their instruments; that could appear to be close to adultery." The voice continued, "I want you to think about this kind of love and hear this statement. But, Pearl, you must be sure to put the word *if* in front of the thought." "*If* music is their *God* then they must be the holiest of men. Who else, what else, gives them such a 'Oneness'?"

Loyalty may not be one of man's strongest virtues, but it is certainly practiced among men and women of this rare breed. Don't think for a minute I was leaving out the "lady musicians." *They are one.* If there is a gripe at home over someone not quite coming through on the gig the night before, don't dare think that you, an "outsider," have the right to criticize or even speak a word against that same individual. That would be called *disloyalty*. You could be eliminated from their society in a quiet, unknowing way.

These are strange, but exciting creatures. And I have in mind *all* musicians: jazz, blues, symphonic, country, whatever. I notice when I do a job with "symphonies" I get an aloof look, as if to say, "Where does she fit in here?" Remember, I don't even think of myself as a musician, although some say, "Yes, words are music." I consider myself a storyteller who tells tales in tune to music. When it's all over, though, both the symphony and jazz musicians are in love with each other. *Neither one has harmed a note*. That's important. That's the measure of a musician.

You might ask, "Pearl, are these guys 'purists'?" Lord, no! It's a bond that is so tightly knit together it becomes a puzzle to the outsider. "Too bad," I think sometimes; "the world should be all musicians because of that bond called love."

When they meet, they embrace as lovers, and they leave each other in the same way. Surgeons, lawyers, merchants, singers, dancers, etc., etc., don't usually do that. Often, as I watch them, I think of a puppy. His master leaves him a moment and the joy he feels when the master returns is unmatched. That's the musicians' unity. Mutual adoration.

They *listen* to other people. They *hear* their own. When you speak to them they look straight into your eyes, "eyeball to eyeball." I always feel they're looking for notes. But you wind up talking to yourself and you don't know it. You ask, "What do you think of that?" "Of what?" they say. How frustrating.

Why doesn't "the rare breed" ever offend or criticize their own kind (at least in your presence)? There is no need to. Should a man play a wrong note, his fellow musician spares him the agony of, "That was wrong." Why? Because *the note* tells him. The *note* says, "I hurt, you have caused me pain, please correct it." That human being will nurse it until it is cured. Yes, these men and women do live in a strange, silent-but-loud world. They are never absent from each other. I'm convinced that the musician dies hearing the angels tuning up for his entrance to the "Heavenly Band." There is always a chair and a part to play. To them a man doesn't die; he simply has a rest written into the arrangement.

# Otto Preminger

In 1958 film giant Samuel Goldwyn decided to produce *Porgy and Bess.* I had never seen the play when it was on Broadway. We were to be directed by the masterful Armenian Mr. Rouben Mamoulian, who had directed the original play. This was indeed an honor for me because once again I would work under the magic of the man who had directed me in my first play, *St. Louis Woman,* in 1946. As it turned out, though, we were directed by Otto Preminger.

The stars of the original play were Todd Duncan, Anne Wiggins Brown, Avon Long, and many of the great Negro actors and actresses of the time. These beautiful voices must have been awesome and the magic of Ira and George Gershwin will live forever.

The stars of the movie version were to be Sammy Davis, Jr., a man whose entire body reeks with talent, and who, at that time, was at the height of his fame. Sammy was to be Sportin' Life. Sidney Poitier, the new, hot movie guy, was Porgy; Dorothy Dandridge, a beautiful girl who had long made a splash in many movies, was Bess; Ruth Attaway was Serena, and a gentleman who had played the role of Crown before, Brock Peters, graced us with his acting ability and tremendous baritone. Also featured was a young lady of about twenty-two who today is a major figure in cabaret, plays, and television — Diahann Carroll. All in all it was a sterling cast who would soon know Otto Preminger. He looked like a general, acted like a general, but usually he was a "pussy cat."

*Porgy and Bess* also meant a lot to me because when Louie and I married in London, a young lady with "the kind of voice angels bestow," Miss Leontyne Price, was appearing as Bess in the London production. Louie (who was playing with Duke Ellington at the time) had flown in from the States. On our wedding night I had to work and Leontyne, who was then married to the great baritone William Warfield (Porgy), came to see us; Leontyne sang "I Love You Truly." No wonder we're still married, having been bound together with such a solo.

The Preminger-Mamoulian dispute was large. Here were two major directors with a top figure of movieland, Mr. Goldwyn, handling talent and directorial differences. We sat and waited it out. The pain and respect I felt was for both men; either way it went, both were my friends. I did, of course, favor Mamoulian; however, all of it was out of our realm.

As soon as that dispute was settled, we were told to be in costumes for inspection at 9 A.M. on the specified day. At 7 A.M. a call came to me at the Chateau Marmont where we were staying. "Don't come near the studio," the man on the phone said, "it is all in flames." The roof had blown and our sound stage was on fire. Had we arrived earlier, it is possible that at least one hundred and twenty people might have lost their lives. We were told the film would be delayed six or eight weeks. On our return a new director was announced: "Otto Preminger." That was a firebrand no one put out. It was my second experience with "The Austrian."

I first met Otto Preminger at a dinner in London. I, the nonsocialite, attended alone, and was seated next to this tall, bald-headed man, a giant with piercing blue eyes. I had seen him in the movies, always playing the villain, the Nazi, whatever. I thought he was German. Well, you learn quickly from Otto, "My darlink, I am not 'Cherman,' I am from Vienna, darlink." (He stressed that issue.)

It was a strange evening because I knew no

one, yet I was trying to fit in with someone I'd feel at home with. One thing for sure I did not feel at home with "the artichoke." Who had brought this disaster upon me? Sitting upright on my plate was this green, oval object with leaves. I'd seen it in stores while doing my grocery shopping, but I never bought one. How was I to know that this artichoke would be an introduction to a movie maker who would someday use me in one of his films.

Somehow this sensitive man Preminger must have felt, "This dear young lady does not understand the object facing her; it's throwing her a curve." He turned to me and said, "Darlink [heavy Austrian accent coming through], pull off the leaf, dip it into the sauce, and eat it." Following his instructions, with pinky finger in the correct position, I pulled off my first leaf, dipped, and tasted. Ah, delicious! Perhaps that was the beginning of Otto's knowledge that *I took direction* and learned easily.

Not too long after, while working at La Vie en Rose in New York, a party that included Otto came to see the show. Afterward he said, "Darlink, you *vere* delightful. I loved you." "Well," I answered, "maybe you'll put me in a movie." He laughed and I didn't blame him; I'm no actress. But fate plays lovely games because a few days later a call came: "Mr. Otto Preminger would like you to play the role of Frankie in *Carmen Jones.*" Cloud nine was not tall enough. This was in 1954.

Getting back to *Porgy and Bess,* everything was going fine on the set, the songs were all recorded (I did my own voice on record); Sammy Davis and Brock Peters did their own voices; Poitier's and Dorothy Dandridge's singing voices were dubbed by Robert Farlane of the Met and the stunning Marilyn Horne, respectively. Of course, Marilyn Horne is now one of the greatest mezzo-sopranos in the world.

One day Dorothy provoked the dreaded Preminger roar. She had angered him about something just before lunch at a rehearsal of the card game scene. He wanted her to show more emotion while singing, but she felt the song another way. The more we rehearsed, the tenser it became. Cameramen, grips, actors, almost everyone felt the fireworks wouldn't be long in coming; somehow a few thought otherwise, as Preminger seemed to be leaning favorably toward what Dottie had been doing. I knew better.

I warned Dorothy after lunch break that she was going to be in for one hell of an evening, "Oh no," she said, "I can handle him." "Use long tongs, Dorothy," I said, "because

327

he's a hot fire." She didn't listen. The aria began at the card table. Otto wanted her to do the scene so that when she reached the peak of the song, she would be weeping; obviously, Dorothy didn't see it that way, or couldn't do it. Lawdy! What he did to that girl.

He kept stopping the scene, screaming, ranting. Then came the wildest thing of all; "You have more lipstick on than you wore this morning," Otto said. "No," said Dorothy. "Yes," said Otto. This debate went on for quite a few minutes, back and forth; no winner. He shot the scene about six more times, screaming until he was hoarse and we were ready to drop. "Damn this man," we all thought, "what is he after?" "Otto the Great" knew. Finally, he wore Dorothy down to a pulp, and angry tears welled in her eyes. As soon as Preminger saw that, he yelled: "*Action.*" At that moment the aria began and Dorothy's chest was heaving. She was furious; as the song progressed she grew angrier and stronger. Poor thing, she was totally overcome with her emotions and could no longer hold back her tears but she kept on and on, mouthing that song perfectly. As she broke down with exhaustion from her feelings, the song ended. "*Cut,*" screamed Otto. He got what he wanted.

He tried one tirade against Sidney Poitier,

who was playing Porgy. That was wonderful to watch. Brute strength and determination were matched; they simply outstared each other and "the show went on."

People have often asked me, "How did you miss the screamer?" Well, I did what he asked, and that was all. Once Preminger knew the other actor I was doing the scene with was wrong, and instead of attacking him, he decided to attack his friend, me. The set was absolutely silent because so many had said, "She is his pet." He sat up on the camera and coldly said, "Darlink, you must be tired." Knowing he was so far wrong and why he was pulling the stunt, I answered, "No, I'm not tired, but you must be — so why don't we all rest." Those penetrating blue eyes met mine with a murderous glare, held my gaze, then he cracked up laughing. "That's a good idea, darlink." Maybe he had thought of the girl who couldn't hold her own with an "artichoke" holding her own against him.

There is no artist, large or small, who worked under Preminger's direction who doesn't have a tale to tell of his or her experiences with him. He was indeed a rare man; a great director, and a good friend. Think of all his great works — *Laura, Advise and Consent, The Man with the Golden Arm, The Moon Is Blue.* He dared to do as he pleased. That was Otto Preminger.

# A Standing Ovation for . . .

*Louis Armstrong*

In July 1971, we opened a road tour of *Hello, Dolly!* at the Shrine Auditorium in Los Angeles. Backstage I received three separate arrangements of white flowers, each different. I remember one especially: a ton of white carnations. Stunningly white. As they were being delivered by one messenger, a thick letter was pushed into my hands by a different messenger. Usually, like most performers, I do not open any mail or telegrams before a show. It's not necessarily a superstition; I guess I just want to concentrate on getting ready for show time. But this letter I opened.

It was from *Louis Armstrong* — and it was eight pages long. Why was he writing? As I read I got no answer as to why; but I got more insight into the life of a man whom I'd known and loved as a person, and who, of course, was the best trumpet showman I'd ever witnessed.

He unfolded tales of his childhood, telling me how his mother would come home from work bringing nice food; he went on and on, mostly in general terms. The more I read, the less I understood why he wrote it. Within two days he was dead. His darling wife Lucille (now deceased) later told me, "Pops [as everyone called him] was celebrating his day, then turned to me and said, 'Get me some stationery; I'm going to write Pearl a letter.' "

I never could explain this; and now they are both gone. I'll always remember Louis Armstrong, an exceptional talent. "Pops" has not been replaced.

*Ethel Waters*

Here is "The Lady" who did it all and did it well. Not many talents can equal her. Miss Ethel Waters was an outstanding singer, dancer, and actress.

I remember that her own funeral featured *Ethel Waters singing*. After a short eulogy at the church in Forest Lawn, a man arose, went to the podium, and said, "All of us know that no one could sing 'His Eye Is on the Sparrow,' the favorite hymn of Miss Waters, better than she did; since no one could do it better, we decided to play a tape of her singing this at a Billy Graham revival." At first there was an eerie silence as she started to sing; then came intervals of sniffling and soft sobbing. Me, I was choking with a quiet emotion for this lady whom I had grown to know in her last days.

I had lived across the street from her at Juan and Rose Tizol's house. Juan was one of the original Ellington men, and his "Caravan" and "Perdido" are two of the greatest-ever jazz tunes. Many times Miss Waters would bring her food over to eat with Rose and me (when I was in California on a picture or club date). She was lonely in her big house. *No company.* So many had forgotten the great lady.

Once I went over to her house. On the wall was a photo that hung practically from floor to ceiling. It was Waters in costume, gorgeous figure and face, as she appeared in *Thousands Cheer.* Few people remember that this lady did the first TV sitcom starring a black performer: "Beulah." Now here she was alone and lonely. Her long, gray plaits hung over her shoulder; there were no wrinkles in her face. No one called her "Ethel," it was always "Miss Waters," as she demanded. This truly was the reigning queen of talent for over twenty-five years. Yes, her eye was on the sparrow and He watched over her.

Not too many years ago, I had the opportunity to play the role of Berenice, made famous by Miss Waters, in *Member of the Wedding.*

It was a ninety-minute movie by NBC. Never had such an honor been accorded me. It was frightening but fulfilling and I hope that I did a worthy job. At the end of the play Berenice sings, "I sing because I'm happy, I sing because I'm free, my eye is on the sparrow and I know He watches me." He did, Miss Ethel Waters.

# "Simi Love"

We sat side by side in Professor Ferguson's art class one semester. The handsome young boy had a warm smile and as I listened to him discussing issues, answering questions that so many of us were lost on, it was obvious he was very knowledgeable in art. He was very astute. One day, while waiting for the professor, we started to discuss poetry. As it turned out, we both loved and attempted to write it. We formed a nice friendship; he helped me in many areas of art where I was having trouble. So I became Aunt Pearl, and Louie (after their meeting) became Uncle Louis. He was my play-nephew "Simi."

John graduated before me with top marks. After graduation, he went on to Loyola law school and did very well. Through the auspices of Georgetown he was able to go during a couple of summers to Fiji to work at the governor's mansion. While in Fiji he used to send me bars of soap called *"Pearl* [brand name]"; then he started sending swatches of gorgeous patterned material made on the island.

Two years later I received an offer from John to invest in his fashion firm. Usually I'm not into any investments or speculations, yet I had the feeling this boy had something worthwhile so I called my accountant. "Tony, I think we have a smart, honest cookie here so what about a few pennies' worth of stock?" Tony listened slowly; he always seems to listen slowly when it involves *money*. You don't talk him into a deal fast. Anyhow we went for it.

John moved up fast in the fashion world, at home and abroad. His styles were being sold at Neiman-Marcus and elsewhere. He was swinging. Occasionally we'd trade poems and letters; however, with both of us being so busy we didn't keep in contact as often as we'd have liked.

I live in Lake Havasu City, Arizona, and although the train station is at Needles, California, forty miles away, Louie and I don't head back east without first going up to Los Angeles to see the doctors (foot and medical), and to visit our children. Unfortunately Louie and I spend very little time at home; it's unbelievable that we're away months at a time. We have promised now, as I finish this book on the back porch over the Christmas holidays, to remedy this situation.

One day while awaiting the train we opened the paper and there, a page large, was an announcement of John's opening day at Neiman-Marcus. I was squealing like a pig with delight. The next morning, as soon as the store opened, Aunt Pearl was there. John inside was awaiting his first customer. Little did he know Aunt Pearl and Uncle Louie would be there to view his fantastic display. I went crazy getting gifts for friends. I even helped corner some customers saying, "Look at our nephew's robes, bathing suits, caps; we went to Georgetown together; he's a genius." I really had my sales pitch going while John stood back and just beamed. His aunt Pearl, he knew, was so happy for him.

Times passed, more clippings came to us about all of John's achievements; his company was making great progress. To this day I've never bothered him about the stock deal; I was just happy for him.

Train time came again and up to Los Angeles we went. We decided to take our usual walk on the jogger's path across from the Hilton Hotel on Wilshire Boulevard. Halfway around we heard a voice screaming, "Aunt Pearl, Uncle Louie, it's me, John." We looked around and pulling over to the curb in that busy traffic was our nephew. "Come around the block, honey, you can't stop or park there," I yelled. Before you could say "boo," a stunning, new red car came swinging over to the corner where we stood. He jumped out, all smiles, and we hugged a lot.

"Aunt Pearl, I found you. I've been meaning to get in touch, it's so important. I'm sick." "You're what?" Louie and I asked simultaneously. "I must tell you I have ARC," he said. To tell the truth, I heard him but couldn't relate at the moment. "John," I said, "you have never looked better in your life" (really he did — and still does after over a year now). "Never mind, Aunt Pearl, I'm sick; I have AIDS." We just stood still, numb with shock, despair, and pain.

"Let's drive to the hotel, honey, and talk," we said. In the car he started to explain his medicine, and by the time we reached the hotel we knew so much about AIDS. As John said, "Aunt Pearl, knowledge is so important, research is necessary; and so much more is government involvement." We parted, holding on to hope. Aunt Pearl told him to keep extreme faith and know that God can cure all.

Every click of the train wheels repeated, "John has AIDS, John has AIDS; he's waiting helplessly for help and no one has the answer yet." It was the closest I had been to the situation.

The first thing that came to me to ask John

about his personal life was, "Do your parents know?" "Yes, Aunt Pearl," he answered. "They are heartbroken but supportive of me." I felt broken-hearted, too. I ached for the boy facing what most have said is a dead-end street; a young man and two older people reaching out for what, we didn't know.

I've come to see that the courage to go on is so needed with this AIDS situation. My admiration for the people who are ill is deep as they continue to seek life's threads; determined to make the world aware of their existence. We should relate to the situation in which those with AIDS find themselves, to let ourselves be touched by what has so far been recognized as an incurable disease. Sad to say, many friends and relatives deny its presence. AIDS patients have to cope with the pain of their mounting expenses, of being denied a job (when medical sources say you cannot contaminate others except sexually, by blood transfusions from someone infected, sharing contaminated needles, or as a hemophiliac being treated wrongly). Everyone longs to be self-sufficient, and to deny a man the chance to be that is morally wrong. AIDS patients do not want to be leaners; they want to be able to stand on their own feet as long as possible, avoiding the embarrassment of being looked upon as lepers were in biblical times.

In Atlantic City recently, I heard a sad story, one that almost made me ashamed to be called a human being. A young worker in the hotel overheard me telling someone about a speech on AIDS I had given at the World Health Organization. Turning to Louie and me, he said, "That's very nice, Miss Bailey, because I had a cousin die last week and our relatives refused to let him be buried in the family plot." I looked at him as though he had told me of an earthquake. "How cruel," I answered him, "how indecent of humanity."

There is an urgency in the voices of the dying to speak to us in life. Frightened people are suffering daily — wanting to talk to *someone, anyone*, who will *hear* them. I can tell by John's recent letters, as he lives with his problem, that it isn't a matter of people just avoiding AIDS victims because they don't care to listen. The victims are not asking us to sit down and get our ears bent listening. They only want us to hear. It's like they're screaming loudly on the "inside," in order to reach the "outsider," and they feel by the actions that have been taken (particularly in government) that no one can hear their screams. And so the pain inside hurts more. They're literally bursting their lungs and hearts.

Thinking more about the cemetery situation, I ask, "Who are we to deprive the dead of a final resting place? Has mankind really reached such depths of depravity?" The dead seek the earth (returning to themselves, as dust). Athough I did not know that young man in Atlantic City, his cousin's words tore at my soul and I, as others do, cry for humanity.

John and I have talked often. I've asked a few questions. He's given me answers to many things I wanted to know but did not feel it was my right to ask. The idea of death never entered my mind because, being the final touch, it was something I did not want to touch upon. The answers I was seeking were those concerning continued life. Medical science and all other forms of research have brought us to realize how terrible this epidemic has become. Further delays in finding a solution to the present crisis can mean only decay to our future generations. If we don't pick up our pace AIDS will roll right over us like a tank; we'll all be trapped. One way we may possibly be able to squeeze this monster back into its "Pandora Box" is to ask the right questions. It is necessary, though, for the victims to open up and let the researchers in; not the probers or the curious; I mean the *carers*. While the search goes on under the microscope, the "source" (victim) needs to be tapped for the final answer. Not after death, but before.

Allow me to share some of John's thoughts with you since he can state things better than I:

July 19, 1988

Dear Aunt Pearl and Uncle Louie,

I've been well — in fact with this new drug from Japan, my blood counts have been significantly improving. I still feel and look great. My trip to Samoa was truly wonderful and I wrote a collection of poetry while I was there, that I've enclosed for you. I'm thinking of getting back into design and I'm looking into how I will do it. But I'm anxious to be creative again.

I had realized that I had been allowing AIDS to limit my potential, and I'm not going to allow that to happen anymore. A year and a half of dealing with AIDS is enough time for me — so watch out world, John is coming back.

Boy! That really made me feel GOOD.

John sent his résumés around.

Sept. 13, 1988

In 1986 I was designing my Simi O'Pago Pago men's and children's lines,

341

and was nominated for the Marty Award for Best West Coast Men's Wear Designer. At the same time I saw an epidemic running through our industry: AIDS. I have seen very close friends die and have been personally touched by this disease. I decided to take the initiative and founded FIFA, The Fashion Industry to Fight AIDS, which eventually became a division of AIDS Project Los Angeles. With the help of people like you, I started the first industry-supported clothing bank of *new* clothing for persons with AIDS.

Through my involvement with AIDS Project Los Angeles, I became aware of the tremendous need for AIDS-related government advocacy. Given my degree in law and my political experience, I accepted a full-time position as a government lobbyist for AIDS Project Los Angeles. In the past year I have been active in advocating on federal, state, and local levels for increased funding for AIDS education, research, and treatment. It has been a challenging and rewarding experience. I feel that I have made a significant contribution to the AIDS battle and now I feel that I am ready to put those energies back into my fashion career.

Sincerely yours,

Time passed. Then John wrote this letter to a priest:

November 11, 1988

It's after midnight and I've gotten out of bed (though I am yearning to sleep) to pen these thoughts to you — perhaps, so they are never lost. I should have been asleep — instead I have been up, crying. I just finished reading a novel by a friend of mine, Paul Monette, called *Borrowed Time*, about the loss of his lover Roger who died two years ago. I know many of the people in the book. I kept putting down the book for weeks, never wanting to read the final forty pages; I knew the ending all too well.

It's funny reading of Roger's final weeks when he had gone blind, his friends had brought him tapes to listen to. I recalled bringing a tape to my dear friend, Adam, who died of AIDS in September. At that time Adam gave me a book to "borrow" — that book was *Borrowed Time*. I cannot help but think that Adam was passing along to me the real commodity; for the past three years he had lived on "borrowed time" and now he was passing it on to me.

I received your letter today and it was really good to hear from you. You mentioned many specifics from my last letter to you, but you did not mention one thing I had written to you about. I told you I had lost five friends to AIDS in the past two months — well, make that seven as of this writing. I can understand one not wanting to address that in a letter; person to person is more your style. But I pray to God you *hear* me when I tell you I've just lost seven friends to AIDS in two months. I am not yet thirty and each day I face life with a virus inside of me that is killing almost all of my friends. I just wish someone from the outside would hear us — would hear me.

AIDS in the Eighties is analogous to Hitler in the Thirties. Only those of us on the front line truly know and understand the devastation of that epidemic, just as only the Jews knew the terror of Nazism before the rest of the world. I hope you hear me tonight; I pray you hear me tonight.

I went to a support group tonight and at one point the facilitator asked me what it feels like to lose seven friends in so short a period of time. I think I am still too numb to know. Every once in awhile it hits me that one of them is gone. I think a lot about why they are gone while I am still healthy and here. I too am on borrowed time.

I'd like to believe that maybe I am of the next generation of persons with AIDS, living longer with new drugs and preventative treatments; but who really knows? So AZT has added an extra two years to my life — who knows how long this truce will last? This is the reality of those of us with the virus. Science has no answers, and the longer I live, the more questions science faces.

Pearl Bailey called me last week very excited. She was asked to be the keynote speaker at the opening reception of the World Health Organization's first world AIDS conference to be held on December 1st in Geneva. She accepted the invitation because of her friendship with me and her desire to share that with many people.

She's going to speak about the personal side of AIDS, a side she has learned of through our friendship over the years. She has been a very supportive friend to me through my illness. She'll be reading my poems on AIDS and distributing them to representatives from over 160 nations. This is what we need more of, and this is why I share my feelings with a friend like you and Pearl.

I just needed to get my thoughts down on paper and I thank you for being there to listen. I pray that you hear me.

All my love,

In addition to his letters, I have found John's heart in his poetry. Like these:

## AT TWENTY-EIGHT

At twenty-eight
for the first time,
I saw my life
    without me.
And I trembled
    'til I cried.
Into perspective
    suddenly.
Everything —
    into perspective
And I began
    to rebuild
This time with
    a clarity
    of purpose —
    a vision of life
    limited (perhaps) by time,
    but infinite in love.

Today
I live more
than ever before.
My family loves more
than ever before
My friends love more
than ever before
I love more
than ever before.
And it shows.
What some never know
I know
now.
I have been blessed
with love
at twenty-eight
*The Ides of March 1987*

## WHAT IS EASTER?

Twenty-eight years a Catholic
and I never really
understood
the message of Easter
until now,
until AIDS.
Nor did I really
understand
why it's called
Good Friday

347

Christ knew death
on that good day,
and without facing death
there can be no Easter
Easter —
a time of hope, joy, new life and
new beginnings.
Those of us with AIDS
having faced death,
can now move on
to hope, joy, new life and
new beginnings.
The day we learn of our illness
is our Good Friday,
and each day of life,
from that moment on,
is our Easter

*4/6/87*

And so I went to Geneva, dear John. Sat
with the ladies and gentlemen, listened, heard,
and prayed. There were participants from
Kuwait, Geneva, Thailand, the United Kingdom, France, the United States, Japan, Aus-
tralia, Malta, Berlin, the U.S.S.R. We read
our speeches and debated and prayed. Let us
hope the trip was not in vain. I share my
speech with you, dear readers, in the hope
that you may never have to live these moments
with any of your loved ones or share the secrets

of others with the rest of the world.

## WE THE SEEKERS SHALL BE THE FINDERS*

It was a long journey here, measured more in love than distance. The realization that the world would be here to listen, speak, and search together has made it worthwhile. Hope, faith, love traveled all the way with me. The "outsider" has to become "insider," on the subject of AIDS.

I've heard it said, "Not in this century will there be a cure." We must say, and believe: "Oh yes there will be." Each nation sitting here has been touched, not one has escaped this pestilence, AIDS. Like the "four horsemen," it is riding the earth, destroying: with no regard to age, race, or sex. Those who say, "Not me," think of all who said the same thing.

In the words of Martin Buber, "Let everyone cry out to God and lift his heart up to him, as if he were hanging by a hair, and a tempest were raging to the very heart of heaven, and he were at a loss for what to do, and there were hardly time to cry out.

*Statement delivered to the World Health Organization on AIDS at Geneva, December 1, 1988.

It is a time when no counsel indeed, can help a man and he has no refuge save to remain in his loneliness and lift his eyes and his heart up to God and cry out to Him. And this should be done at all times for in the world a man is in great danger."

The recognition of AIDS comes closer when it strikes someone dear. I met a young boy who at 25 had reached a large degree of success. At 30, he is reaching out for LIFE. DEATH is reaching out for him. He was caught in the dragnet of AIDS.

Today he is frightened (though he hides it well), questioning, probing, helping others. He wonders why the doctors, scientists, politicians, and financiers aren't doing more: anything so that he can live. The disgust about the speed and inefficiency is eating at his soul. He said in a recent letter to me, "I am not yet 30 and each day I face life with a virus inside of me that is killing almost all of my friends. I just wish someone from the 'outside' would hear it — would hear me." I call him a brave, young man, waking each day asking God, "Is this the day?"

In the Bible we read of the lepers whom men shunned: some brave souls walked among them. So many times we tend to shrug off good, able souls, thinking we can solve situations from a distance. No! my friends we must take a closer look seeing "the faces," and "the hearts." As I looked into the heart of this boy, I sometimes *felt* to ask, "How, little friend, did this occur? Can you help us so we may know more? We are trying to help you. Give us a clue as to the beginning." I remember him telling me of his first knowledge. He said, "When the doctor told me first, I cried; then I spoke to the priest." Then he said, and he laughed, "I started to sell all my possessions." "One day," he said, "I looked around me and discovered I had sold my bed." I knew then he was telling me *all*. He was getting ready for death. How dare a disease prepare us in such a cruel, inhuman way.

I thought, *it is not fair* for you to have this disease. It is not fair for us to sit here in darkness waiting for answers without even a clue. We need help, too.

In some *bosom* there is faith: In some *mind* there is a key to open the door. We must falsify the lie that AIDS is "unconquerable." Somewhere in the world a man or woman will, by the grace of God, become filled with the knowledge that will save humanity.

Through our combined efforts it can and must be done if mankind is to survive this terrible pestilence. God created mankind.

We must not allow AIDS to destroy it, or force us to destroy ourselves. The cry for help grows louder, and louder every day. Our ears must grow sharper to the sound of "H E L P."

Yes, this trip is worthwhile for mankind's sake. Let us gather together often in love for mankind's sake. Let us seek no reward other than life. Let us try to find the truth.

Time is not on our side. God is.

We must keep searching until we find a cure for AIDS.

# The Twisted Creature

It was 1 A.M on a summer night when the Limited came to a screeching, jolting halt. One car was slightly tilted on its side resting; it was ours. Louie was in the upper bunk (he hasn't cared for them since); I was in the lower bunk reading. Simultaneously with the jolt was my feeling of veering off to the right; the train kept moving, slowly but sideways. It had definitely left the track.

There was dead silence at first. No screaming, no panic. I sat on the leaning brink, putting on my tennis shoes swiftly, covering my gown with a thick caftan robe. Louie clambered down slowly. He seemed to be still figuring out what was going on. For sure it was no "Zildjian Cymbal Crash." Just like a woman, I took my purse, urging Louie to hurry up. My big concern was for gas leakage or explosions. What the hell, I'd read about train wrecks but never experienced one. By this time the crew was busy trying to explain to people what to do. Remember, at that particular hour most of the passengers were asleep. Me, the reader, was deep into her book. Louie started pulling on his socks. Pearl left. I was the first one off, climbing up a grassy steep incline on hands and knees. My hands were now trembling. There was a baby next door to us and I kept asking, "Where's the baby?" Then the mother and baby appeared.

At the top of the incline was a very large platform: the entrance way to a maintenance building. The passengers kept moving out, onto the platform, bunching up like little children back by the high fence behind the building. Folks were finally aware of their plight and were frightened; really frightened. Still no panic. It was more a disbelief than fear; they could now *see* this train.

When we go down the walkway at the station to board a train we notice our size against it and think, "Boy this is big" — when you turn over on a train and see from a distance that monster lying on its side, it looks like a huge dinosaur getting ready to devour you. This baby was smashed, twisted, and angry. It looked like something in agony; its metal had been hurt, crushed. Instead of looming larger than you, the train was suddenly like a child put into perspective by some unforeseen thing, either stronger or more clever than it.

So different from tearing down that track as "King of the Road."

Many passengers were middle-aged, so the crawl up the hill wasn't easy. Many of the crew had been hurt. Propping my foot on the slope, I assisted the crew, who were working diligently. Stopping to take a rest, I heard *someone*, somewhere, say, "Heh, that's Pearl. You all right, Pearl? Let me take your picture, Pearl." Were they hurt or insane? It really irked me because this was no celebrity moment, *this* was a bad train wreck.

"Come on, folks, let's forget the celebrity stuff — come over here, hold hands, and let's work to get the rest of these people off the train." Some then came over and our work proceeded. Funny things happen, I imagine, in these kinds of circumstances.

It happened in Mansfield, Ohio. That place deserves all the praise one can give. In approximately six minutes after we crashed, firemen, paramedics, Red Cross, and hospital ambulances were there; everyone was working hard. I'd say their swift arrival accounted for the lack of panic among the people. Inside the maintenance building, we were given coffee, chairs, and comfort. Louie and I drive a lot and are often in the state of Ohio. Recently Governor Celeste gave us the Governor's Award. I'd love to pass it on to the city of Mansfield.

Since I'm a "road hog," I can discuss this night with a great deal of *geography* in mind. As you know, when you pass into the State of Pennsylvania you are coming into the Allegheny Mountain area (Pittsburgh, Allentown, etc., etc.). You also are going to do an *ess curve*, which is very famous and, my dears, *very* high — the Horseshoe Curve. Had the accident happened an hour or two later, this would have been our territory. God was more than good.

Once off "the monster," we all stood and surveyed the scene. And we truly prayed. The only thing that saved us was that slight incline and fortunately the very high hill on the other side. It formed a backdrop for the tired, embarrassed sleeping giant.

The people started up again. "Pearl, pose with me. Where are you going? Sing us a song." Here I was about to "weewee" myself and these people who were as nervous as I were kibitzing. The emotions were coming up in my stomach; and although I sensed we all were tense, I could not let their emotions get me into a nervous dither. So Louie and I walked toward what had been the engine.

Upon inspection, we could see the problem. A large, flatbed truck piled high with long steel pipes had been on its way to the factory, on the other side of the tracks. A man was standing there surveying the scene. He just stood quietly looking on in amazement. Turning to us, he said, "You know the truck just stalled; I heard the whistle and I jumped out." He was the driver. He was probably looking at his whole life. All I could think of at that moment was the comic strip of "Beetle Bailey," when the sergeant beats "Bailey" to a pancake. Here was a "metal pancake," flat to the track. When these two powerful forces met, one destroyed the other.

Walking back we felt a soft summer rain; not much. It didn't wet, it warmed. People by now were laid out on stretchers (some were beginning to feel aches and pains); an ankle turned or broken, etc., etc. The most extreme thing seemed to be (among the elderly ones, particularly) "chest pains." Them I could relate to.

One little lady about eighty was giving the nice paramedics a hard time. Lying on the stretcher she was refusing to let them take her to the hospital. Her chest pains concerned them. The more they begged, the more determined she became (only aggravating her situation). Bending over, I asked her, "Please let them help you."

The bluest, fiercest look greeted my brown eyes. She held my gaze for about three minutes. "Don't I know you?" she asked. "What's your name?" "Pearl," I answered. "Pearl! Pearl Bailey!" Keep in mind, my mad, multi-colored caftan robe with the straw hat and scarf, long sleeve gown — I was most un-attractive, but warm. Kneeling down to the lady was beginning to take its toll on my back. I thought to myself, "Lady, if you don't want to go with these men, please get up off this stretcher and I'll go." Pulling me closer, she whispered in my ear, "Pearl, I hurt, but what do you think I ought to do?" I looked at this lovely lady. "Honey, if you want to see a doc-tor then go with these people, if you want to see a lawyer then stay here. My idea would be to go with them — that way you might get to see *both*." She left with the paramedics, who roared with laughter at my logic.

For two years I was chairman of the Ameri-can Lung Association, and on this particular trip was on my way to do some posters for Rich Jachetti, the promotion man at Tavern on the Green in New York. By now the news had hit the nation about the terrible wreck. Next morning at Holiday Inn, where they had so courteously opened the doors to us, Dan Rather's people at CBS (along with local media) were in the lobby. Phones were ringing.

Keeping my promise, Louie and I rented a car and took off for New York — about five or six hours away. Rich had heard the news, and although he was happy about our safety, he still had a job to do. He had asked a charming lady inside having lunch if she would stand with our posters. "Certainly," she was kind enough to agree.

We arrived as they were posing this beauty. I mean a beauty. Although I didn't personally know her, she is one of my loves. Dolly Parton. We posed together and talked, "Country Girl" and "Gospel Girl" — both Southerners.

I still love trains, love the warm rain, respect and love Mansfield, Ohio, and give a large salute to an Amtrak crew who, although in pain themselves, worked their fannies off.

And I met Dolly Parton. We may not match "up top," but I overpower her on the *bottom*.

Amtrak is up on its feet and Train-riding Pearl rides again.

# The Bear's Home:
## Russia

Charles Wick, head of the USIA (United States Information Agency) called. "Pearl, would you and Louie like to go to Moscow and entertain at the U.S. embassy?" How would we like it? We'd love it! Russia! The Big Bear. The closed door was opening a bit wider and we were going in. I had experienced one meeting with a Russian years before at a diplomatic affair given by then Secretary of State William Rogers at which I performed.

The last selection I did was a number in which I walked between the tables relating to each country; I'd sing a bit of a song about it. At the front table near the stage sat a sedate man with a short crew cut. "Where are you from, darling?" I asked, placing my hand upon his shoulder. "California," he answered. His voice was as stiff as his hair. Everyone in the room started to snicker. Immediately we struck up the tune, "California, Here I Come." The audience howled. The lyrics

360

turned out to fit this man's situation; but how were all of us to know that? I couldn't figure out why this moment was so hilarious. Why? The man was H. R. Haldeman, "the biggie" of the White House, after President Nixon, it was said.

I turned from Haldeman and started to mount the stage to end the song when suddenly a large tall figure bounded onto the small dance floor, grabbed me, and spun me around. We went into the wildest dance sequence. The audience went mad; he was madder. It was Ambassador Dobrynin of Russia. What we call behaving boisterously is to the Russians just letting their hair down, having fun. Dobrynin was really having fun. He recently went back to Russia after staying in the States approximately twenty-four years.

After our great display of virtuosity, I closed the show and was invited to Dobrynin's table. His wife sat there in a plain blue dress (not evening attire as everyone else was wearing). With the Russians, it seems, they *do* and *dress* as they please. The ambassador kept up a constant stream of tales and jokes. Half of the people sitting there (including me), didn't understand a damn word he was saying, but they kept laughing anyway. Mrs. Dobrynin kept telling me she was a pianist, all the while listening to her vibrant, entertaining "Big

Bear." One thing Dobrynin did not do: give away any state secrets. All of this came to my mind as we prepared for our second trip to Moscow.

The USIA had difficulty getting the visas, although the Russians had approved the trip. First, it was a "go"; then a "maybe"; then it didn't exist at all — as far as the Russians knew, they said. The Russians have been known to issue a visa, then revoke it; and as you unpack to stay home, they issue it again.

School break was coming up at Georgetown University, and that was the only time I could go, plus Louie and the fellows had other bookings. Charles Wick, being a former musician, knew the circumstances; yet *no one* rushed the "Bear."

Friday was departure day (some of our people had to come from different cities to D.C.), so on Wednesday I said, "No visa today, then the trip is canceled." I went on to study for a mid-term examination. That afternoon when I came from school, the visa had been okayed. Glory be! We were on our way to Moscow and Leningrad.

We left on an American carrier, stopped in London to rest a night, then proceeded to Moscow the next day on Aeroflot, the Russian airline. Having been to the Middle East, we were seasoned travelers, but this was a completely new adventure. Personally, I know that although I was happy, I was also scared. We all longed to be assured (by whom, heaven only knows) that our freedom would stay intact. We did not want to make any mistakes so as to be detained in Siberia or some far-off place in the Soviet Union. Home was a long way and we were getting farther by the minute. *No one slept.*

A voice came over the intercom: "You have now crossed the Baltic Sea; you are in Soviet air space." My fanny tightened a bit. I kept praying that the "Bear's" claws had been clipped. We started to descend. More flip-flops of the stomach occurred. Looking down from the small window of the plane, one could only see vast, barren space, not one tree or house. We came in from the north. I imagined already that it was Siberia, of course. The plane seemed to linger in some spots longer than others, as if to give the passengers (everyone else looked as apprehensive as we) *the full measure* of what we were coming into. Strains of "There Is No Place Like Home" rang in my ears.

We touched down with mixed feelings: joy, anxiety, and questioning, "Should we have come?" Strangely enough I had had this feeling in no other land. I suppose because our two countries have been in so many tight situations, as the superpowers, it's natural that we fear, mistrust, and are wary of each other. Anyhow, we were here and *that was that.* We gathered our belongings and proceeded to the exit gate. There was no need to wonder where or how you moved because soldiers were everywhere to rush you along. They were *not* smiling.

We marched into a bare, unfriendly-looking building. One word hits you, *"Card"* (landing card). Naturally, if you're nervous or afraid, you fumble for the card. Then the word hits harder, "Card." Aha! I found it. The soldier took it, handed it back, and waved me on to another soldier at the passport window. "What the hell, everybody is a soldier," I thought.

Spotting some people giving a tiny wave (it was more a wiggle of the finger) on the other side of the railing, I figured them to be our contacts from the embassy. *They were;* but they were also about as helpless as we were to hurry things along. *Nobody* gets pushy there. Playing it cool is the best way to deal with an entrance into *any* country. Waving a hand could mean you're sending a signal, so watch it. It's even dangerous to do in some Western countries.

The first "floor show," as I call it, began when I reached the passport window. Sitting there was a clean-cut young man, looking all of twenty. He was in uniform and, unsmiling, said one word: "Passport." I handed it over.

Let me digress a bit, so you can appreciate the show. I was wearing a brown pantsuit, a snap brim brown velour hat, with my large tinted glasses. I thought I looked pretty spiffy. I handed over my passport containing what, in my estimation, was *the ugliest photo* I'd ever taken in my life. I had begged in America, "Please spare the Russians this photo."

The soldier looked long and hard at the photo, then glanced at me through the small glass window with the little hole in it. His eyes flicked up and down two or three times. "Glasses," he motioned. I took them off. He repeated the same procedure, eyes flicking up and down, looking again to the photo. "Hat," he motioned. Another order. Instantly I removed the hat. I was getting nervous. Up — down, up — down. Was this going to turn into a slow striptease?

Suddenly it hit me. I said, "I know why you don't believe that picture is me. *I am not that ugly. I have never been that ugly. I don't intend to ever get that ugly.*" You'd never guess the consequences. The young man, who had acted as though he did not understand or speak English, almost fell off his stool laughing. Actually, he howled. He had understood every word I said. Inside, at customs, I went through more.

The customs man also gave me that cold scrutiny, then grabbed my hand and said, "Carats." He caught me off-guard for a second. Oh! I'd forgotten *the ring*. Before I could tell him, he had whipped out a jeweler's glass and placed it over the ring.

Milton Hinton, dean of all jazz bassists in America, and truly one of the greats, has a large green bass case which looks like it contains a mummy. As with all musicians when it comes to their instruments, he guards it with his life. It is sealed when he travels overseas. *They never opened it.* Look at a diamond ring, but leave a mummy case closed. Not too fair, is it?

John Beyrle and Jocelyn Greene finally piled us into a van and limousine and we sped off to the hotel. Arriving at the hotel, Jocelyn, Louie, and I went through "floor show number two." I was wearing a long necklace of round gold beads. *It broke.* As I started to rise from my seat, beads rolled on the floor, down my sweater, in my bra. Later we found some missing beads in my pants. The dirty snowbank outside contained a few. This show was a doozy.

There were a lot of men standing talking in a group outside the hotel. Cab drivers were cracking up at our frantic scramble. I said,

"These beads are gold." The magic word. The search now became a mob scene. Gold was rolling around in the streets of Moscow. Every bead was found and returned. What a grand entrance into Moscow!

Check-in was "floor show three." A short account of that would be impossible so let's just say we made it to our room. That was not exactly easy, either. I don't know how John and Jocelyn had survived this diplomatic bit for so long; they were good at it, *and still young*. Your room key is on a piece of metal, which if it were hung around your neck, or even put in your pocket, would pull you to the floor, it is so heavy. Never fear, though, because you don't get a chance to carry it around that much. They keep it for you.

Before entering the elevator there's a small vestibule. Three or four people are there at a table to check your green card. *No green card* (which is given at the check-in desk), no entering the elevator. Picture that in the United States. *Bedlam.*

Our small suite held a plain hard sofa, a small coffee table, and an extra armchair. Four stairs led to an upstairs bedroom. The tiny twin beds were hard (no feathered mattresses, I assure you). No grandeur here but that didn't bother us. Everything was very clean. Louie and I have very few wants so we make out fine no matter what the situation. It makes for happy traveling.

Next stop was Spaso House, where Ambassador and Mrs. Arthur Hartman lived. Sentries stand in boxes outside. They are tall, real tall; not smiling. They had offered us the luxury of living at the embassy, but we preferred the hotel. Frankly, the embassy in Moscow is not a highly decorated or pretentious place.

At Spaso House the press awaited us, eager to pounce on the unsuspecting naive Americans. Most of the press was from the United States. Americans don't show up too often in Moscow (entertainers especially). Only a few, like Louis Armstrong, Benny Goodman, etc., had shared the hospitality of Russia. Things are changing, though. Now more people, including entertainers, are having the privilege of going to Russia and coming back *amazed*, *delighted*, and more knowledgeable about the Kremlin. Even President and Mrs. Reagan learned things I suppose they never imagined about that ancient land.

The press man pounced, "What do you think of Moscow?" The man had short, curly hair and he peered at me intently through thick, horn-rimmed glasses which made him look terribly important. I wondered, "Is he friend or enemy? Is this the question and answer which will get me thrown out of the country?" He acted as though he were the political writer and wanted to get on with the heavy stuff before anyone asked about show business.

Calmly and slowly, I answered: "We just arrived an hour or so ago. I've been no place yet, sir; and whatever my opinion is I shall keep it to myself until I leave." That fixed him, but not for long. Pausing and studying me, he shot back, "Well, Miss Bailey, for as long as you've been here, *what do you think?*" "Sir," I answered, "I told you my thoughts have not lingered on Russia at all. I've been too busy thanking God that we arrived safely. For your information, if it will help you, I am able to adjust easily so whatever I come across, I'll face at that time. Perhaps then I'll even find you and give you a firsthand opinion of what I think" — I paused — looked at him — and added, "As I leave Russia." He squirmed. I enjoyed. And we got on with the press conference. Short, sweet, and safe. I had not brought a coat warm enough for Siberia.

The others seemed to get a kick out of that. This, they knew, was no "new kid on the block." We discussed issues for about an hour and a half over coffee and cakes. It turned out well. My political friend learned that show people don't just entertain; *we also have intelligence.* Our likes and dislikes get squashed early in our careers after facing all kinds of audiences. The ladder of success which we climb is filled with broken rungs, so we learn the tricks of the trade as we climb.

I learned what, how, when, where to say things years earlier in the United Nations. Both Soviet and American people have been structured to mistrust each other. It's like a football game. *Offense. Defense.* The spectators are the other countries (or peoples) who are watching. The "Bald Eagle" (U.S.A.), and "The Russian Bear" (U.S.S.R.). Both heavyweights. The important thing in life is to know in what division you play; and in my encounter with the press man, I stayed in my division: *I was a guest* in another man's country and behaved accordingly.

Show time, the real one, came the next night. Spaso House holds only so many, but Ambassador Arthur Hartman and his dear wife Donna accepted the requests of many important people in the Russian government they had not expected. The guests were packed in like well-oiled sardines. There are so many types of Russians, from different sections of the country; they prefer to be called "Soviets." For a while they were so quiet we wondered (although they applauded) how we were doing. We soon found out. Spaso House rocked at the end. I went down the aisle singing one

370

of their favorites, "Dark Eyes." This song spaces them out.

Louie had blown their minds with his drum solo; Milt and his bass had them screaming; Remo Palmier's quiet guitar touched their sensitive souls; and Roz Claxton's style of stride piano-playing amazed them. These guys were a tough act to follow. The audience would not stop applauding, so we started to applaud them, Russian-style.

Finally Hartman and Donna came on stage, gave us accolades and flowers; a Soviet jazz figure had written a parody of "Won't You Come Home, Bill Bailey," asking me to return. (Pearl Bailey, won't you please come back?) As soon as this was over, the audience yelled for more. The ambassador said, "Pearl, they want more." "Well, Ambassador, I always do a special song at home to close the show — it's sort of religious. I know there are religious differences here," I said softly to him. "Do it, Pearl," he said, "they love you." So I did. "Let There Be Peace on Earth." *Tears flowed*. We all fell in love with God in some form, I know.

Then the beads broke again — after Louie's restringing job. Soviets, Americans, the ambassador, Donna, and everyone ended the program searching for gold. At that particular moment I would have let anyone keep those beads. I had found a better gold; I had found the wonderful wealth which cannot be measured in ounces. It was in the hearts of men and women far away from home, where some had taught me it did not exist. I found it in Russia. The political writer touched my arm and said, "Never mind what you think about Russia; *Russia loves you.*" How warm.

Spreading out into different rooms we mingled and had a beautiful evening. The buffet was modest, to say the least: potato chips, pizzas, popcorn, and some little meatballs. We all ate as if it were caviar, chicken, and prime rib. It served the purpose. Of course there were beer, "hard" nips, and champagne. And yes, vodka! My silent prayer was, "Let brotherly love continue." We parted, hugging and promising one another to meet again.

We got up early the next morning — excited again. We were going to Leningrad, the bastion that Hitler wished he had never heard of. That city and its people will long go down in history for its sacrifices and the glory it bestowed upon Russia. The people of Leningrad seem to walk taller than those in Moscow. They have a distinct pride. They know what they did to Hitler, and probably saved Mother Russia.

What a ride we had on the famous Red Express. Amtrak has finally met its match.

Both are *old, loud rattles* and need tons of repairs. Amtrak has a heating system (it fails a lot, ask me), male and female car porters, better beds, and better food *but* it arrives most of the time (lately) behind schedule. The Red Express has a lady (our stoker was nice and plump like a "Perdue" chicken), a potbelly stove in a corner at one end of the corridor, chilly compartments, and one bathroom for all at the other end of the corridor.

Berths on the Red Express are actually boards with not-too-thick mattresses that are pulled down from the side wall. A small table is attached to the window. Picture-taking from windows is forbidden in certain areas. You are told that, specifically. This is primarily because enroute to Leningrad we pass by military areas. Of course, lots of this happens at night. However, who feels like disobeying so far from home? The Red Express outdoes Amtrak on at least two points: it *arrives on time*, and *porters* are right there *waiting*.

Tom, the consul, a tall, nice-looking, and pleasant man, met us at the station. There was an instant warmth. We went to our hotel — lovely, large, beautifully furnished, a nice lobby, a souvenir hall for postcards, etc. It was so different from Moscow. The whole air of Leningrad was of a different culture. On our sheet of what to bring to Russia (items we were informed they possibly did not have) were deodorant, toilet tissues, soap, etc. My dear, they had Yves St. Laurent deodorant, the softest of tissues, plenty of soap, etc., etc. (So much for the travel brochures at home.) What they do love is instant coffee, tea, and candy. When you offer some they smile and say *"Nyet";* if you extend your hand they take a small bit. And if you give more, they fairly bubble. No tips accepted. At least that was the case in 1984.

At the hotel dining entrance "Dark Eyes" came into play once more. Thank heavens for that song. We arrived at the door, where sat a short, very plump lady checking receipts. Not realizing the time schedule, we asked to have some breakfast. *"Nyet, nyet."* We asked, "Just coffee, maybe, lady?" *"Nyet, nyet."* I knew I shouldn't force the issue.

Then I started humming "Dark Eyes." The cold eyes looked up — a few more bars — the eyes warmed. In a split second this lady got up, fairly dragged me into the large café, down a middle aisle (there were booths on each side), summoned a waiter, called the kitchen help to bring back food to the buffet warmers, and said to me, "Eat, eat." We ate.

Next came a large bottle of champagne (at 11 A.M.), *and the dance.* Before Louie, E.B., or I knew it, the Hostess and I were fairly sailing down the middle aisle, doing a duet. We swirled all over the place as late diners clapped their hands in unison. Broadway was never like this. *All of this for my two hard-boiled eggs.* We were "Royalty." And she was the "Royal Bear."

We got a free day in Leningrad and Louie and I were given a car with a young Soviet driver, Igor. He did not speak English, but he was very pleasant. He was in civilian clothes, so it gave us a sense of not being watched. He could have been KGB; however, he acted as though he was as happy as we to get from under hammer and sickle.

The three of us took off for L'Hermitage. We have had the pleasure while abroad of seeing the Louvre in Paris and the Borghese Gallery in Rome. At the entrance of L'Hermitage are wide massive stairs (as wide as a three-lane street). You enter a huge lobby; I mean gigantic. In Russia you can exhaust yourselves on the adjectives meaning "large." Just begin to think in terms of "gigantic" *everything*. Up a few stairs you see the most gorgeous chandelier the eyes can behold. Gaping at that piece strains every neck muscle.

There's so much: sculpture, paintings, tombs; it's too much to drink in on a short visit. We bought books and slides in the museum shop and left, hoping someday we'd get a chance to return to see this wonder again.

As we emerged from the museum we saw an entire regiment standing across the street, overlooking a freeway. The streets are about four to six lanes wide. The soldiers looked over at Igor, Louie, and me taking photos. They began to stare, so I waved; they stood like stones. I made a motion, could I take their photos? A man whom we could see was their commandant shook his head, saying *"da,"* yes. I began my photo taking; the next thing I knew, we were being photographed by them. I danced, they laughed. They would laugh uproariously at everything I did. Finally, we waved good-bye, got in the car, and started our shopping tour. All the time Igor was having as much fun as we — only he sort of stood apart. He must have thought, "These Americans are queer people."

Next were the souvenir shops. All the stores, small and large, contain some of the most reasonable, yet the most beautiful souvenirs that I've seen in any country. The hand carvings and the painted, lacquered boxes are exquisite. What's great about the Russian souvenirs, or for that matter anything, is no matter what store you go in, *the prices are the same.* They must be, it's the law. *Good law,* thank goodness. I've been in countries where virtually everyone, in every place, gives you the business. To make a profit is one thing; to cheat people is another.

The Russians have the finest amber in the world, with no specks. And Louie in his generosity bought me a sable hat. *Seventy-five dollars*. It would be at least three to five hundred here.

The salespeople don't hassle you. In fact, they hardly move unless you point to something, or address them. They are very courteous. The shopper picks up his basket and walks along the aisles, selecting articles; then he goes through a turnstile to get checked out. It really is like an American Piggly-Wiggly store. I had noticed this particularly in Moscow.

Back to the car we went, looking like Santa Clauses. "Igor," I asked, "is it possible to go see a synagogue?" He paused, thought about it, then said, *"Da."* (I kept wondering how could he say *da* and *nyet* to what he did not understand.) He probably understood English better than I thought. We were taken to one of the oldest synagogues in the world. A fence almost six feet high surrounds the place. There is no grass, and it looks cold and barren. When we walked into the yard we had a feeling of intruding upon the lives of a hidden people. We mounted the stairs and came to a tall, heavy wood door with a large iron knocker. A man opened it slowly and, without saying anything, waved us in. Igor was not with us. He dared not come. He had parked across and down the street a bit. The smell of chicken soup (penicillin, the cure for everything, they say) wafted across our nostrils. Ah! It smelled so like my house where I prepared chicken soup every day. Out of a large double door came a tall man with a long white coat, such as physicians wear. He and the other man began to converse rapidly in Hebrew.

I tried, by using one word here and there to say, "*We — Americans — like to see* [pointing to my eyes]" and meet them. After about six attempts one man shook his head in a knowing way and led us into where the services were held. A tiny man with a broad-brimmed black hat followed us. He was about the size of a seven-year-old child. As soon as we got inside, the big man took a key on a circular ring and locked the door. Oh, my lord! What was going on? The little man said nothing, nor did we.

We began to knock on the door so we could get out. Back came the man to let us out. He shook his head again that he now understood and marched us across the hall into another room. Again, once we entered, he locked us in, and the little man too. Immediately I could tell where we were: it was the wedding chapel. "What the heck," I thought, "he's late, we've been married [at that time] thirty-two years." This was in 1984. Rattling his keys, he returned and released us.

Finally a lady came down from another floor. She was a very dignified person, reminding me of the great Golda Meir. She could speak broken English, so we got our message across. They embraced us as she translated our words. We had a lovely session. Later that night Louie and I talked of those people forced to live behind that high fence. Somewhere in the world, it seems, someone is always behind a "High Fence of Hatred."

Our day with Igor was filled with much love, understanding, and, in a sense, sadness. We take so much for granted; and so much is lost on us. Americans need to see how other people live — the advantages, yes, and disadvantages. There's a lot to learn — and enjoy — from seeing things that were created by hand, hearing the music of the masters years ago, viewing works of art, and seeing the buildings (palaces, castles) as we did. It makes me think, "Are we going backward or forward?" Igor was reluctant to leave us; he would have continued all day. We knew we had made a friend. All day he had laughed, and we treated him like a brother or a son. We gave him a tiny gift as he would not accept money. We could feel his emotions, and he felt ours, when we parted. Louie, Igor, and Pearl.

Contrary to all beliefs, the Soviet people have to be the friendliest you'll ever meet. There appears to an outsider a longing for freedom, to be loved. Their government is another *unwritten story,* but I did not come in contact with it. (Little did Louie and I know that at a later time we would meet their supreme leader.)

The love got turned on that night in Leningrad at the consulate. Show time came again. A packed consulate awaited, filled with Soviets and the staffers. Midway through the first song, "On the Road Again," I halted. That face. I had seen that small, bouncing blond figure on the front aisle seat before. "Honey," I asked, "haven't I seen you before?" He grinned, speaking no English, *"Da."* Of course. He had been at the embassy in Moscow jumping too; a jazz saxophone player. We continued. Later that night he jammed with Louie and the fellows.

The boy is now in America, married, going to school, playing his horn. Music draws them all together.

As usual my feet were killing me. I pleaded

lovingly with the audience, *"My feet,* I'll do all you want — more and more — just tell me who wears a size nine?" A lady in the back yelled, *"Da."* Well, folks, somewhere in Leningrad, or worn back to the States by a "staffer," is a pair of Pearl's new hurting shoes.

It was cold when we left the next morning, but the glow of the night before lingered and kept us warm. Tom, our friend, waved us off, we took photos, then on to our stoked, potbelly stove, and the *Red Express* to Moscow.

When we arrived we had some time to see more. We walked the streets observing the people and their fur hats (by now I had one too, compliments of a loving husband). I wondered at the pressure these people live under. The people of a free democratic country would reel or revolt under their restrictions. On the subway trip we observed the people, those standing and those sitting, conveniently avoiding any eye contact. They never seemed to relate to one other.

In my opinion, if their eyes had met they would have communicated the message, "I want to be free, to think, to love, don't you?" How could people exist like this? I wondered. Well, they do.

They move around in the magnificence of those subways like robots. The subway almost appears to be designed for these people. Gorgeous chandeliers, mosaic walls, stained-glass windows, massive clocks that tick with such precision. A train came and went every two or three minutes. Walkways wind all through this underground tunnel. It's a maze. Escalators — the steepest you can imagine — take people up to the sunlight. Seven million people a day. *It's Plato's cave theory again* — into the sunlight, back into darkness.

We gained so much from this visit. A knowledge of a people about whom we had heard the worst, *not the best*. A chance to experience our own way of freedom versus another's. Fears can be established or clarified in some of these experiences. We Americans dare to walk freely, yet I must admit there is much to praise in the Soviet Union. We shall soon see what advancement is made under the new regime. We learned that so-called "strangers" can be drawn together with common bonds like music, dancing, art, sciences.

The trip back home was quieter than the one going over. It was reflection time. Each of us was living our own special moments. We had been to Russia. For me now, it was a return to school; for the fellows, back to their music.

Early one December, just before leaving for my job at the United Nations, I had a call from the White House. "Pearl, the President and Mrs. Reagan are inviting you and Louie to the state dinner for Chairman and Mrs. Mikhail Gorbachev." What? I knew only a select few would make that one. The whole country had been waiting to see this man. December 8 was the day.

About two days before the eighth, another call came, "Pearl, Mrs. Reagan wants you both to attend the ceremonies in the garden." I told the President when I passed him later in the day, "If you had held a luncheon, I could have slept over and spent the whole day here." He roared.

That night was a great accomplishment. Gorbachev, of course, had stated that he *would not* wear a tuxedo (although it was a state dinner). His wife wore a simple long dress. He also had requested a short dinner and an even shorter entertainment program. Mrs. Reagan had complied with this, I'm sure.

Well, sir, it turned out differently. The receiving line bit was funny because by now, as I said, Louie and I — as some others — had been there, on and off, all day. After shaking hands, the President turned to Gorbachev and said, "This is our Pearl, a great entertainer and person." I said something in Russian, "Hello" or whatever. He looked, answered, and laughed. I don't think the President knew what I had said, but he enjoyed the warmth.

Mrs. Gorbachev shook hands; however, her smile is not that forthcoming. I'd say she is cordial, but he is more forthright and open. She studies each person she meets. There is a lot of *clever brain power* in that lady. I bet she can crack a whip. Their personalities are different. Being with them is like standing between the Polar Bear and the Black Bear: *both to be considered.*

At dinner, I was seated at a table with Chief of Protocol Mrs. Seliva Roosevelt, Charles Wick of the USIA, Senator Robert Byrd of West Virginia, the fiddler who later said to the table, "We need more Pearls in the world." (Don't get too many, Senator.) Also at our table sat a man high on the power list in Russia. He seemed very interested in me.

The evening was a howling success. Louie and I have had the occasion to attend many dinners at the White House, but this was a rare evening. You could feel it in the air; the emotions were there, I'm sure, because of these particular guests. Gorbachev, having a ball, was sitting with Mrs. Reagan (Raisa sat with the President). The Chairman was talking, laughing, sipping; I'm telling you he was really partying. I said to Wick, "That child is having such a good time, he may never go home." Those at the table heard it and almost passed out laughing. Gorbachev's man said, "Maybe we'll come back." I answered, "Sir, you'll be here so often they'll think you live in Jersey." That did it. Our table was a pip. Funny thing, he laughed harder than everybody else. I'm sure so many of these people speak English, at least enough to understand us.

The President looked over at me and smiled. He was pleased at the way the evening was going. I mouthed, "Love is in this room, it's so relaxed." He didn't get it so he beckoned me over. I didn't go because I thought it would be intruding. Then Charles Wick said, "Pearl, he said come over, so he means it." I went over, stooped between him and the brilliant GU professor, ambassador, and lovely lady, Jeane Kirkpatrick. After I told Reagan my thoughts, he said, "I think you're right, Pearl. There is something different and warmer." Folks, whether it was the idea of never having met the Russians head on like this (all of us in the room); being glad that we were at least touching; or just tension releasing, *it was* a different evening from any most of us had experienced. Here were the two world superpowers either *growing apart* or *get-*

*ting together*. That remains to be seen.

The entertainment was superb. Van Cliburn, a favorite of the Russians, and of course one of our treasures, played. At the end, as usual, the President and Mrs. Reagan went to the podium to thank him — which usually means the end of the evening. *Not so that night*. As they and Van Cliburn were leaving the stage, Mrs. Gorbachev arose, walked over to Van Cliburn, and spoke (he too speaks Russian). No one, not even President and Mrs. Reagan, knew what was going on. The interpreter who had been nearby ran around quickly to check it out. Mrs. Gorbachev was requesting a number. By this time, Mr. Gorbachev was also in the act, while Reagan and Nancy stood by trying to figure it all out — as was everyone else in the room. It turned out they wanted Van to sing and play "Moscow Nights."

Van Cliburn spoke to Reagan, who told him, "But of course." Van Cliburn said to the audience, "I'm not really a singer," then smiled and proceeded. When it dawned on the American audience that they too knew this song, they chimed in. We all sang. George Will was there and Chita Rivera; it was great fun — and relief.

Usually no one follows the President's act but Raisa Gorbachev did. The Chairman had already stayed well over the time he designated. The dinner and entertainment were not as scheduled, I assure you. Which was good, because it meant everyone enjoyed the affair.

For the benefit of those who would like to know if the Gorbachevs enjoyed themselves, ask: "Didn't he return?" He sure did. *But not from Jersey.* Unfortunately, he couldn't stay, due to the tragedy in Armenia.

We have learned in these times that when God shakes the earth (earthquakes, tornados) man's plans are altered. A large quake ended Gorbachev's last visit, and he went home immediately. As we think of that event we learn something, all of us. If men of all races, creeds, and colors could have bent down and together tried to hold the earth still, they would not have questioned their abilities to get along. They would have only joined hands; the entire world could gain from this.

I learned that a *size-nine American shoe* can fit a size-nine Soviet foot. The numbers may not match, but the feet are the same. *They're just feet. We're just humans.*

# Great, Gentle, Sad, Strong: Africa

*Touch the arm* of an African. There is no give and ripple — just strength. *Touch the heart* of an African and find it is gentle to its family and friends. *Touch the soul* of the African and learn it is sad at the loss of its continent to strangers from other shores. Strangers who daily try to push the Africans back into the earth from which they emerged. *Touch the inner strength* of an African — find a people who are going to hold on forever to what is rightfully theirs by the grace of God.

Years ago on my first trip to Africa, on landing in Senegal, I thought I was in Virginia. The smell of peanuts pervades the air. In Senegal also I first saw and touched a leper. It was only after I had bent over, rubbed his head, and held his hand that someone said, "Pearl, he is a leper." All I could see was a human. I imagine, had I known, perhaps my emotions would have led me to draw back. I'm so glad I didn't know.

Going to the small hospitals on the outskirts of Dakar, the capital, we were able to see and touch many of the sick and lame. All the helpers at these places were busy — happily preparing the rice, fish, stew, and delicious soup for the young and old ones. There was not an abundance of food, but plenty of loving care — as if they were preparing a feast for a king. After we all shared a meal, they sang and those who could dance danced. I must say there was one thing they all did, one thing in common: they smiled.

I wish the world would awaken and realize what Africa really represents. It is the second-largest continent after Asia. It is also one of the richest in minerals (gold, silver, platinum, diamonds, coal, uranium); a continent from whose earth springs corn, pineapples, yams, rice, greens. Nigeria alone has a population of over 50 million people. Egypt, land of the Pharaohs, has over 30 million. Camels, elephants, lions, tigers, freely roam the jungle; they are not penned in cages. Africa covers much of the world's surface and yet its people are not free. Why?

Daily, during the General Assembly at the United Nations, I sit and hear the voices speaking out, literally crying out, "Give us back our land, our freedom which we so rightly deserve. Give us our land to live in as we choose. Stop the raping of our women, beating of our children, torture and jailing of our men. Stop feathering your nests with our birds." How painful and agonizing it must be to see such things. It makes me angry. Angry because I as one human being can do so little to stop them.

How many times I watched faces as the Africans lost vote after vote. The plotters and planners whispered encouraging words to some of the African nations, knowing full well they were meaningless words. True, politics does make strange bedfellows; I have slept with a few and thank God had sense enough to exercise the right to have "twin beds of thought," so that I didn't get too close. I got up and washed. They stink.

There are so many outstanding and brilliant African people in and out of the United Nations whom I had the opportunity to meet. One man who certainly requires attention is Ambassador Paul Bamela Engo of Cameroon. When he sweeps into the Assembly your head has to turn. He is a large, striking man in his outfit and wears a different cap every day — at just the right angle. I think he realizes what a handsome figure he cuts.

His entrance is matched of course by the eloquence of his speeches. A lawyer, trained in England, he really lays the king's English on *thick* with a touch of his own dialect to sweeten the pot. As he reads, his eyes sweep over the audience as if to say, "Do you people get my message?" "Ambassador," I say, "they sure do; the trouble is they don't always act upon it."

Once, after delivering a magnificent statement in the Security Council, there was silence. It was as though everyone was either stunned, was thinking, crying, or ashamed. *For sure they weren't asleep.* It was difficult for anyone to swallow, so "choked up" were we by his speech.

The African's kindness is shown in many ways. He does not speak simply for his own country; he speaks *to* and *of* the world. I suppose the Africans are trying to tell us, "If you learn to care about us, then you can care about others." It's as the Bible says. You can smell the love and empathy they have for each other. It burns in their eyes and reflects through their souls. Even when they disagree, they agree on one thing: freedom. Their bond is one which must not loosen.

I referred elsewhere in this book to an incident with the Zimbabwe delegation. It will help you understand, as I came to understand, the nature of the African people. Long after the incident, I turned in my seat and fully met the eyes of the ambassador. He looked at me, then shook his head lightly as if talking to himself, "This woman is a different kind of diplomat, she's either a nut or a clown." A moment passed; he smiled slowly. No teeth were shown. I grinned what I call a pussycat grin.

Africans possess some unmatchable talents. My husband Louie — master drummer and creator of the double bass drum technique — points out to people that African drummers are the greatest in the world, bar none. Hard to dispute. Theirs is a God-given gift, a rhythm within the soul of a people which passes on from generation to generation. In America, the Negro gave the only original art: music (blues and jazz). Unmatched. The spirituals and blues seem to link our Negro people to their heritage from Africa. Souls blending into souls. It's a continuity of trying to loosen chains of bondage.

Once in a deep forest I went to a center to see some native children. We went inside their one-room building and they started to dance. I joined in and did what was popular in America at that time, The Hustle. Believe me, by the second go-round they joined in and outhustled me. Any sound or beat is caught immediately in the African ear; the talent is inborn. When the session was over, those children had heated that building so with rhythm, it's a wonder the forest didn't catch on fire.

Another time, in Abidjan on the Ivory Coast, there was a conference with the Ecosoc (Economic and Social) group from the UN. We were invited to the theater for a musical presentation. Drummers, dancers, and audience were all *one*. Every nation in there was swinging. Their beat seems to say, *"Feel us, know us."*

My eyes grew wider as my trip continued; each place was a new experience. After hearing the drummers, I sent Louie a wire (he was in the States): "Louie you talked about these drummers all your life. Do yourself a favor and come hear them." He *came*, he *saw*, he *flipped*.

In Abidjan, Louie and I met Bernard, a taxi driver, who became tour guide and dear brother. Not the "slap-hands-heh, brother!" bit we practice here. Our camaraderie was a reality. "Person touching Person." Bernard took us to Tresihville, the famous "souk" (marketplace). There I experienced another lesson on man's inhumanity to man: the exploitation and profiting from other people's land and labor. Red mud wet from the previous night's rain and open sewers made us slip and slide as we made our way to the flight of steps leading to the top level. The market had a roof overhead; and though all the sides were open, there was a terrible stench inside. I heard numerous dialects, but French is spoken by most of the population. Tourists pored over the precious goods and bartering was at its best. On that day buyer and seller were having a brain tug of war. Who was wiser? Who would win?

All the goods were displayed on large square wooden tables, merchants working side by side. You had to keep ducking your head under racks of caftans, tie-dye shirts (for which Africa is famous), and cloths of the finest cotton. Also on those tables were ebony wood carvings such as the eye has not seen in our country. We pay dearly for those articles when they reach our shores. It's a pity the salespeople in Africa don't receive what they should. These tables are uncovered — no tablecloths — despite the valuable things being shown for sale.

All the while we were shopping, I kept saying, "Louie, I know there are a lot of bodies in here, but I smell a distinct odor of 'poo-poo.'" "Honey, it's an outdoor market so you're probably also getting outdoor smells," he told me. *How wrong he was.*

After looking around, we gathered all we wanted from one table. Then we awaited the seller. No one was in sight. My feet, per usual, started to ache (yes, even in sandals they act up), so I bent down to ease them off a bit — and there found the seller.

A handsome brown-skinned woman with the most beautiful eyes was sitting on the floor, underneath the table. One ample breast was bare and being suckled by a small brown baby. The child was enjoying the meal so much that the tiny hands were patting the breast lovingly. I also found "the smell"; for under that table were spots of dried dung. (Later, when leaving, I noticed it in many other places.) *Humanity in dung.* Oh, my lord. That was not only new to me, it was sickening.

Quickly I dropped the curtain without speaking, and Louie and I continued to wait. She could still see our feet so she knew her goods would be bought. But she just kept nursing her baby. Louie and I were filled with uneasy thoughts. We discussed the insulting way humanity was forced to live. Riches on top, and humanity underneath — in dung! The sifting and sorting of people. What is the world coming to? If we see this firsthand, how can we swallow our own spittle without choking? If we take a long, hard look at "us," our throats will be raw from the scraping of our inhumanity to each other. I feel an urgency — for all of us — to do something *now*. Or we may someday wish we had never tasted of life at all.

I shared these thoughts with my husband and we discussed it while waiting to pay the woman. Bernard, our dear brother, kept up his usual happy patter, joking and smiling. He, too, was ashamed of what we had seen, but he was proud of the lady. Touched by our sense of caring, he drew even closer to us. That day lives with me as vividly as another: the day of the funeral.

An African funeral has to be witnessed, especially if it is in a small village. Riding out with a couple of new friends to a large village in a Land-Rover (a good van for bad road travel), we came across a clearing in the woods. There lived a group of people, maybe sixty or seventy. A young policeman had been shot and killed; A man in our party who knew the villagers asked us to wait until he paid his respects to the people. We got out and entered a tent where people were sitting on long picnic benches. Well, folks, I almost died of fright that day.

A giant black, spiderlike, crawling figure jumped out of nowhere and landed in the middle of the room. Oh, my lord, where to go? What to do? He began a frenzied dance as the others watched. They were not afraid. It was as if they expected him. At that moment I would have settled for Arizona, Virginia, or anywhere. He disappeared suddenly, as he had come.

Down from the hill came more people; they were returning from the grave site. Just as the last person was down we heard a loud sound. Drums; the mighty drums.

An old lady of seventy or eighty started to dance and the crowd formed a circle around her. It was rhythmic, and the others stood and watched her respectfully. She danced like a sixteen-year-old ballerina, but this was the "Queen Bee." Perhaps she was the mother or a relative of the dead man. Looking over, she beckoned me to join her. Now, I am a dancer, but, honey, forget it. This was no soft shoe; this was a dance of the *feet, heart,* and *soul*. She was barefoot, and I *gladly* took my shoes off. This lady taught me a lesson: "Sit down and watch a 'Mistress of Her Trade.' "

By now there were about three drummers; and looking at Louie's eyes, I could read his mind, "Oh, to be a part of those men." I nudged him forward and he began tapping his fingers lightly and then he too joined the frenetic pace. Everyone was into it. After a while some stopped to watch this strange man who dared to join the masters. But the dance caught on and they kept playing; in fact, it went on until we all practically dropped.

*Louie was in heaven.*

That night at the hotel (still smiling because he had been a part of those drums), he said, "Honey, they touched me." And they had; they literally picked him up from the ground because of his ability to play as they did. "Honey," he repeated, "when you get the admiration and respect of the African drummer, you are on your way." He slept that night with a smile on his face. A couple of times during the night I awoke and his fingers were keeping a beat on the bed. He was still smiling.

Someday we pray to return to Africa, a free Africa, to see more of the land and people. To be able to walk over all parts of that glorious land, holding hands each with the other; unafraid. Then and only then will I, for one, begin to believe that humanity is trying to find itself. Louie wrote a line and asked me to add his feelings. He said, "Only those who search discover the open laughter and hidden cries of humanity." I say, "Africa weep no more. God shall one day dry your tears."

# Aging

This great country will reach its full potential when it becomes aware of the elderly. The senior citizen has too long been ignored, lost in the shuffle of governmental affairs. Some forces in the government appear to be against everything that is conducive to the survival of the elderly. Have they forgotten that they too are growing older each year? How long are we going to allow this action to happen? We must recognize the needs of the people who brought this country to its height, through all kinds of tribulations, years ago.

Older people are sinking into "bags of pity," becoming afraid of what should be the "glory years," aging beautifully, being treated with respect. The years are coming, of course they are, that's what time is. There are so many things that can be done toward making the later years of one's life the most beautiful and memorable.

In these times if a person can keep his or her health, without going to the poorhouse to pay for it, and be allowed to keep a job, it's a miracle. I believe as long as one is able to function properly and still be perceived as a useful citizen, he or she has it made. Sit in your rocking chair, dear hearts, and rock enough of these people who sit in their offices judging who is useful and who isn't. Someday they too will sit and rock, unable to rise from their chairs. Why can't they relate to *"themselves"* of the future? Yes, now they are prosperous, are still working, have someone to take care of them. But it's a long road ahead. Riches do not stop the aging process. *They* are not the ones who *allow* us to live. God already gave us that right; they're too late.

We seem to be saying to our senior citizens, "You are worthless, you do not fit into the scheme of things in this modern world; you older folks are out of touch." I say to them, you lie! There *are* things for our citizens to do, places to go. "Go hide your heads, you 'stiflers of freedom.' And beware, the numbers on you are moving in."

Further, I say to them: "Many who are doing the jobs now are too inexperienced; perhaps because they are too young." The time taken away from elderly people should be given to the young; maybe it will help them to get that needed knowledge. Stop killing us off (I'm one of that over-sixty group); honey, we have qualities needed in the work force today. How do you think we got so tired, so early in life? Hard work and experience.

Have you recently walked into a bank, department store, or supermarket, and gone through the agony of trying to get service from one of the *young* newcomers to the work force? I have.

You walk into a department store that's almost empty, and you saunter over to a counter for service. Behind that counter stand two lovely young girls or men talking (Lord knows about what). They have no idea *so far* that anyone is waiting for them. They keep on talking. You stand for a while and wait to be noticed. At this point, one of the salesmen turns and gives you a look that could kill a lion. How dare *you* (customers) intrude upon our privacy? We were right in the middle of a juicy conversation. Oh well, here goes. They *glide* or *slide* (whatever step they choose) over and their first word is, "Yes?" Generally I respond, "Yes, what? Honey, I didn't ask anything yet." Next words come heavily, "Do you want something?" Now I ask you, readers, "Why are you in the store?" Either to look and buy, or to steal.

You state your case. "I would like to buy a pair of panty hose. I'm aware that this is the cosmetic counter, but could you perhaps direct me to the department where they are sold?" You will get a look that will go down in history. "This," the young one states, "is the cosmetic counter." If your memory serves you right you realize that was made clear by you only moments ago. You try again: "I know it is the cosmetic counter, but could you help me?" Why you asked that you will never know, because suddenly your helper has disappeared in the background and been replaced by the other conversationalist, who utters, "*Yes?*" By now you are getting a bit irritable; but fear not, for the "younger-than-they" manager is on the way over. That famous line again, "*Yes?*"

I tell you, *red* is the only color you now see. At ten years old you were not this far off the mark. Someone yells down two counters, "Sarah, do you know where the panty hose are? This person [at least you now have some identity] wants to know." As soon as Sarah says the magic word, "I think," you get a shove on the shoulder which sends you down to Sarah. If you have never experienced this, do try it and you'll wish there were some older person with an ear trumpet, glasses, and a cane who would take the time to help you. Lack of experience, friend, lack of experience in common courtesy; first taught in homes, then practiced abroad.

Backward we drift, thinking technology can lead us to where we want to go. Technology, according to society, belongs only to the young. The brains of the elderly are not being challenged enough to find out if their skills still exist. "This is out of your scope," others tell them. Why can't older ones be tried out?

New computers, of course, rid us of the older methods and older people. There is nothing wrong with seeking progress as long as we don't destroy what is tried and true. Great minds, *not* machines, led us to where we are at the present time. Yet some business people can't seem to calculate simple math without a computer. Let the machine break down for us older ones; we'll count in our heads. I remember in school many times when the teacher said, "Let's eliminate the pencil and paper today, and do arithmetic in our heads." What a task, but we made it.

Let me recount a computer story: I went to give a lecture in Columbus, Ohio, at one of the finest hotels in the city. Upon arrival, after driving over three hundred miles from Washington, D.C., my road manager, E.B., approached the desk and asked for the rooms. Click, click, click, click, click; then a pause, then a voice, "I'm sorry, but Miss Bailey is not listed for a space here." E.B. gave them my married name, the lecture peoples' name, etc., etc. He gave everything but my birthright. We also gave them the name of the group that set up the registration for the lecture. No help. After much deliberation among what had now grown into a group of four or five, E.B. decided to ask for his room. The task of getting checked in was a deepening horror, so finally I said, "The lecture is here, I am here, and it is my job to be here."

Then one of the brilliant minds in the group spoke up, "Ah! we have you, Mr. Smith, but not you, Miss Bailey." E.B. asked, "How can you have me and not her? I work with her so there'd be no need for me to be here, if she's not present." If this is beginning to sound confusing to you, think what was happening to us in Columbus. So I decided, "Good-bye, folks, I'm on my way back to Washington. Tell the lecture people I arrived, *but wasn't here.*" Halfway up the long lobby a screaming voice sounded, *"Miss Bailey, Miss Bailey, we've found you."* How lucky could I get?

That incident in the lobby was my opening statement at the lecture and the people almost fell out of their seats laughing. I tell you, it's hopeless and frustrating to have a machine call you a liar.

I don't think any of us is unaware that as the years come on, we tend to get slower, a lit-

404

tle forgetful, maybe quicker to frustration; however, that is not a thing just for *special people*. In time it happens to us all. I've had my share of "things forgotten."

One day, coming home from classes at Georgetown, I had a burning desire for a baked potato and a steak. I put the potato in tinfoil with some oil and garlic, to make it tender and soft. The steak wouldn't take long because it would be a quickie (pink). The potato would cook approximately thirty-five minutes. During the cooking time, I started my homework; this was my daily ritual. Thirty-five minutes became about one hour, and yipes! I screamed, "My potato!" Running into the kitchen I quickly opened the oven door; *it was as cold as ice. I had never turned the oven on.* It was the first time my memory failed me like that. By the second, third, and fifth time I knew, "Ole girl, start your thinking process a little earlier so *you'll* get the message quicker." Now that I'm pulling that stunt frequently, it's not so funny. It's interesting as hell, though.

I've had a few other slips, such as pouring the coffee in the cup when only the saucer is there. I console myself when thinking of the generation gap, "At least I know how to *make* coffee; some of the young ones don't. Ha! Ha!"

Admittedly, as the people in the work force who hire us older citizens say, "The old ones forget." Well, the young forget too; and at their ages they don't even have a lot to remember. They seem to forget some of the things they shouldn't — things and people of value, hard work, right attitudes. Things that we older people could *never* forget because they were instilled in us years ago. Thank God.

Some of the fault for young people not being as concerned as they should be rests upon the shoulders of older people. There are many talented, intelligent, and respectable young people out here in the work force. Just as there are many young people who have a deep respect and love for the elderly. It's just that when they see their government sometimes treating these people badly, they develop an "I-don't-care-either" attitude. They are not totally to blame.

It's beautiful when you see in the work force young and old ones working side by side, smiling, talking, *learning* from one another. "Age is wisdom," and we can be the "wisdom of the ages" to the young.

Years ago we called a "senior citizen" the "older" lady or gentleman. Now of course we have the mighty label. Why should gray hair set you so far above the crowd that you feel left out? I remember when gray hair was a badge of honor; now it means you just blew the job.

To me, the great heartbreaker for so many elderly is the nursing homes. There comes the time when we think about Mom, Dad, Auntie, Uncle, and those we cannot cope with in our homes — either because of our work hours, or because we feel unable to handle their particular medical situation. The family then sits down and figures out where is the best place to put *this person* who somehow, in an odd sort of way, is *in the way*. This has nothing to do with whether one is *loved or not;* it's all circumstances, necessity.

For the elderly's first few weeks in the nursing home visiting relatives pour in with roses, kisses, and wonderful memories. Then, strangely enough (in many cases, not all), the visits decrease, flowers don't come as often, and the person starts to feel lonely without his or her family around. Nurses and personnel in general are usually hard-working, caring people; yet there is laxity in many areas. And they're *not family,* anyway. Then the *person* becomes the *patient.*

After a while, during visits, you start to notice their lack of memory, loss of recognition, and withdrawal from those they love. They feel forsaken. Unless you've been in one of these homes, you cannot feel the loneliness, the hurt, the pain. I don't know anyone who doesn't desire *to be home*. If there is *any way* that a family can deal with the medical problem of an older person in the home, please, I beg you to do it. Something is taken from human beings when they're put in a home. Louie and I made a promise to each other not to put each other in a home. Lord, I pray we can keep that promise.

Jacksonville, Florida, opened another door to me about senior citizen care. On arriving there via Amtrak, I was met by two lovely sisters, Hortense and Gertrude, both connected with that fantastic organization, the National Association of Negro Women. This organization was founded by a remarkable lady, Mrs. Mary McLeod Bethune, who was a close associate of Mrs. Eleanor Roosevelt. I was in Jacksonville to speak at the opening of a new senior citizen home and center.

As we pulled away from the station in the limousine, I noticed a white building with a high wire fence around it. Behind this enclosure I saw people in chairs, sitting very still, not speaking, immobile. They looked like seated stone statues. "What's that?" I asked Gertrude, the older of the two sisters. "It's Sun Ray, Pearl, a home that our group has been trying to maintain for the elderly." "But,

Gertrude," I said, "they're just sitting there, doing nothing. They'll die, they have nothing to do." "I know, Pearl," she said sadly. "Gertrude," I asked, "please allow me to stop here tomorrow before I get on the train."

We had a glorious time at the new center; the photos, speeches, everything went well. As soon as my work was done, E.B. and I took off for the shopping area. We marched straight into Woolworth's and had a great time. All the salespeople helped us pick out socks, underwear, anything we saw fit to buy to please those people behind the fence. We continued on to J. C. Penney's, where we bought checkers, dominoes, needlepoint and embroidery kits, cards — things so their hands would not be idle. Off we went to the train station with our plastic bags of goodies. I also brought a beautiful bouquet of yellow irises that had been given to me by the people at the Big Center. Santa Claus couldn't have loaded up any more than we did.

When we passed through the gates of Sun Ray, the figures were still sitting there, staring ahead, listless, doing *nothing*. Hortense, Gertrude, and E.B. started passing out the goodies. I went inside. The rooms were very dark and gloomy, with tiny bulbs (what appeared to be about twenty watts) in the lamps. Going from room to room made me so depressed. Suddenly I stopped at a doorway. An elegant lady was sitting stiff and straight in her chair. She sat so high that I imagined if she stood she would have been six feet. A little lady with a loud voice kept following me. "She's blind," she roared. "Yes, honey, but she's not deaf," I said gently. I sat on the edge of her cot in front of her chair and slipped one of the long-stemmed irises between her clasped hands. Then I moved on.

"Pearl," Hortense reminded me, "you're going to miss your train." "Well, Hortense," I said, "I'll just have to catch another, my work is not through here yet." As we passed the elegant lady's room again, she was still sitting in the same position, with the flower upright as I had placed it. She had not shifted her position. I sat down again at the foot of her bed, placed my hand upon her knee softly, and said, "Lady, you are not blind, I am, because I see that yellow flower with the green stem; you see more than that flower; you see God." She didn't budge; she knew. I left.

Meantime out in the yard, checker and domino games were in progress; some were putting on their new socks; a sewing class had begun. No one really had time for Pearl; they were too busy with their newfound treasures. It was a beautiful picture of useful humanity. They waved as we started our journey.

But outside the yard I stopped. "Pearl," the sisters said, "we'll be late." "One minute, honey," I said, "I have an idea. Whose land is this?" I asked. "Well, it belongs to us." "Honey," I replied, "your place is on the highway, you have the land, why don't you let the people plant seeds and sell their wares on the side of the road? That way they could earn money toward their own upkeep and their home." Our idea became reality.

After arriving back home, I had my secretary Dodi buy seeds and send them to Sun Ray. The seeds were planted. In season we received a letter reporting on "Pearl's Gardens," as they had named it. It is now an ongoing project. This is what can and should be done at places like that so that the in-patients can have air, exercise, and feel wanted. It helps their mind, body, and soul. The last time we were there the building had been newly painted, and everyone still had their long, white socks. The ladies who run the home were so proud — and showed it in their smiles. It's a good lesson for all of us: we should never "decide" when someone else's usefulness ends.

# For Those Who Have Nothing Left

I awoke suddenly one morning in Chicago. I was angry. The anger grabbed me in the pit of my stomach and twisted my guts real hard. I had to get out of the bed. It was 8:43 A.M. Thoughts had begun to race through my head and they became as tight as my insides. The churning suddenly was just knotted balls.

So long has the message existed, my mind told me, so long has nothing been done about it. The politicians have talked and talked, reaching no conclusions. As long as the people of this land sit back and gripe, groan, sing songs, give charity benefits but don't actually get involved in this issue, it will continue. Why is there not a stronger demand for a cure to society's ills? *Because frankly there are too many who don't give a damn.* One of the reasons is mankind usually cannot see himself, *ever*, in the same predicament; so we sit back and wait for others. We've excused ourselves and blamed everyone else. Each one of us in a sense is guilty. Of what? "The present conditions in our world," I answer.

Men and women lie upon the streets of our nation in the same positions in which they were born. Curled-up fetuses being passed by straight and tall fetuses. We all emerged from the womb, so we certainly can relate. In walking by these curled-up creatures on the streets of our country, why can't we see ourselves? We all should stop and take a long look; it is you, me, the world, when we all stop caring.

How exactly did all these people get on the streets, benches, church steps, hallways, trains, and bus stations? We, all of us in a sense, allowed it to happen.

Going into other places like Africa, the Middle East, and Europe we used to look at the beggars, lame people, mentally ill, and thank God we didn't see this in our country. Well, we sure see it now. In the 1930s this country experienced a depression, (bread lines, soup kitchens) but never have we seen a degradation of mankind such as we are seeing now.

Talking and praying about it *is not* the solution. Getting it done by deeds is the answer. In this democracy that we call ourselves, unification, communication, and love are needed. Measurement of each other as to the

413

length and breadth of our needs is a drawn-out process. We are already measured in God's eyes as human beings. Categories can get in the way of humanity's cries and needs. Labeling this person or that one crowds our path of thinking. "Labels belong on cans," a friend named Shirley once told me in Florida. How right you are, darling Shirley.

My prayer is that perhaps some readers will start to move toward making progress in reaching the human beings who sit in alleys, lie in doorways, stand weakly on corners, and pick in the trash for a morsel a day. They, the mentally and physically ill, the sick, the hungry await us.

America is slipping away into darkness, losing our people in the fast hardening cement of the times. The "fetus position" on the sidewalks must stop. We walk the streets daily and see exactly what is wrong, yet we move on to our "own selves." Never mind the others. Not all of us, but far too many. I and others may not be expected or able to pick these human beings up in our arms and carry them home. We may not be charged to dip into our purses, wallets, or pockets to give them all we have. But how about trying for some small part of us? We should reach out and touch these human beings as soon as we can. Stop, give a word of encouragement and hope.

Some have been away so long from the reality of being treated decently or living among their family or friends that they have become dangerously angry. Some may spit in your face. It's a terrible thanks for what you're trying to do; but many of them feel that the rest of us have been spitting in their faces. True, their situation does not belong completely on our shoulders, but we have to remember that the life of nothingness and noncaring changes people. They begin to behave like animals in the jungle whose territory is invaded. Their territory is "poverty"; they claim it as their own.

How nice that hot bowl of soup, cup of coffee, or good meal tastes to us. How nice it will taste to the homeless. What the hell, half of us walking the streets, jogging, playing tennis to lose weight could lose a bit more by fasting a meal, giving it away to a hungry person. I for one will be happy to give my pounds of flesh.

"But, Pearl, are you aware they're going to buy whiskey, beer, and drugs with my hard-earned money?" "Yes, I am well aware; I've been taken like you." However, keep in mind that while we are judging them, God may be judging us.

Frankly I do not care to take my money and pass it on to someone so that he can further his destruction. I feel I have sinned. Neither do I care to enter a posh restaurant, spend money on a meal that will choke me with its richness as we sit and discuss the plight of those persons we just passed.

Friend, I and you should and do get furious and be insulted. We avoid someone who sits on a church step day after day awaiting the lucrative ones, while heaping abuse on every passerby. Some even threaten us and they look capable of doing what they threaten. I know you're asking, "Well, are you saying in one breath 'do it,' and in another 'these people are taking us for a ride'?" "*Yes and no.* What I'm trying to convey is a debatable issue which must be seen in the right perspective; then accept the fact that whatever the case, we have come to a point in America (for that matter, in the world) when the debate within 'self' will have to stop. A time when we'll accept 'There but for you go I.'"

A man on Madison Avenue almost made me change my thinking, but I pressed on to "the awakening," the knowledge that this familiar sight would have to be acted upon. When I watch the pill popper, washing his important vitamin down as his hand shoots out toward me for the donation, yes, I waver. All of these are tests of "Can we see ourselves?"

The "tall tales" our street people tell melt

your heart; some even test Shakespeare's skill. How many hours a day we spend analyzing their stories; some are masterpieces. On the way to work at the United Nations I used to buy bananas. A large man sat on the concrete, bullying everyone who passed. One day, feeling he might want that early morning breakfast, I offered this nourishing fruit. Not only did he refuse; he insulted me. All this time he was puffing on an expensive brand of cigarette, which he withdrew from a freshly opened pack.

"What's your name?" he asked one morning. "Heh!" he followed up, "ain't you Pearl Bailey?" I stopped. "Yes, do you want a banana?" "Hell, no," he said with a biting sarcasm, "you should help me because I've been sitting here nine years." I told him, "I know someone who is not quite on the streets but has been sitting on their fanny for nine years, comfortably in some friends' houses, taking it easy, leaning on others. Why don't you try to help yourself?" He gave me his favorite sneer and refused the banana. Well, I thought he didn't dig that for breakfast.

Moving on, I still pondered over whatever condition had made him like this; he was a bitter hunk of misery. This is the kind of person who might bring out the worst in you. Unscrew the heart valves a bit more and love on. What to do? we ask. What and who put him on the sidewalk?

A once lovely lady sat on Lexington Avenue, and every time we went to dinner on Third Avenue, we took that route home. That poor darling woman looked so lost. One particular night I stopped. Louie lingered just ahead; he had given me a dollar. To me, scrounging around for money in front of people embarrasses them (I know it does me), so I get my offering together before reaching the person. It somehow lends a bit more dignity to the person asking; he's not begging, you're giving in love. Be that as it may, this is my personal feeling. Everyone has emotions and again I picture myself, my friends, or family asking for help.

Approaching the lady, I asked quietly, "May I give you a dollar?" Without looking up, she shook her head, "No." Walking reluctantly away, I returned, "Please allow me to," I begged her. Denying me a look at her face, she held out her hand and made a weak gesture, only moving her fingers as if to say, "Give." Bending over her I said, "I am so sorry, so very sorry that you are here. God will help you. He sees us and knows *what we're doing* and *have done.*" She kept her head down. I moved on. I could see that this lady had not long been on the streets by the way she was dressed and the way she acted. It was new to her. She was learning the ways of the street, and finding them distasteful. "Dear God," Louie and I choked.

Every person has pride and Louie and I were reminded of that as we took a leisurely stroll through Central Park. That day I received one of the strongest rebuffs ever. In our path, bent over, busy as all hell, was a handsome, young, bearded man scrounging in the wastebasket for anything edible. The sight of a human being digging in that trash among the dog poop and every other filthy thing sickens me.

It was a gorgeous day, sunbeams bathed everyone, even my food-seeking friend. Blankets were spread out, lovers shared lunch as they shared a bench; picnic baskets were being unloaded with goodies. Leftovers from previous eaters were filling the trash bin with more "pickings." Ants were busy as ever gathering goodies for their meal later. With so much food being wasted in this country they were reaping a large harvest.

No one bothered to look at this man, searching in the trash (a sight all too familiar); they were too busy opening picnic baskets, brown paper bags, and sipping their cold sodas. There was no time for a hungry stranger. I approached him and asked, "May I give you something with which to buy a meal?" "No," he said sharply, "go away." My head rattled at the sharpness of his tone. I moved away toward Louie. "Come on, honey," Louie said, "he obviously doesn't want help." Looking back at him, I noticed he kept peering after me. Suddenly he discovered a goody in a bag. He looked it over, made his choice, and started shuffling off, probably to enjoy some leftover french fries. Everyone else kept eating as if he never existed. Again, that sickening feeling overcame me. We walked slowly back home without saying a word; humanity's pain hurt us.

Later that night I said to Louie, "Honey, now I understand what happened in the park today. That young man did not mean to be cruel to us. He was not trying to insult me. He was trying with all the decency he had left to save the one thing left: his *pride.*" Without saying a word, he was telling the world, "Leave me something, lady, leave me something."

That young man left *me, you, all of America,* something that day *to think about, do something about.* God help us if we don't.

# The Pains No One Knows

Our bodies speak to us; there are times when they speak clearly, yet we don't listen and sooner or later pay the price. Many times it's a heavy price. Dr. Levy, my late, beloved physician, always said, "You pay for what you get and you get what you pay for." How true. Years ago, during a visit, he told me: "You've drained yourself physically and mentally; all you have left is spiritual strength. In this material world, lady, you've hit 'rock bottom.'" Little did we know then that the bottom had yet to come; that would be in 1972.

In 1946, the real big break came (I'd been working before, but in a minor frame). I went into the Zanzibar Café on Forty-ninth and Broadway on the bill with Cab Calloway, Bill Bailey (my brother), plus the chorus girls. At that time it was truly "Broadway." The Latin Quarter and the Paramount, Strand, Capitol theaters; the greatest of the great performers graced these stages. These were the war years and after. We were doing three shows, seven

421

days a week, plus benefits in between. Even at my young age (along with the excitement of being in "big-time" show biz), it was too much.

I started losing my balance and was getting depressed. Mr. Howard, the club's owner, recommended that I go to a famous doctor he knew in Philadelphia. I did not notify my family, who lived in Philly — the young still have that bad habit. This man looked like Abraham Lincoln. I sat on the table as he knocked on my head, knees, elbows. Pearl didn't know what was going on. All the time he kept asking me about the show, etc. He finally asked, "What songs do you sing?" I named them: "Fifteen Years," "That's Good Enough for Me," "St. Louis Blues" (fast tempo), and my encore, "Tired." "Stop," he said, "tell me the words to 'Tired.'"

> Tired of the life I lead
> Tired of the blues I breed
> Tired, counting things I need —

I continued into the next eight bars. "Stop," he said again. "Young lady, you are extremely tired [no other complications] and you are telling yourself this every night, so much that you are beginning to believe it *because it is true*." Lincoln or not, I thought,

422

"This man is *off*." However, *he was the doctor, not me*. I took the song out of the show as advised and in a week or so I was all new again. Thank God I listened to him.

There were moments in *Dolly* which called for some serious thinking. After doing more than my scheduled contract had called for, my body started talking to me hot and heavy. But who listens to the body? Nobody. It rebelled. I fell. Often. While on a road tour, I asked those involved to listen to my health problem. Heh! There's a show to do and money in this. In vaudeville it was only yourself and your musicians involved (it's called "one on one" now); in legit show business (plays), there's an entire group of people depending on your presence. They flip out if you're not there. They don't care to see the understudy. *Neither does your audience*. (People have been pleasantly surprised when the understudy turns out to be better than the headliner.) My pleading went unheeded. I kept falling until it was almost too late. Was it to be my *health* first or *show business?*

Many people are unaware of the pressure that can be put upon a performer when a whole show is involved. Everyone has heard the saying, "The show must go on." Well, I found out — and so have many others — that the show *will* definitely go on *with or without you*; should the understudy take over to get the job done, and the audience thoroughly approves, *it's your fair fanny*. When you return the next day, you're jobless. Strangely enough in my case, in 1946 I filled in for Sister Rosetta Thorpe at the Strand, and carried on from there. (Luckily for me the understudy in *Dolly* was not well received and so I kept at it. Fate plays a helluva game of cards, folks.)

Dodi, my "play" daughter and secretary, was with me in Houston, Texas, at my lowest ebb. The more she had said, "Stop, and listen to these physicians," the longer I played. She was furious with me, but more upset with those who refused to understand. I talked her into going home to California. Reluctantly she left; she pressed an envelope in my hand. I read her letter later; even now I tell Louie, "If Dodi had never told me she loved me in all these years, her letter left no doubt about how much."

I always pray to God to give me that "extra zap," to finish what I've started. I feel a surge of "energetic love" pushing me in the back, giving me that chance to carry on intelligently. It allows me to lean against buildings, or sit on benches, yes, I've even sat on curbs! Whenever I realize the pace is too hasty, I simply close the door of myself and sit and listen to God. He gives me rest and fortifies me for the world. "Amen."

I've appeared in every condition: bandaged feet, sore eyes (I wore dark glasses once in *Dolly* after having an eye exam), flu; you name it. Folks have said, "We were at the show, we were so angry because you were not there." And I respond, "Forgive me for causing you such pain, I was in the hospital. Had I known you were coming perhaps I could have held off being ill." *Just one human feeling for another.*

I heard Mr. George Burns, a master showman, say on a television interview, "Whatever you feel when that light hits you, somehow you come alive out there and do the job." He just turned a beautiful ninety-two. I loved his Gracie too.

Again after a turn in the *Dolly* road tour, I suffered a setback. Then I received a letter from one of the most eminent heart specialists, Dr. William Hitzig (he's now deceased). Doc and I had become devoted friends. His medical help to me did not surpass our great devotion to each other. Once after he had tended me, he wrote me a letter. I had it put in a special frame.

Dear Pearlie Mae —
    As you already know I was one of last

night's standing ovationists who were both literally spell-bound and amazed by your unbelievable performance. It was a rare experience to view your two hours of hard work and endurance which I can only describe as a phenomenon and an inspiration. I say this only because I know more about what "makes you tick" than anyone who graced your appreciative audience. I was deeply impressed by your courage which far outweighed your tremendous talent and brilliant performance. Only few who have your guts and self-discipline would have dared your efforts to bring pleasure to the gathering and for this I admire you. It was the right thing to do — and only brave men and women who know themselves and their physical limitations would have done it your way. And I believe in it — that is, to meet life's challenges head-on till the bell tolls — for I am not unlike you. In this way we share a common destiny with joy, and with understanding, come what may — even though our paths take us along different routes — you as a hard working brilliant performer who brings pleasure to the masses and I as a hard working (12–20 hours per day) country doctor on Park Avenue who attempts to bring

426

health to the community. We have chosen this way of life even though our lot has not been dissimilar for we are both victims of having given so much already — and are now members of the "coronary club." I would never have dared to stop your hard work for you enjoyed every minute of it and you did it so well. It's the only way to stay alive — build up accessory blood vessels — and only then will Peace come through us. I practice that way. There is no surcease for those of us who can and want to serve. If I am in town I will come again with friends who need to be inspired as I was last night.

Affectionately,
BILL HITZIG

*What a classic.* These things, folks, are what keep me alive. These and your devotion through the years.

In 1972, God gave me a rest. *Medically I was declared dead.* I have never questioned the how or why. It is not for me to know. All I *do* know is, *I go on because I must.* God sets the time; He winds the pieces and He decides when "the ticking" should stop and when "the ticking" continues.

Doc Levy once said to me after a bout with

fatigue, "You did it again." "Doc," I said, "you mean I stepped on that merry-go-round?" "No," he answered sternly, "you didn't step, lady, you took a flying leap." We all do. We go off on a tangent of living (good or bad) and seem to think that life *has* to be a continuity *without breathing*. Most of us don't even realize what's happening. Some of this stupidity (and it is just that) is to please others. Others who, most likely, are running too.

My devoted friend and a true saint — Dr. Peter Rizzo, orthopedic man at St. Vincent's Hospital, was tragically killed in New York. Once while my leg was in traction, he said, "The people at the theater keep calling every morning to see if you will make the show tonight. I've been answering them. Suddenly I said to them I'm not going to answer you about Pearl anymore. She is my patient and her illness is private." He added, "Pearl, I'm not in your business, but I sure learned a bit more about the selfishness of man." Doc, how little you know. We miss you.

Of course my current doctor, I call son, brother, mentor, everything. Laurel, his dear wife, is just as close. Many people have gripes about dentists, physicians, nurses — most often over the *bills* they get. Let me tell you, I've seen more sick doctors walking halls of hospitals than there are patients in bed. They do care. There are noncarers in every business. All I know is there has never been a moment that Louie or anyone has called Dr. Rood and that young man has not been interested. Sometimes it was: *"Now what's wrong, nut?"* But then, in his own affectionate way, he'd say, "Mama Pearl, if you need me, I'm on the way."

# Washington VIPs

Getting in and out of cars, on and off planes and trains, many people stumble. Oddly enough, it seems that one can sit so comfortably while in these vehicles then emerge for that graceful entrance or exit and go "Bloop." A real "boo-boo." And if you happen to be the President of the United States it's a "fumbler."

We all pray that the world is not looking when we stumble along the way, mentally, or physically. As for myself (a dancer), I would like everyone to simply disappear from sight, *don't be so helpful,* and let me silently, stiffly crawl (and I do) out of a limo. Years ago the move was a breeze, now it's a hurricane. The driver pulls, I push; somehow I remain in the same spot. "Spirit of Grace." So for Pearl. Now how about heads of state going through these gyrations? Awaiting them are cameras, guests, etc., etc.

If Gerald Ford is as clumsy as is written,

then I ask how come he does the Charleston so well? (Also his fox-trot is smooth and his waltz step will fit any Wayne King music.) I once did the Charleston with Jerry (as friends call him). I sat with this man and his family as they watched an election go down the drain; and I remembered the attempted assassination. We had applauded him when he first took on the presidency of this great nation. He could have stumbled. He didn't. Later, we all watched, lived his emotions as he sat by his wife's side when she announced to the world, bravely, her drug problem.

A lot of men stand straight, yet stumble. A lot waver. Some simply go down and give up. President Gerald R. Ford *didn't* and doesn't. He deserves a salute.

While we stand for that salute let's give a big one to the lady by Ford's side, my sister Betty Ford. Women so many times are judged by their affinity for one another; some think our world is filled with petty jealousies about men, women, children, fashion, etc., etc. Hold your breath.

We women "glue" at "glue time." Situations arise that can draw us more into sisterhood. *We are not* an "order." We become a "Oneness" of understanding. Bickering, dickering, scratching, and clawing all the way, with or without each other, we can make it. The dangerous and slippery steps are what intrigue us all. Standing with and behind those we love — husband, children, friends — when the road gets rocky. Somehow we always feel we *must* be there, learning, understanding, bearing, loving; standing for, standing against; speaking out, seldom holding back; afraid and courageous. And all the while *paining*. Women call it "being a woman." And by golly, I'm sure that describes the noble woman, Betty Ford. Knowing and loving Betty as I do (we're Aries girls — April 8, March 29), I can feel much of her inner soul.

As the picture comes clear, I see another lady with whom I've had some relationship, Barbara Bush. Time will cover "Lady Barbara"; she will probably be spoken of as the Civil War figure I read about in school, Barbara Fritchie.

When the Bush family lived in the Vice President's house, Barbara gave an affair to benefit "Reading Is Fundamental." (This helping-children-read thing is no newly inspired bit with her.) There was a large lovely tent in the yard, filled with so many people involved with "RIF," including Anne Richardson and others. Present, too, were two famous children's authors, and your friend Pearl, author of *Duey's Tale*. We were to do a reading and demonstration. Secretary of Education William Bennett, now "Drug Czar," gave the closing remarks.

As the affair closed, Barbara Bush took my hand and we slowly strolled down the driveway. The Secret Service sauntered a bit in the back allowing for woman talk. Louie hovered behind with the guys. All of a sudden Barbara stopped, gave me a hug, and said a few private words (subject matter between God, Barbara, and Pearl). It harmed no one yet can help all. "Pray." Just simply "Pray, Pearl." I do — I pray that you all meet and know a Barbara Bush in your world.

Does a person have to be judged without even being known, as Rosalynn Carter came to be, at certain things? Are we from the South all going to be the soft-spoken beautifiers of gardens as was Lady Bird Johnson? No. Each individual is himself or herself.

In the case of Rosalynn Carter and President Jimmy Carter, whom I met at a reception given for a George Wein Jazz Event (Louie played there), we touched. I watched little Amy excitedly running down the hall with her playmates among the dignitaries. They were looking for something to do. They would gaze into faces, dismiss them in their childlike minds, move over to the "goody tray," then take off again.

Even then I suppose Amy was searching our souls. The young do seek to find us; we had a chance to read about and observe Amy doing that same seeking in her college days. In that big white house that girl probably had *seen* and *heard* humanity and had come out into the world of ordinary men and women either to *carry on* or *rectify*.

You might ask, "Does Amy belong in this chapter of 'VIPs'?" *Yes.* Because what *was* and *is* was found by that child in "The Large House," and was brought out. She perhaps saw and lived more than any of us; as a matter of fact, as I reflect upon this, the children of the White House families are really "the seers."

President Carter, to me, had a strange smile; he appeared to bare his teeth so it could have been called an "inward smile." Somehow, his smile did not encourage you to return it — as an Eisenhower smile would. Ike gave out, Carter absorbed.

Because Carter was not a "projector," it seems most of us missed the man. The work, love, energy, and travel that Jimmy Carter and his wife Rosalynn have put into serving humanity throughout all parts of the world is to be commended. How many of us have witnessed these people in Harlem, in different countries, helping the needy, repairing or building houses, down on their knees in the middle of humanity? That's love in action.

What a pity that this love was not related to in different ways during his presidency. Assuming that this was the message he was trying to get across, it was not understood. Probably no one was really tuned into his kind of simplicity and plainness. He was a Man of the Sea. Pity we missed his "boat of efforts." Anyhow, both of these people are still at their labor. Bless them.

I met Lynda Bird Johnson soon after she married the marine Chuck Robb at the grand apartment of the most fabulous woman in the world: the "Hostess with the Mostest on the Ball," Ambassador Perle Mesta. This was our lady ambassador to Luxembourg. What an appointment. What a "grande dame." To be on her list of friends (there were some enemies, too) was a must. *Anything* that was Washington society or government, she was a part of. I held her hand in Tulsa, Oklahoma, a few years back when she passed away. "Sing me a hymn, Pearl," she said. For two hours she never turned two of my fingers loose as I sang the hymns.

I'll never forget on my first ever trip to

entertain at the White House. I wore this black chiffon dress with a boa feather train trailing about three feet behind me. Don Loper, the great designer had made it for me.

Mrs. Mesta insisted (by now I was her adopted niece or something) that I sleep at her apartment the night before. When I dressed for the affair that night, she was sitting in the living room to look me over. "Turn, Pearl, turn, Pearl." "Lord, Miss Mesta, what do I do with this long thing in back?" She threw it elegantly over my shoulder so that it dripped down my back. Honey, I was "piss-assed elegant." Oooops!

Another time on a visit to "The House," Perle Mesta gave a prereception for me at her apartment. Before the guests arrived I was out in the hallway, dipping my knee a bit (she had a few royal guests), holding out my hand to be kissed; folks, I was "*how*dy-*doo*ing" all over the place. I felt like a seasoned "debutante." It's the first time I had "grits" for dessert. She was Oklahoma via Texas or vice versa — and oil dripped along with everything else she had. She was strong, kind, brilliant, loved; and disliked by some who were seeking to sit in her place. She ruled the roost in D.C.

On this night I met the whole Johnson family. Lynda and Luci are two strong girls in character; Lynda and I still correspond. Her husband Chuck became governor of Virginia (my home state) and is currently a U.S. Senator from Virginia.

President Johnson gave off an aura of authority; with a capital "A." Power seemed to encircle him in the Senate and as President. He liked it. I'm sure at the breakfast table it was the same. He was a "take-charge man."

He died alone. He probably wanted it that way so that no signs of weakness would show. The "Giant from Texas" rode high in the saddle. And Lady Bird beautified not only the parks, but his life.

President Nixon played the piano with the fervor of the great Art Tatum and Artur Rubinstein combined. Unfortunately, he did not possess their skill. Still he played. I sang — *whatever he played.*

As the President stepped on the platform in the East Room before the audience of people gathered in honor of the visit of Chancelor Willy Brandt to thank his "Ambassador of Love" (he had officially credited me with that honor), I said, "Mr. President, you play the piano. No one has had a President as their pianist. Would you give your guest the privilege of witnessing this feat?" Why did I ask? Barely were the words out of my mouth before he was seated at the grand.

Before I could choose the song, he took off on "Home on the Range" — in *his* key. "Sir [I tried to stop him], I want to sing, not ride a horse." The fervor continued. "Sir, the key is *too* low." Let me tell you, the audience was lower — to the floor, almost bent in half with laughter. Only Richard M. Nixon was totally serious, smiling at his achievement. We *struggled* through the song. "Thank you, sir," I said. *The audience* heard me; *the President didn't*. He was already well into his encore, "God Bless America."

Somewhere in America exists a tape which should forever be in your library. (It has been shown on TV.) President Nixon and his Ambassador Pearl in concert at the White House. A true American classic.

To come from a large family, or in this case a "Dynasty of Rulers," is cause for pride; it is also a burden. About two years ago Nancy Reagan's secretary called and invited us to a state dinner for the man who came from a dynasty.

The body, form, and face of this man dwarfed everyone in the room. His Majesty King Fahd is the ruler of the Kingdom of Saudi Arabia. He had everyone's attention and so (as I watched the ladies) did his handsome nephew sheikhs.

I met another handsome man over thirty years ago at a Friars affair. It was one of the greatest that was ever held. On this night the male-only Friars (as it was at the time) was honoring Sammy Davis, Jr. Never before had this honor been bestowed upon a member of our race. The dais included (I'll miss a few) Tony Martin, Humphrey Bogart, Jack Benny, Eddie Cantor, George Jessel, George Burns, and my favorite cowboy, Gary Cooper.

One man there ended up being the President of the United States. An actor leading the country. This same man nominated me to be a delegate to the United Nations in 1987 and 1988. (President Ford had placed me there in 1975 and 1976.) This man and his wife invited me to their home (the White House) so much in the space of eight years that I just started telling folks, "I'm going to 'The House.'" Each time I went for any President, rest assured the favorite of all was often there. Wonderful Bob Hope, married to that gorgeous singer, Dolores.

President Reagan bestowed the Presidential Medal of Freedom upon me October 17, 1988. This is our nation's highest civilian award. I was in the company of three widows — Mrs. Jean MacArthur, Mrs. J. Willard Marriott, Sr., and Mrs. Malcolm Baldrige —

Chief Justice Warren Burger, Mr. Irving Brown, and Mr. David Packard. We were all beaming and grateful.

Reagan, *the actor, treaty maker*, ex-baseball announcer, *was* and *is* one of the greatest communicators of all time. Whether you liked him or not, somehow you listened to him. Doesn't hurt to be able to read and act out a well-written script; I've watched people do it every day in the UN.

Reagan charmed them all: Gorbachev, Thatcher, kings and queens. Nancy Reagan watched everything and everybody with the most enchanting eyes you'll ever see. Her eyes at once engulf, hold, dare, understand, defy: whatever *you* want to read into them. As for myself, I read, "She likes and trusts you, Pearl." Good eyes, Nancy.

I wouldn't be surprised after these eight years if one day we tune in the news to see Reagan as anchor man or hear him as sportscaster at the ball game. We might see Ronnie and Nancy off to China, Russia, Arabia; watch them riding at the ranch, or perhaps saddling up to ride across some desert. No doubt we'll see them at Maggie Thatcher's house in England. Wherever he is, President Ronald Reagan will be communicating. He played his role, which the nation thrust upon him for eight long years; and if we called him tomorrow I think he'd return to catch up on what he thinks he should have done.

Eight years at the helm is one thing; but serving under such a person is a tough job too. Ask George Bush. He did time; his burden will be heavy.

Lionel Hampton, world renowned vibra-harpist, who played for Bush's twenty-first birthday party, once said to me, "Pearl, this is a helluva decent man." I like decent people. Lionel and Bush are as tight as they were on their first meeting. I told Louie I make a bet Lionel will be in the White House "House Band."

Bush, the pilot, UN ambassador, ambassador to China, representative to Congress, is off and running. So we pray he'll catch the fish he seeks, and ring those "horseshoe pegs."

# "*Sweet*" Memories of Youth

I can remember catching lightning bugs as they flickered in the dusk of summer evenings, childlike pulling off their lights (a child's cruelty I suppose), putting their lights on my ring finger — my diamond. I never wanted more than one stone, so I'm sure I'll be forgiven doing in one lightning bug every now and then.

I remember buying those long white pieces of paper with button candy on them. You picked the buttons off one at a time and relished them. If you had a special friend then, he or she got treated to a small strip which you carefully tore off — so as not to give them too many. Even a best friend can get sick on too much candy.

I remember the small, round, silver pans of soft candy with a little spoon to eat it with. It tasted good. I wonder why I ate it then and wouldn't care for it now?

I remember "jaw breakers." Two cents, I think they were. They lasted a real long time. And your jaw stuck out so that you looked like the grown-ups when they had a toothache or the old men who sat and played checkers, with their cheeks puffed out.

I well remember the two chocolate cupcakes for a nickel. Hot dog! They tasted good. Chocolate anything used to be (and still is, whenever I indulge myself) my favorite flavor.

Ah, do I well remember snowballs; with all the flavors. Raspberry, blackberry, grape, strawberry (it was okay), and, of course, chocolate. They were five cents for a good-size one. We once had a snowball stand outside our house. The iceman would bring a block of ice for the icebox, and one for the snowball stand. I loved to scrape the ice, whenever he'd let me. I wasn't tall till I was twelve. I'm only five-six now. Sure would love to scrape a snowball now.

My favorite thing — mmm, mmm, mmm — sour pickles. I got into dill pickles later. If only every day I could have had a sour pickle, my life would have been complete — over with by twelve. The greatest of all was when I could afford a peppermint stick to push down in the center of the pickle. The combined flavor of the peppermint and vinegar was sheer heaven. Dill pickles and green tomatoes from Mr. and Mrs. Max's store across the street from us, were my treat. Once I got a licking from Mama for going over and telling Mr. Max, "Mama would like a pickle and a peppermint stick." Never mind that I said it — it was *how many times* I said it. When Mama went to pay her weekly tab, it was twenty-one dollars. Now twenty-one dollars then would be like a hundred dollars (I guess) now. "Pickles, Max," I ordered, "pickles." Mama knew the culprit. Needless to say, my taste for pickles declined until I could afford them on my salary — years later. When Mama cured you, she cured you well!

I remember being a top-notch "double dutch" rope jumper. The single rope was a breeze. We played salt, pepper, mustard, vinegar (the slow start), then the pace was picked up and you had to jump real fast to keep up. But "double dutch" called for the master touch. Turning "double dutch" was not easy because you had to really know how to get those two hands moving in a special rhythm. Some who turned the rope broke the rhythm. Then when you learned to jump it backward (the ropes going outward), you were looked upon as somewhat of a genius.

The train left Philadelphia at 7 A.M., I well remember, for Washington, D. C. That meant we were going to visit Virgie, my oldest sister, who still lived in Washington, and Mama's old friends. A whole day of joy. It returned at 7 P.M., which meant either I slept all the way back or was awfully sleepy in school the next day. Most of the time, though, I did sleep — being all of ten or eleven years of age. The price of the excursion was $3.95. The price of an Amtrak ticket now, round trip, is an inch or two over $100. Gee whiz, time does change. Prices too.

The hair stylist now will probably want to say the mannish cut is all the rage, but I remember having one at ten years old. That was sixty years ago. Mama always plaited my hair. Some of the girls had their hair hanging loose. I liked that; so when I got to the school yard, I opened the plaits, then redid them before going home. Somehow I couldn't get it the way Mama had put it together and she knew something was being done. For punishment she "corn-rowed" it. (That is another thing that the stylist, "Bo" Derek, and a few others said they started. Actually it's African.) I had never worn that style before;

in school we used to laugh at the children whose families did it to them. Now me! I was heartbroken. How could I go to school and be humiliated by my friends. My stepfather (wonderful Mr. Walter) begged Mama to spare me. In vain.

The next day at school I suffered deeply. That night my devoted brother Willie saved me. He was six years my senior and had a job selling candy at the Pearl Theater, on Ridge Avenue, so he could be near the profession which he eventually entered. (I had a chance to see his peers: *Bill "Bojangles" Robinson, Eddie Rector,* and *John Bubbles* of the famous team "Buck and Bubbles.")

Although he was known as Bill Bailey, his name was *Willie Eugene Bailey.* A teacher once threatened to send me home for what she called "sass" (talking back to her). She had asked the class for "names" and "nicknames." "Charles" was "Chuck," "Steven" was "Stevie," etc. I raised my hand, "Willie" was "Willie." "No, Pearl," she said, "William is Bill, and Willie could be Bill." "No, ma'am," I said, "Willie is called Willie at home." Oh, that got me in trouble! But I loved my brother so much and no one was going to "fancy up" Willie. My love and trust in him paid off, for after the great "corn-rowing" scene, he took me to the barbershop and I received a "mannish cut."

Putting his cap on my head, he rushed me out of Mama's sight so I could go to bed, without her checking me out. No such luck. In our house you were checked out *coming* and *going*. Mama had a roaring fit. "Willie, what have you done?" "Mama," he said, "this is the latest style and she looks cute." Mama loved all of us dearly (three girls and a boy), but her boy (we girls knew it) was her heart.

She griped a bit more, then quieted down. One thing about my mama, she was not a "*screamer*." She had a soft, gentle (not whiny) voice. People just loved her. I almost got "braided" again because now with the short hair, when I finished playing in the school yard, and with the wind blowing, when I arrived home, my hair was really standing on end. Mama said, "One more day coming home like that, young lady, and you're braided for life." Lawdy! Talk about a little girl arriving at the front door brushing and slicking down her hair; that was Pearl.

I remember our graduation speech from John F. Reynolds at Twenty-fifth and Jefferson in Philadelphia. My father, the Reverend, and Mama constantly burned these words in our brains as a discipline lesson so I knew them even before reciting them at school. I've never forgotten them and try to live their message every day of my life:

1. Though I speak with the tongues of men and of angels, and have not charity, I am become as sounding brass, or a tinkling cymbal.

2. And though I have the gift of prophecy, and understand all mysteries, and all knowledge; and though I have all faith so that I could remove mountains, and have not charity I am nothing. (1 Cor. 13:1-2)

*You don't have to graduate to know that Charity is Love.*

I remember some summer evenings Mama and I (by now Eura was married, and Virgie still lived in Washington) would sit on the white concrete stairs — everyone in Baltimore and Philadelphia has white front steps. Mama would say, "Dick [my nickname], how about some Chinese noodles?" "Great, Mama." The Chinese restaurant was around the corner. We had already had dinner, but this was a taste instead of ice cream. Mama would splurge for a box each; fifteen cents plain, twenty with pork. With plenty of soy sauce, Mother and baby girl sat and "people-watched." We would laugh at some, moan about some being fat or skinny. That was our party time.

Blindman's Buff. Who can't remember that? Marcella Smith was my first ever girlfriend. Marcella lived two doors away and Mama had lived at their house when she and Papa separated and she went to Philadelphia. I've often wondered how did Mama ever pick Philly? Had anyone recommended it? She was born in Virginia and had lived in D.C. I thought that was the end of Mama's world; however, she became a lover of the "City of Brotherly Love." Mama is buried in Philadelphia, not her native Virginia.

On weeknights after homework, and of course after the chores had been done, I was allowed to go to Marcella's and play Blindman's Buff. One obstacle I never overcame. The deadline for coming home was 9 P.M. I suppose children get so carried away when they're playing they lose all sense of time, or they figure if the parents are such good friends they'll be forgiven a small disobedience. But when Mama said, 9 P.M. *sharp*, she meant every word. We were raised in a home where Mama and Papa taught us, "Your word is your bond." I had given my word, *To obey*. But I miscued. Invariably it was 9:15, or 9:20. What happened to our clock I don't know. Fate was on Mama's side. I suffered and missed a few nights of my pleasure. Marcella and I sat on the front steps and moped.

It is so beautiful to think of all these things and know that someone, somewhere is reliving these moments with you. Volumes could be written about our childhood joys and pains. Our first time sitting on the steps with a boyfriend or a "fellow" (as they were then called), playing hookey (if you did), your favorite Western movies or the Pearl White serials, the trips on Christmas to Woolworth's to spend that whole dollar and fifty cents.

So, so many cherished moments . . .

# The Two of Us

Whack! Whack! The golf balls soared into the air. They didn't go far. My first one never left the tee, nor the second and third. The fourth went three feet at least; I was elated. Louie did better, ten or twelve feet. "Did you see that, honey?" we echoed each other. So where was the prize? What should have been asked was, "Did we feel it?" Our bones (me, a dancer, Louie the ambidextrous drummer) had the sound of someone cracking ice. All this for two little balls. Mine was orange. I was showing off. After all, it dawned on us, although we live on the golf course, it had been twenty-three years since we smacked a ball. Worse yet after thirty-six years of marriage, traveling over so much of the world, driving, flying, sailing, we had never taken a nonworking *vacation. Ever.*

Louie finished the last day at Disneyland with his big band on June 19, 1987. We decided to take an honest-to-goodness vacation. We said, no Charlie the dog, no music, no writing paper (for me); we didn't want wake-up calls, dog walking — anything — just a "loose living, for-real" vacation. We went from Disneyland home to Arizona to go through the house (we do our own cleaning, yard work, cooking, etc.): we went to our closets and found casual clothing we had never worn. Shame on us.

"What had we been doing all these years?" you ask. Working, traveling, writing music, giving lectures and seminars (Louie), going through Georgetown (Pearl), big band, small band gigs (Louie) — we did it all. We got home occasionally, but not as often as two people should have. Even our mail was handled mostly on the road. With all our happiness together, we truly stand guilty of not "taking time to smell the roses."

Were we relaxed? Oh yes. I stay that way, more so than Louie. I'm a real "homebody" even on the road. Many times I stay in a hotel or motel room sitting by the window looking out at humanity, reading (all the time), doing needlepoint, crocheting — nothing but *something*.

Louie has to walk outside every day, so he gets the papers (I read all in every town we go to); he gets the tidbits we need. Whenever I go out it is a floor show. Everyone feels (and I'm glad) they can speak to me; I return their feelings. After a few hours out in the streets I feel as though I've done a full day's work. I love folks, but, honey, love is draining too. So in I go. I need company with God. He replenishes me and then I'm ready again for the outside. Now Louie and I were ready to give *ourselves* a treat.

We, as I said, have done so much traveling to different parts of the world, but each time we'd be doing some form of work (charity or personal). We climbed happily into the car (Charlie was most disappointed with his mistress and master; we dropped him at Doc Litchfield's, his buddy) and off we scooted like teenagers. I drove. I get a kick out of driving up to places, shocking the doormen. "Miss Bailey, where is your limo? Your chauffeur?" Are you kidding, fellows, I drive myself. Whenever you see me in a limo, someone sent it. I just love driving. On trips I do four or five hundred miles with a smile. Louie drives well *but* if a note enters his head he drives right past the road signs; sometimes he begins to *doze* (although he says he doesn't); in no time Pearl is at the wheel. You've got to watch the speed demons — those who, as E.B. always says, just look for *space* and take it at any one's expense.

Now we're not prudes just because we've taken no vacation. Louie never drank or smoked (maybe a glass of wine at his mother's); I smoked once (never inhaled) and ended up two-year chairman of the American Lung Association. And I really loved a *cold draft beer* once in a while. *Come to think of it, it's been thirteen years.* We decided we were dried prunes.

Boy! How we used to go hear the bands, singers, and shows, but, honey, it's not like "the good old days," so I think we fell into the pattern of staying home. That was all over though on that June day. We were swingers again.

The doorman at Caesars Palace greeted us warmly; Louie overtipped, I thought, "The ole boy is showing his girlfriend [me] what a sport he still is." Inside, Louie's sister Dee-Dee (my daughter is her namesake) awaited us. She had been at Caesars sixteen years in the "Baccarat Circle." "Finally you two joined the human race," she said. What the hell she was talking about we didn't know because Big Dee has *never* had a vacation either. In 1988, after over fifty years of working, she retired and is having a ball in her mobile home.

Immediately after checking in we took off for the Desert Inn golf driving range. I had worked there three years before I married Louie. The staff of old-timers who remembered us observed us as though we had just come from the dead.

Out to the driving range. The man who sold the equipment was also an old friend. He too thought we were "unwrapped mummies." Boy! Had it been *that* long since we socialized or fraternized? He *gave* us the buckets of balls. Two *large ones*. We went berserk. Louie bought two more large buckets. Folks, talk about two sore but happy humans. We talked all night about our achievements. Next day we went back. And the next.

Dodi had made reservations for us at the fantastic Hotel Del Coronado in Coronado, California (across the bridge from downtown San Diego). This hotel is old, and has to be visited to be appreciated. It is one of *the* places to live beautifully by the Pacific. We spent five or six days there. The owner, Mr. M. Larry Lawrence, makes your visit worthwhile.

We found the golf range at once and took off. Okay, folks! I'll astound you. *We walked* to and from the golf course.

That's one thing Louie and I like to do. In front of our house we easily walk three to five miles a day. But we do it at 6 A.M., before the heat — 90 degrees at least. Our temperature in summer can reach 115 to 120 degrees.

In the early evenings, we enjoyed a fantastic

455

dinner at the Harbor House restaurant across from the hotel, watching the boats tie up at the dock. This was living. Returning to the hotel, we removed our shoes and headed for the beach.

Louie discovered from two young boys how to get the big pretty clams out. We sat on the rocks, watching sand crabs, small starfish, children covering fathers with sand, watching the sunset.

At night Louie was like a child Michelangelo. He decided to shellac the shells of the clams (they were huge). One would have thought he was going to open a clam shop. His art work is displayed on our front porch.

## The Laguna Beach Art Festival

We had been invited by dear Sally Reeves and her husband Douglas to the Laguna Beach Festival of Arts. That should be another "wonder of the U.S.A." Don't miss it, you "stay-at-homers." The whole town participates, babies and all. Laguna is a fascinating place with all its many festivals.

While in San Diego we had met two fellow Arizonans, Pete and Janet, and invited them to join us at the festival for the Pageant of the Masters. Luck was with them because it is usually a sold-out affair from the day the pageant closes down in the fall until it opens the following year. Our children and friends have adored it.

We lingered in Laguna, eating with Frances (our Chinese love) at the Golden Dragon, and still hitting the golf ball; friends Gordon and Ruth, being true golfers, hung on with us. Bucket after bucket disappeared. By now I was swinging my *butt* off and feeling like Babe Zaharias — like my Babe Zaharias clubs. She was the greatest; I was finding my way.

At Laguna we had a verandah that appeared to almost hang over the ocean. It was a bit *too close* for me. The sounds of those powerful waves at night were frightening. I had a feeling inside of their power. My mind drifted to "what if those waves wanted to continue their journey?" *Nothing* or *nobody* could stop them. They were "Power" magnified.

One day a phone call came, from a man I call my son and friend, Tony Fantozzi. He worked at the William Morris Agency. He *had* to see me personally although he said, "I know you and Louie are on strict vacation." Well, we never refused Tony. He came, we sat on that verandah. The deals all sounded like money in the bank. As it turned out they all fell through. Now as I ponder, I'm so glad.

At Laguna, Louie and I had found what was important: more clams, golf, more friends.

At that point, who needed or even wanted all of the "speculators" or "speculations" about making a buck? We were already rich living with nature; the sea. Anyhow, Tony meant well. That night as we lay in bed a poem ran through my head and heart as the sea knocked at our door. Vacation unspoiled in my mind, I got up and wrote it down on motel stationery.

## TO THE PACIFIC

Why am I not asleep,
Am I afraid —
Afraid that you will come upon me
And cover me?
There is no escape
There's too much of you
Overpowering
I hear and see you coming
Yet I'm unable to escape
To Move.
What would be the use?
For you would only follow me
Whether I'd want to go with you or not
Would not be my choice.
Yet you are kind, for you warn me
That you are coming and I'll be going.
I'm afraid, perplexed, in love with you. I
    can't take my eyes off your majesty.
    My hands cannot hold your fullness —

— My feet are washed with your cool-
ness.

You turn yourself over, thunderously
And engulf my soul — You
Where do you come from?
Where do you go?

After returning home, Louie and I recalled
one day, sitting under the tree, sipping a cold
drink in Vegas, talking about what in the
world had we been doing, ignoring all of this
fun, working too hard, not joining in with
friends who had begged us to make trips with
them. That summer day in 1987 we decided
this *must never* happen again.

So far we haven't kept our word. We've
traveled far since then, but no vacation. We
haven't even been sitting on the back porch
much lately either. But at least we're healthy
and happy, thank God.

As I write this (February 1989), we're
preparing to leave with our group for the Sinai
Desert (North and South), Haifa, and the
Mediterranean (to entertain our sailors). On
April 26 Louie is taking a group to the Berne,
Switzerland, Festival. I'll watch the Alps, and
read. Then on to Italy (the museums for me),
then home to the back porch. When we're on
the golf course, Charlie can watch over the

fence. I'll put a low fire under a pot of lima beans, and we'll go outside to Whack! Whack! those little white balls.

We *will* take another real vacation someday, God willing. Maybe with Charlie this time.

| ML | DATE DUE | | |
|---|---|---|---|
| | | | |
| | | | |
| | | | |
| | | | |
| | | | |
| | | | |
| | | | |
| | | | |
| | | | |
| | | | |